jump the shark®

jump the shark®

Jon Hein

DUTTON

DUTTON
Published by the Penguin Group
Penguin Putnam Inc., 375 Hudson Street, New York, New York 10014, U.S.A.
Penguin Books Ltd, 80 Strand, London WC2R 0RL, England
Penguin Books Australia Ltd, Ringwood, Victoria, Australia
Penguin Books Canada Ltd, 10 Alcorn Avenue, Toronto, Ontario, Canada M4V 3B2
Penguin Books (N.Z.) Ltd, 182–190 Wairau Road, Auckland 10, New Zealand

Penguin Books Ltd, Registered Offices: Harmondsworth, Middlesex, England

Published by Dutton, a member of Penguin Putnam Inc.

First printing, September 2002
1   3   5   7   9   10   8   6   4   2

 REGISTERED TRADEMARK—MARCA REGISTRADA

LIBRARY OF CONGRESS CATALOGING-IN-PUBLICATION DATA
Hein, Jon.
    Jump the shark : when good things go bad / Jon Hein.
        p.   cm.
    ISBN 0-525-94676-4 (acid-free paper)
    1. Popular culture—United States—Miscellanea. 2. Mass media—United
States—Miscellanea. 3. Errors—Miscellanea. 4. United States—Civilization—
1945—Miscellanea. I. Title.

E169.12 H44 2002
306'.0973—dc21   2002021253

Printed in the United States of America
Set in Helvetica Neue

This book is printed on acid-free paper. ♾

For Debbie, my true love, who inspires me daily
and keeps me from jumping.

For Rachel and Emily, my girls who make life worth living.

For Mom, Dad, and my brother, Kevin, who knew that watching
all that TV would eventually amount to something.

Contents

Sports 231
Hall of Fame 232

Politics 287
Hall of Fame 288

Introduction

It was my sophomore year at the University of Michigan in 1987, and I was living in a dump at 807 South Division with four other guys (not that there's anything wrong with that). We were trying to figure out what to do that night in Ann Arbor, and quickly realized we weren't getting off our asses . . . again. A few Schmidts later, the night's discussion started to meander to our usual topics . . . sports and women.

But on this particular night our chat went down a different path. With Nick at Nite setting the mood, we started to reminisce about something near and dear to us all . . . classic TV. What, we asked one another, was the precise moment that you knew it was all downhill for your favorite show?

Love Boat? Vicki. *Flintstones?* The Great Gazoo. *Happy Days?* "That's easy," said Sean Connolly, my perennial college roommate. "It was when Fonzie jumped the shark."

Silence. No explanation necessary. The phrase said it all.

"Jumping the Shark" refers to a moment on *Happy Days* when Fonzie, fully clad in his leather jacket while on water skis, literally jumps over a shark in the Pacific Ocean. Anyone who was watching knew that very instant that the show would never be the same. It also happened to be during a three-part vacation episode, another sure sign that the show was going to jump the shark anyway.

We spent the entire night searching our collective memories for the moments when TV shows jumped the shark, fiercely debating each and every one. On the days that followed that fateful evening, we would apply the phrase to practically anything.

"You see the game last night? The Wings jumped the shark."

"The history final? Yeah, I jumped."

"Roy brought who home? Definite shark bait."

Fast-forward one decade. I needed to learn HTML, the lingua franca of the Internet, to teach a class at PC & Mac Central. I was a partner in this computer-training firm, and the Web had fallen into my domain.

The only way to learn anything on a computer is to sit down and just do it, so I decided to build a website and boost my skills as I went. My college buddies were spread throughout this great land. What better way to stay in touch than to extend our Jump the Shark discussions to the Web?

I posted www.jumptheshark.com on December 24, 1997, with approximately two hundred television shows and votes from all my friends in low places. A few months later, the *Los Angeles Times* published an article about an April Fools' episode on *South Park* and wondered if the show had jumped the shark. The phrase hit a nerve, and now the site boasts millions of votes on over two thousand programs.

Everyone watches TV. It's the common denominator of today's culture . . . and we all have strong opinions on what comes across our screen. Jump the Shark is not just my take on the history of television. Passionate opinions from a variety of contributors shape and mold the site. I simply provide a forum to debate when programs take their fatal leap. Okay, I stick my two cents in on every show, but the site would not have succeeded without user votes and feedback.

Why does Jump the Shark work? For one, the votes aren't all "*Buffy* rules" and "*Emeril* sucks." There's thought and feeling behind each comment. We all grew up with these shows and feel betrayed when they jump. We'll also defend them to the death if we feel they never took the plunge.

The essence of Jump the Shark is this impassioned debate, and it's not just limited to television. Music, sports, movies, politics . . . all of pop culture is subject to strapping on the skis. We're just along for the ride.

I didn't expect millions of people to vote at Jump the Shark. I didn't expect the press to grab a hold of it. I didn't expect the television networks to follow the site. But I'm certainly glad that they did. It's nice to know that the folks behind *Pink Lady and Jeff* and Milli Vanilli are listening.

Which brings us to the tome you now hold in your hands. These pages will serve as your guide through the finest Jump the Shark moments in television, music, sports, politics, and celebrity life. Believe me, it was tough to narrow down the list.

I have the utmost respect for all of the entities covered within these pages. These are the opinions of one guy and his quirky website. Great debate is at the core of the shark (along with an old, chewed-up Louisiana license plate), so feel free to e-mail me at shark@jumptheshark.com if you agree, disagree, or wonder why *St. Elsewhere* had to end that way.

We all know that there's a moment . . . a defining moment when something in pop culture has reached its peak. That instant when you know from now on . . . it will never be the same.

Ready to jump in?

Jon Hein

jump the shark®

Television

"The man is absolutely right . . ."

—Garry Marshall on Jump the Shark
with Craig Kilborn on *The Late, Late Show*

A new cute kid suddenly moves in. Someone is pregnant or getting married, maybe both. The cast spontaneously breaks out into song. Next week's show is billed as A Very Special episode.

You feel it in your gut. You know that your favorite TV show has jumped the shark. Even the great Garry Marshall admitted he knew it when he sent Fonzie out on those water skis . . . *Happy Days* would never be the same.

There are a variety of ways that programs can jump, and I've narrowed some of them down into common themes or categories specific to television. Here's a brief sampling with a prime example included:

Same Character, Different Actor—Mike Evans and Damon Evans play Lionel on *The Jeffersons*

Death—Henry Blake's plane home goes down on *M*A*S*H*

Puberty—Kevin Arnold's voice cracks on *The Wonder Years*

Singing—Linda Lavin belts out a Broadway showstopper at Mel's Diner on *Alice*

Birth—Avery is born on *Murphy Brown*

Live—Tina takes down Colby at the *Survivor* finale

I Do—Jeannie and Master tie the knot on *I Dream of Jeannie*

They Did It—Niles and Daphne get together on *Frasier*

The Movie—Mulder and Scully *Fight the Future* on *The X-Files*

Moving—Meathead, Gloria, and Joey move out on *All in the Family*

Special Guest Star—Nancy Reagan just says no to the cast of *Diff'rent Strokes*

A Very Special . . . —This week, on A Very Special *Blossom* . . .

1

New Kid in Town—Seven moves in with the Bundys on *Married . . . with Children*

Hair Care—Keri Russell cuts her hair short on *Felicity*

Graduation—The class turns the tassel on *Beverly Hills 90210*

Exit Stage Left—Dr. Joel Fleischman leaves *Northern Exposure*

Color—No more black and white on *The Beverly Hillbillies*

Vacation—A trip to Italy for *Everybody Loves Raymond*

Each new season, we can count on television writers to try and pull off one of these plot devices, and few, if any, succeed.

Some jumps are more brutal than others. I couldn't possibly cover the two thousand plus shows that are currently posted at www.jumptheshark.com, but I've detailed my favorites in this chapter.

Hall of Fame—Television Wing

The most blatant shark jumps in television history (excluding Fonzie's leap, of course) are:

10. David and Maddie finally get together on *Moonlighting*
9. Bobby Ewing takes a shower on *Dallas*
8. Coy and Vance show up on *The Dukes of Hazzard*
7. Any show that casts our patron saint, Ted McGinley
6. The move from Milwaukee to L.A. on *Laverne & Shirley*
5. Cousin Oliver joins *The Brady Bunch*
4. Dick Sargent replaces Dick York as Darrin on *Bewitched*
3. Barney Fife leaves Mayberry on *The Andy Griffith Show*
2. Scrappy Doo joins his uncle on *Scooby Doo*
1. Mabel Buchman is born on *Mad About You*

All in the Family

1971–1979 Saturdays on CBS

jump the shark?

"Boy the way Glenn Miller played/Songs that made the Hit Parade . . ." *All in the Family* was the first sitcom that dealt with real-life issues in a brutally honest way and made us laugh (mostly awkwardly) at both the show and ourselves.

> **Meathead, Gloria, and little Joey move to California**

CBS aired a disclaimer prior to its premiere episode warning of the blunt humor Norman Lear was about to bestow upon us. Archie Bunker was an outspoken working-class bigot surrounded by people he despised. His "dingbat" wife, Edith, was the antithesis of Archie, but loved him just the same. They shared their house with their daughter, Gloria, who was married to the Polish unemployed liberal Michael, who Archie referred to as Meathead.

REVELATIONS

Jean Stapleton really doesn't talk like that? Here are some classic real-life surprises . . .

1 *Golden Girls'* Estelle Getty (Sophia) is younger than Bea Arthur (Dorothy).

2 Bob Barker's hair is gray

3 Mr. Rogers does all the voices in the "Land of Make-believe"

4 Olivia D'Abo (Karen) on *The Wonder Years* is British

5 Sam Malone wears a wig

You think it got testy on *Crossfire*? *All in the Family* was a breeding ground for opinionated characters who couldn't help but irritate Archie. Who could forget George, Louise, or Lionel Jefferson (before they moved on up to the East Side), Edith's cousin Maude, or that special smooch from Special Guest Star Sammy Davis Jr.?

All in the Family started slowly and needed a season to find its audience. CBS didn't support the show until it realized it had a groundbreaking hit on its hands. It survived the departure and subsequent spin-offs of *Maude* and *The Jeffersons*. However, when the Italian neighbors the Lorenzos moved in, we spotted a fin. This happened to coincide with the first time we heard Jean Stapleton's real voice during an awards acceptance speech.

The next season Mike shaved his mustache, Gloria announced she was pregnant, and baby Joey was born. Following his birth and an unforgettable diaper change, Archie got laid off

BIGOT EXPRESS

Who's a bigger bigot, Archie or . . . ?

1 Rush Limbaugh

2 Ralph Kramden

3 Tony Soprano

4 George Jefferson

5 Morton Downey, Jr.

MOVING ON UP?

Moving is a sure sign of jumping, especially if California is the destination. Fatal moves:

1 *Laverne & Shirley* head to L.A.
2 The Ricardos head to Connecticut
3 Mary Richards changes apartments
4 Oscar and Felix upgrade apartments
5 *The X-Files* set moves from Vancouver to L.A.

and the Bunkers took in Teresa as a boarder. The Stivics moved out, Archie bought the bar, Danielle Brisebois joined the cast as Archie's long-lost niece Stephanie, and the shark was jumped. This was also the season that Edith almost got raped.

As the focus shifted to the bar (later *Archie Bunker's Place*), we found ourselves longing for the Stivics to return from California and stir things up with Archie. Unfortunately, "those were the days."

When did

The Andy Griffith Show

1960–1968 Mondays on CBS

jump the shark?

The Andy Griffith Show was set in the perfect southern town of Mayberry and began with a leisurely stroll down to the fishin' hole, whistlin' that memorable theme. Sheriff Andy kept the peace with help from his cousin, faithful deputy Barney Fife, while Aunt Bee and his son, Opie, were at home.

Barney Fife decides to leave town.

GROWIN' UP

Ron Howard will always be Opie in our eyes. Our favorite childhood stars:

1 Kristy McNichol
2 Rodney Allen Rippey
3 Adam Rich
4 Keisha Knight Pulliam
5 Butch Patrick

The first five seasons in Mayberry were chock filled with aw shucks, golly gee episodes. Who can forget Howard's trip to the Caribbean, the bowling and baseball games, anything involving Aunt Bee and a pie, and getting to know Opie, Otis, and even Gomer Pyle? Mayberry dealt with hula hoops and miniskirts, hippies and NASA, and of course, the misadventures of Deputy Barney Fife.

At the end of season five, Don Knotts's contract was up and he had the opportunity to make film classics like *The Ghost and Mr. Chicken.* The five-time Emmy winner and counter to Andy's low-key personality decided it was time to leave Mayberry. When Barney Fife departed the laughs went with him, and *The Andy Griffith Show* was never the same.

Gomer's brother Goober acquired a more prominent role, Helen Crump became more of a nag, and Opie joined a rock 'n' roll band. Jack Burns's turn as Deputy Warren Ferguson left us clamoring for Barney when the show went to color in its sixth season. Ironically, Don Knotts would experience that very same feeling when he replaced the Ropers on *Three's Company* as Mr. Furley.

Barney returned to Mayberry later in a special guest appearance, but the damage was done. If you look closely at the fishin' hole, you'll see a fin slowly swimming away.

When did
The Beverly Hillbillies

1962–1971 Wednesdays on CBS

jump the shark?

"Come and listen to a story 'bout a man named Jed . . ."

This classic fish-out-of-water story happened in the town of Beverly and we couldn't get

It went from black and white to color.

enough of it. The Clampetts hailed from the Ozarks and struck it rich when an oil well sprouted in their front yard. Black gold. Texas tea. Jed, Granny, Jethro, and Elly May loaded up their truck, moved to Beverly, put a few million into Drysdale's Commerce Bank, and bought the mansion next door to Mr. Drysdale.

As Drysdale and his assistant Jane Hathaway tried to keep tabs on their most valued clients, wacky hijinks ensued.

The Beverly Hillbillies was unpretentious, silly, and unbelievably popular. Society didn't get the Clampetts, and the Clampetts certainly didn't get society, but it didn't matter. The shark warning signs went up in the third season when the Drysdales got the Clampetts involved with a movie studio. Jethro tried to be a playboy, Elly May dated a movie star, and Granny kept on yelling "Jed!"

However, when we started seeing the Clampetts in color instead of black and white, we knew the shark had been jumped. The Clampetts just got stupider, as did the plots, and that innocent intrigue wasn't there anymore. Jed was now singing (seriously), Jethro had gone beyond Hollywood, and Granny was still yelling "Jed!" Even Pat Boone put in a special guest star appearance as himself.

We can thank the *Beverly Hillbillies* for rural classics such as *Green Acres* and *Petticoat Junction.* Unfortunately, all the money in the world couldn't stop the shark from visiting the Clampetts. Y'all come back now, you hear?

Beverly Hills 90210

1990–2000 Wednesdays on FOX

jump the shark?

The zip code of the nineties was *90210* . . . not bad for a show that most "experts" figured would last only a few episodes. This Spelling gang proved that, like their hangout the Peach Pit, they could keep it going way after dark.

Brenda goes abroad.

Beverly Hills 90210 was a lethal combination of good-looking young (but not quite teenager) actors, California sun, a creator named Star, and an Executive Producer (plus a so-called actress) named Spelling. The show revolved around the Walsh family, who had just moved from Minneapolis. Brandon and Brenda were midwestern kids trying to fit in at West Beverly Hills High . . . and fit in they did.

The original *90210* alumni, including Steve, Kelly, Dylan, Donna, Andrea, and David, got advice at "Casa Walsh" from Brandon and Brenda's parents. In later years, Peach Pit owner Nat took over the mentor role (and actor Joe E. Tata finally made the opening credits) when Mom and Pop Walsh moved to Japan—leaving the house to Brandon, Steve, and vampy cousin Valerie, as well as a host of quickly made and fast-forgotten college friends. Over the decade-long run, we saw a host of interchangeable beautiful young actors literally come and go with problems that grew increasingly "serious." Who could forget Emily trashing the float, Andrea's balding husband Jesse, the hit on Dylan's wife, and Donna and Val's singing, abusive boyfriend Ray!

We spotted a fin when Dylan inherited millions from his mysterious, and now dead, father and David hit puberty and began to rap. When the original cast graduated from high school ("Donna Martin graduates!" is still ringing in our

---

GOING POSTAL

We love when shows somehow involve the U.S. Mail. Our favorites:

1 02134 (*Zoom*)
2 Cliff Clavin (*Cheers*)
3 Newman (*Seinfeld*)
4 Speedy Delivery (*Mister Rogers' Neighborhood*)
5 Mailbox (*Blue's Clues*)

EXIT . . . STAGE LEFT

Shannen Doherty proved it doesn't have to be old to be a classic exit. Our faves:

1 Barney Fife
2 Dr. Joel Fleischmann
3 Dr. Doug Ross
4 Diane Chambers
5 Richie Cunningham
6 Flo
7 Vinnie Barbarino
8 Chrissy Snow
9 Jill Munroe
10 Bob Vila

BYE-BYE BEVERLY HIGH

The College Years . . . a sure sign of jumping the shark. Our favorite institutions of lower learning:

1 Carver High—*The White Shadow*
2 Sunnydale High—*Buffy the Vampire Slayer*
3 JFK Junior High—*Saved By the Bell*
4 Jefferson High—*Happy Days*
5 Eastland Academy—*The Facts of Life*

ears) and attended California U., we sensed the leap to come.

Brenda's exit to study acting abroad (good advice, Shannen) signaled the start of a *90210* exodus, and the show had finally jumped the shark. Cousin Val had Brenda's bite, and she was easier to hate because we had no loyalty to her. Still Kelly Kapowski—even with new "assets"—couldn't fill Shannen's shoes. All of the Walshes would find greener pastures elsewhere, Dylan (Luke Perry) would leave searching for a film career, only to (surprise!) return three years later. Even newcomer-turned-regular Clare put away her handcuffs and jumped ship in '97. Brandon and Kelly sort of got married, Donna's quest to remain a virgin continued (unsuccessfully, in the end), and classics like the Peach Pit After Dark became prominent features of the show.

90210 paved the path for not only *Melrose Place* and *Models, Inc.,* but also for the film careers of Luke Perry and Jason Priestley and a talk show for Gabrielle Carteris. Thank you, Beverly Hills—quite a legacy.

When did

Bewitched

1964–1972 Thursdays on ABC

jump the shark?

Dick Sargent replaces Dick York as Darrin Stephens . . . affectionately known as the Dick switch.

"Bewitched . . . Bewitched . . . You've got me under your spell." Yes, there *were* lyrics to that jazzy opening theme, but the creators of this witch tale were wise enough to spike them.

Bewitched centered around the life of Samantha Stephens, played by the really-hot-at-the-time Elizabeth Montgomery. Sam attempted to abandon her witchcraft in order to fit in at home with husband, Darrin, whom she wed in the first episode.

YOU LOOK . . . DIFFERENT

A classic way to jump the shark is to replace the same character with a different actor.

1 Becky (*Roseanne*)
2 Marilyn (*The Munsters*)
3 Lionel (*The Jeffersons*)
4 Chris (*The Partridge Family*)
5 Vivian (*The Fresh Prince of Bel-Air*)
6 Miss Ellie (*Dallas*)
7 Quentin (*Grace Under Fire*)
8 Claire (*My Wife and Kids*)
9 John-Boy (*The Waltons*)
10 Fallon (*Dynasty*)

The rigors of domestic life presented Sam with little else to do than twitch her nose and stir up trouble while trying to solve family problems. Sam's parents—Endora and Maurice—Uncle Arthur, and Aunt Clara could not fathom why she stopped using her powers and chose to marry Durwood. Frankly, neither could we. Ad agency boss Larry Tate and his wife, Louise, also kept things interesting for the Stephenses.

The writing was on the wall for a jump when Tabitha was born during the second season, but the wacky comedy didn't take itself too seriously yet. At the beginning of season four, Dick Sargent was brought in to replace Dick York, with no acknowledgment. Granted, they had a great excuse—she's a witch, after all.

Following the Dick switch, Sam began to portray her evil cousin Serena. Esmeralda, who was also a witch, was brought in as a housekeeper. The Stephenses had a second child, Adam, who looked nothing like Dick York *or* Dick Sargent. More of the focus shifted to Tabitha, and who could forget the calls to Dr. Bombay.

Bewitched had gone from chronicling an intriguing couple with occasional visitors to a wacky family of four with historical figures often dropping by. No Dick could have prevented the show from taking its fatal leap over the shark.

SEASON OF THE WITCH

Classic witchcraft:

1 *Charmed*
2 *Sabrina*
3 *Friday the 13th*
4 *H.R. Pufnstuf*
5 *Tabitha*

When did
The Brady Bunch
1969–1974 Fridays on ABC

jump the shark?

"Here's the story . . ." There were only five seasons of *The Brady Bunch,* but it feels like the longest running show in the history of television. Syndication brought this crew into our homes repeatedly, and brainwashed us into loving the Bradys.

> **Cousin Oliver joins the bunch and throws its tic-tac-toe symmetry completely out of whack.**

Mike Brady was busy with three boys of his own when he met Carol, who was busy with three very lovely girls. Mix in Ann B. Davis as Alice the housekeeper and a hideously de-

signed home by a "professional" architect (one bathroom for six kids), and you've got the Brady Bunch!

The Brady Bunch managed to sidestep the shark as the kids matured ("When it's time to change . . .") in memorable ways. Whether it was Cindy's lisp or the sudden disappearance of Tiger, too much Sam the Butcher or too little Jan without her glasses, the show was masterfully adept at shark avoidance.

Plenty of Special Guest Stars happened to drop by the Brady home portraying themselves, including Joe Namath, Don Drysdale, Davy Jones, and of course, Desi Arnaz, Jr. Their involvement typically revolved around a prom, big game, or some other major event at F, F, F-I-L, L, L, L-M-O,O,O, O-R-E, Fillmore Junior High. Still, there was nary a fin to be found.

The Brady musical careers were prime shark bait. Alice might have been the only one in the house who didn't want to have a professional singing career. It started with the kids belting out the opening theme and grew like a fungus from there. The Silver Platters. Johnny

BRADY HAIR
The Bradys battled the shark at every turn, even at the hairdresser:
1 Mike's perm
2 Cindy's braids
3 Carol's mullet
4 Alice's rock
5 Greg's afro

Bravo. Cindy's "Good Ship Lollipop." Carol's holiday tunes. If you look closely, you can see Robert Reed holding his, uh, ears in the back of the kitchen.

Nothing could top a Brady vacation. The trip to Hawaii featured Greg's surfing accident, taboo (!), and Special Guest Star Vincent Price. Who could forget the calls of "Bobby! Cindy!" when they were lost in the Grand Canyon? And of course, they're still looking for Mike's architecture plans at the King's Island amusement park. Somehow, this wacky sextet managed to pull it off every time.

Evil twins and stolen playbooks, exploding volcanoes and Greg knocking the egg off the cone, the Bradys still marched on. This show was so camp that nothing could make it jump the shark. Enter Cousin Oliver.

In an attempt to up the cute factor as Bobby and Cindy matured, Robbie Rist was brought in to play Cousin Oliver. Even the Bradys couldn't escape the plight of the most surefire way to jump the shark—a young relative with unexplained origins.

The Bradys continued to march on with variety shows, stage plays, TV reunion movies, successful theatrical releases, and more. They truly became "America's Family" . . . but we'll never accept Oliver as part of the family picture.

ALL IN THE FAMILY

Our favorite relatives who suddenly appeared on the scene to sink a show:

1 Roger (Ted McGinley) on *Happy Days*
2 Jeremy (Ralph Macchio) on *Eight Is Enough*
3 Scrappy Doo on *Scooby Doo*
4 Dawn on *Buffy the Vampire Slayer*
5 Olivia on *The Cosby Show*
6 Vicki on *The Love Boat*
7 Seven on *Married . . . with Children*
8 Sam on *Diff'rent Strokes*
9 Stephanie on *All in the Family*
10 Albert on *Little House on the Prairie*

BELT IT OUT

The Brady kids aren't the only ones who sang their own theme song:

1 *Walker, Texas Ranger* (Chuck Norris)
2 *The Partridge Family* (David Cassidy)
3 *Fat Albert and the Cosby Kids* (Bill Cosby)
4 *Happy Days* (Anson Williams)
5 *T.J. Hooker* (William Shatner)

Buffy the Vampire Slayer

1997– Tuesdays on UPN

jump the shark?

Riley and the Initiative.

Buffy saved the world . . . a lot.

Thanks to Joss Whedon, *Buffy* is a rare gem that has proved to be better on the small screen than it was on the large one. Much better. The show manages to deftly mix comedy and horror with much success and its tongue firmly planted in cheeks and other orifices.

Buffy began when she moved to Sunnydale with her mom, Joyce. She had a fresh start in high school before hell literally broke loose. Along with pals Willow, Xander, and Cordelia, Buffy is charged with protecting everyone from the vampires and other demons who emerge from the Hellmouth, as librarian Rupert Giles faithfully watches on. At the end of the first season, Buffy took care of the Master, died, and was revived by Xander, kicking off what would become a pattern of strange behavior.

Buffy managed to survive Spike and Drusilla, Angel's death, rebirth, and exile to L.A., Oz getting written off and on and off, Faith, and the snake of a Mayor, all within its first few seasons. *Buffy* creators aren't afraid to tempt the shark in different ways, and succeeded early on in steering clear of the fin. But we spotted shark bait when the Scooby gang graduated high school at the end of the third season.

Trying to recover from losing Angel, Buffy enters college and meets up with Riley and the Initiative. This mysterious underground lab beneath the college streets catapulted the Slayer right over the shark. Spike's chip, Willow ditch-

---

THREE IS A MAGIC NUMBER

Like Sarah Michelle, the shark loves celebs with three names:

1 Courtney Thorne-Smith
2 Jennifer Love Hewitt
3 David Ogden Stiers
4 Rowdy Roddy Piper
5 Sarah Jessica Parker
6 Soleil Moon Frye
7 Tiffani Amber Thiessen
8 James Earl Jones
9 Anthony Michael Hall
10 Rodney Allen Rippey

PASS THE POPCORN

Buffy is one of the best in translating from the movies to a hit TV show. These aren't:

1 *Delta House*
2 *Clueless*
3 *Stir Crazy*
4 *Parenthood*
5 *Foul Play*

ing Oz and his wolfman side for Tara (not that there's anything wrong with that), and Faith's body switch were too much for us to handle.

Our fears were confirmed the following season when, like Ralph Macchio on *Eight Is Enough,* Buffy's mysterious sister, Dawn, showed up. Granted, there have been some brilliantly written episodes since the destruction of the Initiative. Buffy has sung, danced, died, and come back again. But regardless of the power it may possess and its ability to repeatedly avoid the shark, no program could survive a move to UPN anyway.

When did

Cheers

1982–1993 Thursdays on NBC

jump the shark?

Who wouldn't want to be in the bar where everybody knows your name (and they're always glad you came)? *Cheers* defined must-see TV during the eighties.

> **Exit Diane Chambers . . . enter Rebecca Howe.**

The show was billed as a comedy about hanging out at a sports bar with a washed up Red Sox pitcher and his buddies. Few people tuned in the first season to follow the exploits of Sam, Diane, Coach, Norm, Cliff, and Carla, but that changed in a hurry.

Bar events included classic visits from Carla's ex Nick Tortelli and his wife Loretta, Al (the old guy in the back of the bar), Paul (Cliff and Norm's bar buddy), Andy Andy, Gary, Cliff's mother, and many others.

Cheers had an uncanny knack for bringing in new characters that were even more interesting than the ones they replaced. Coach (Nicholas Colasanto) died after the third season, and Woody was successfully brought in behind the bar. Diane fell hard for Frasier Crane, a pompous psychologist who, following a memorable snipe

VISITING BEACON HILL

The Bull & Finch, the real *Cheers* bar, is a huge tourist stop. Other attractions:

1 Tom's Diner—*Seinfeld*
2 The Brady House—*The Brady Bunch*
3 Nicollet Mall—*Mary Tyler Moore*
4 1049 Park Avenue—*The Odd Couple*
5 Pacific Princess—*The Love Boat*

hunt, ended up becoming a bar regular.

The sexual tension between Sam and Diane coupled with the situations involving the gang was a winning combination. The show managed to thrive after Sam and Diane finally

got together, an action that sends many shows pole-vaulting right over the shark. Although *Cheers* withstood the death of Coach, it could not survive the fifth season when Diane chose to finish her novel.

Sam sailed around the world and returned to find Rebecca running the bar. Suddenly there were too many competitions with nearby Gary's Oldtown Tavern. Robin Colcord bought the bar, Sam became an employee and was no longer "cool," Lilith and Frasier became the focus, and Carla married Eddie Lebec.

After its final episode, the regulars appeared to be totally smashed on *The Tonight Show*, confirming that *Cheers'* great run was over and the shark had moved on to its next victim.

The Cosby Show

1984–1992 Thursdays on NBC

jump the shark?

We all loved Bill Cosby's stand-up when he told stories of life with Camille and his children ("Stop touching me!"). In the mid-eighties, he parlayed those experiences into *The Cosby Show* and built a monster hit while establishing Thursday night comedy for NBC.

> **Rudy hits puberty and cute little Olivia joins the Huxtable clan.**

The Cosby Show centered around the Huxtable family, who lived in a Brooklyn brownstone. Cliff and Clair helped Sondra,

Denise, Theo, Vanessa, and Rudy navigate the trials and tribulations of eighties life.

Cliff and Clair's parents were frequent visitors, and Special Guest Stars like Stevie Wonder, Dick Vitale, and a variety of jazz musicians stopped by the Huxtables' pad. And there was never a shortage of Hillman references or funky sweaters for Cliff to wear.

The kids, and the series, began to show their age as the years went by. Sondra went from being Chuck Cunningham to having a prominent role on the show. Denise went off to college and encountered *A Different World*. Theo attempted all sorts of hair care statements, failing each time, but matured in his own way. Vanessa grew into her own talk show. Adorable little Rudy wasn't so lucky.

Realizing that puberty was sucking the cute factor right out of their child star, the writers brought in Raven-Symone as Olivia. Sondra had married Olivia's father, Elvin, and borne twins named Winnie and Nelson (not after the Rockefellers). The opening theme song changed once

THURSDAYS AT 8

The Cosby Show built Thursday nights for NBC. Before the Huxtables moved in, you'd find:

1 *Gimme a Break* (1983)

2 *Fame* (1982)

3 *Harper Valley* (1981)

4 *Games People Play* (1980)

5 *Buck Rogers in the 25th Century* (1979)

again, and the impromptu singing jams devolved into horribly staged shows for the grandparents. The family had outgrown the brownstone, and Cliff would never again find the success he had had with these Cosby kids. Hey, hey, hey . . .

When did Dallas

1978–1991 Fridays on CBS

jump the shark?

"Who shot J.R.?" Even if you never tuned in to find out what was going on at the Southfork ranch, you couldn't help but wonder who put a bullet into Major Nelson on this classic evening soap.

Dallas brought the primetime soap opera back to the airwaves in the eighties with its unscrupulous characters, piles of money, battles over power, and plenty of sex to go around.

> **Bobby Ewing appears in the shower and the seventh season was just a dream.**

Jock Ewing, an oil magnate who was married to Miss Ellie, had three boys of his own. The eldest, J.R., was utter scum and married to Sue Ellen. Bobby, the antithesis of J.R., was married to Pam, daughter of Jock's rival Digger Barnes. Gary was literally nuts, so they spun him off into *Knots Landing*. His blond daughter, Lucy, stuck around Southfork and never met a man she didn't like.

The first few seasons of Dallas featured everyone trying to screw someone at the ranch. Cliff Barnes kept searching for ways to bring down the Ewings, as J.R. sunk lower and lower each week—even trying to force Sue Ellen into rehab for alcoholism. At the start of the fourth season, Dallas was at its peak in popularity and we all tuned in to find out that Kristin was the one who pulled the trigger. As Dan Patrick would say, you could not stop J.R. Ewing . . . you could only hope to contain him.

As the marriages, divorces, and remarriages began to pile up, we sensed a jump coming soon. Following Jock's death, Miss Ellie married Clayton Farlow, cousin Jamie teamed up with Cliff Barnes, and Bobby Ewing was killed in a hit-and-run accident. But the show was slipping, and the creators realized they needed to bring Bobby back.

In traditional soap opera fashion, the 1986 season opened with Bobby in the shower, alive and well. Turns out the entire season was simply a dream of Pam's. Even for a soap, this was one of the most blatant shark jumps in the history of television. "Let's just forget about last year and move on?" This was an insult to the intelligence of the viewing population, even those who watched Dallas religiously.

Donna Reed was portraying Miss Ellie, the supposed ghost of Jock Ewing was on the scene, and J.R. was off looking for a blonde who lived in a bottle. Mention the phrase "shower scene" and some naturally think of the film *Psycho*. But even Hitchcock could not envision the horror of Bobby's return and the subsequent leap of this classic soap.

When did Dawson's Creek

1998– Wednesdays on the WB

jump the shark?

This is the school district I want my kids in, because Dawson, Joey, Pacey, and crew speak better than most Nobel laureates do. Emphatically.

> **Dawson and Joey kiss . . . again.**

Dawson's Creek is a teen soap that takes place in Massachusetts, where we follow the lives of Dawson, the would-be filmmaker; his best friend and former tomboy, Joey; and Pacey, whose vocabulary I'm still trying to understand. Sex and thesauri are always on hand.

Dawson and Joey . . . will they or won't they? *Dawson's Creek* began with the childhood friends at the height of their puberty and Dawson falling for, and getting dumped by, Jen. By the second season, Dawson and Joey had kissed and forgotten about everyone else in Capeside. Pacey, Andie, and Jack began to figure into the mix and jealousy reared its beautiful (nothing is ugly on *Dawson's Creek*) head.

The third season brought some shark sightings as Dawson got together with Eve, Pacey hooked up with Joey, and Jack planted his first same-sex kiss. But the fourth season lifted the Creek over the shark as the cast grad-

TAKE ME TO THE RIVER

Take a dip:

1 *Voyage to the Bottom of the Sea*
2 *Seaquest DSV*
3 *Sea Hunt*
4 *Sigmund and the Sea Monsters*
5 *China Beach*

WHAT'S IN A NAME?

Pacey's a guy. Joey's a girl. Traditional?

1 Pat (*Saturday Night Live*)
2 Monroe (*Too Close for Comfort*)
3 ALF (*Alf*)
4 Gazoo (*The Flintstones*)
5 Gonzo (*The Muppet Show*)

18

uated high school, Jack planted another same-sex kiss, and Dawson and Joey smooched once more.

In a nutshell, Joey likes Dawson, Dawson likes Jen, Jen dumps Dawson, Dawson likes Joey, Jen still likes Dawson, Joey dumps Dawson, Dawson looks for some new girls, Joey likes Dawson *again*. Repeat till fade.

When did The Dick Van Dyke Show

1961–1966 Wednesdays on CBS

jump the shark?

> **Rob steps around the ottoman during the opening theme instead of tumbling over it.**

DVD and MTM make a lethal comedic combination. Mix in some great writing, Morey Amsterdam, and Rose Marie, and you've got one of the best family comedies of all time.

The pilot, "Head of the Family," began the chronicle of the life of television writer Rob Petrie. Rob would encounter strange situations at his suburban home with his wife, Laura, or at his writing job for *The Alan Brady Show* with Buddy, Sally, and their boss Mel Cooley. Rob would always find himself in impossible predicaments that could miraculously resolve themselves within the half-hour.

Some of the most memorable episodes of *The Dick Van Dyke Show* featured flashbacks, a technique not often used at the time and a serious form of shark bait. Rob's marriage proposal and late arrival to his own wedding, Rob and Laura's subsequent honeymoon, and Rob's fear that he brought home the wrong baby were all flashbacks, but they were done well.

Other mystifying aspects of *The Dick Van Dyke Show* included comedy writers who weren't particularly funny, Laura's jealousy over various women cast on *The Alan Brady Show,* Rob hardly ever getting jealous of Laura, and

---

UNREALITY TELEVISION

Like *The Alan Brady Show,* these fake shows aired within real ones:

1 *Tool Time*

2 *FYI News Network*

3 *The Six O'clock News on WJM-TV*

4 *Krusty the Klown*

5 *The Larry Sanders Show*

the fact that Mel Cooley looked just like Mr. Slate of *The Flintstones* and Mr. Cogswell of *The Jetsons.*

The show eventually jumped when during the classic "Honey, I'm home" opening, clumsy Rob smartens up and sidesteps the ottoman he had always tipped over. Use this revised opening as a signal to change the channel or you're taking your chances on a Rose Marie songfest.

But we're admittedly nitpicking here . . . *The Dick Van Dyke Show* was classic comedy at its best.

When did
Diff'rent Strokes
1978–1986 Wednesdays on NBC

jump the shark?

"Watch-oo talkin' 'bout, Willis?" This signature line made Gary Coleman more than just a kid from left field.

Diff'rent Strokes began with the rich, white Philip Drummond and his daughter, Kimberly, adopting two black orphans, Willis and Arnold. Mr. Drummond's wife had passed on, so Edna Garrett (yes, *that* Mrs. Garrett) took care of their house.

Mr. Drummond remarries and little red-haired Sam joins the cast.

The show dealt with racial issues in a traditional sitcom setting, but what set it apart was Gary Coleman. In the early episodes, his cute factor was sky high and people tuned in each week just to see what would be coming out of little Arnold's mouth.

The show survived the early departure of Mrs. Garrett (off to Eastland Academy to take care of some girls) and some Very Special episodes that

dealt with issues from child molestation to drug usage. The cast didn't exactly pay attention to the latter episode.

We were on alert when a plethora of Special Guest Stars dropped by the Drummond household, including but not limited to Nancy Reagan, Muhammad Ali, and Mr. T. Janet Jackson, who visited *Good Times* in her early days, and Kim Fields (Tootie), stopped by to see Willis and Arnold from time to time. But as puberty began to rear its ugly head (actually three of them), the urge to add a new cute kid could not be resisted. To add insult to injury, Mr. Drummond decided to marry Maggie McKinney and adopt her young son Sam, portrayed by Danny Cooksey.

The next season, Maggie fell victim to our "Same Character, Different Actor" category as Mary Ann Mobley replaced Dixie Carter. In other words, *Diff'rent Strokes* acknowledged their leap over the shark. But then again, the world don't move to the beat of just one drum.

The Drew Carey Show

1995– Mondays on ABC

jump the shark?

Drew is a funny man. Drew is an ABC man. Drew is a wealthy man. If only he wouldn't sing so damn much on his show.

The Drew Carey Show is anything but a typical sitcom. The show takes place in the offices of Winfred-Louder, a Cleveland department store where Drew and his office nemesis Mimi (the fat one with the makeup . . . no, not Drew) work. Drew is "the" single guy who likes to hang at the Warsaw with Oswald, Lewis, and the prerequisite sexual tension pal, Kate.

> **Drew and crew belt out "Cleveland Rocks."**

The first season opened with "Moon over Parma" as its theme and we familiarized ourselves with the quirks of the cast. Mimi never got over Drew's choice of Kate to work the makeup counter, and tormented him every chance she could as Mr. Bell's personal assistant.

Shark warning signs appeared as early as the second season as the store got sold, Drew and Lisa moved in together, and the theme song changed to "Five O'Clock World." The jump was averted as Drew and Lisa broke up and Mr. Wick proved to be a capable replacement as Drew's boss.

"Cleveland Rocks" was the opening theme for the third season, and the shark was jumped. Drew had always spent time reminding us how fond he was of his hometown, inundating viewers with references to Cleveland and the surrounding suburbs. The theme simply pushed it over the top.

Drew has since been married and dead on the show a number of times. Kate and Drew "did it." Every April Fool's Day features a "What's Wrong with This?" episode with mistakes aplenty. There have been live episodes and mu-

---

OPENING NUMBERS

Cleveland doesn't rock, but these do:

1 *The Rockford Files*
2 *S.W.A.T.*
3 *Barney Miller*
4 *Night Court*
5 *Hill Street Blues*
6 *The Greatest American Hero*
7 *Monday Night Football* (the original)
8 *The Jeffersons*
9 Any theme not written by Alan Thicke
10 Any theme written by Mike Post

BESPECTACLED

Future's so bright . . .

1 Sergeant Bilko
2 Jan Brady
3 Radar O'Reilly
4 Anne Robinson
5 Howard Stern

sical numbers, but somehow Drew keeps on having a good time—despite having starred in *Gepetto*. After the third season, the episodes became less creative and more gimmicky. At the rate they're going, there may soon be an episode with Drew in a leather jacket on water skis . . .

When did

The Dukes of Hazzard

1979–1985 Fridays on CBS

jump the shark?

"Just some good ol' boys . . . never meanin' no harm . . ." That was until the boys held out and CBS gave us replacement Dukes. But I'm jumping ahead.

The Dukes of Hazzard chronicled the travails of the Duke cousins, Bo and Luke. Boss Hogg, who owned the town, couldn't stand those Duke boys messin'

Coy and Vance Duke move to Hazzard County for a season.

up his plans, so he charged sheriff Rosco P. Coltrane and his deputy Enos to stop those Dukes. Boss Hogg wasn't crazy about the Dukes' Uncle Jesse, but we were all crazy for their lil' cousin, Daisy Duke.

Each show opened with Waylon Jennings's narration and his belting out the classic opening theme. The true star of Hazzard County was the General Lee, an Orange Dodge the Dukes adorned with a confederate flag on its roof and an "01" on either door.

The episodes from the first four seasons went something like this: The Dukes race the General Lee, Boss Hogg is scheming, Daisy overhears the scheme and tips off the boys, the boys almost get caught, Rosco and Enos foul up, Uncle Jesse points the Dukes in the right direction, the General Lee jumps something, and Boss Hogg is foiled again. Mix in some Waylon and you've got the most popular show on television during its run.

In the fifth season, the show made a fateful jump with new cousins Coy and Vance Duke. These Duke boys were brought in when the actors portraying Bo and Luke, Tom Wopat and John Schneider, walked out during a contract dispute over merchandising royalties. Despite being dead ringers for the original Dukes, who returned the next season after their holdout, Coy and Vance were the death knell for this show. Soon thereafter came episodes featuring Waylon Jennings as himself, the Dukes as Hollywood stunt car drivers, and aliens in Hazzard County! A self-titled spin-off for Enos proved beyond any doubt that the shark had indeed been jumped.

ER

1994– Thursdays on NBC

jump the shark?

Michael Crichton got bored with dinosaurs and decided to write a show based on his experiences as a med student. The end result was *ER*.

> **Dr. Doug Ross leaves Cook County for good.**

ER hit the ground running as it followed the lives of its doctors and residents, and literally never slowed down. Its pilot, "24," is one of the best ever made and can be seen in syndication on several networks late each night.

DOCTOR, DOCTOR

Our favorite doctors:

1 Dr. Kildare
2 Dr. Who
3 Dr. Shrinker
4 Dr. Katz, Professional Therapist
5 Dr. Quinn, Medicine Woman

We loved to watch doctors Greene, Benton, Carter, Ross, and Lewis, and Nurse Hathaway rush about the ER, weaving their relationships and saving patients' lives. The cast changed as time went on, but the level of drama never wavered.

ER survived the exit of Dr. Lewis, the divorce of Dr. Greene, the maturation of Carter the perennial medical student, the many moods of Dr. Benton, and the womanizing of Dr. Ross. We went on alert when the over-hyped live episode occurred at the start of the fourth season, and things started to get just plain weird from then on.

Chief of Staff Dr. Morgenstern resigned and was replaced by the nasty Dr. Romano. Benton, still a surgical resident, now cared for a deaf baby while hooking up with Dr. Corday. And everyone on the floor seemed to either acquire a life-threatening condition or be assaulted by a whacked patient somewhere along the line.

ABBREVIATED STAYS

Love those short titles:

1 CSI
2 ALF
3 V
4 WIOU
5 E/R (a medical comedy)
6 M*A*S*H
7 CHiPs
8 Cops
9 V.I.P.
10 UFO

The show finally took its leap when Dr. Doug Ross said goodbye to Carol Hathaway and the rest of the ER at the end of the fourth season. A torn Carol decided to stay, and it got really messy in the ER. Lucy Knight was killed by a crazy patient, Carter's drug addiction was revealed, Kerry Weaver decided to play all fields (not that there's anything wrong with that). To top it all off, Sally Field was a Special Guest Star not once, but twice, during the same season. Get me to the ER, stat!

When did The Facts of Life

1979–1988 Wednesdays on NBC

jump the shark?

"You take the good, you take the bad, you take them both and there you have . . ." this tale of four young ladies and their perilous journey through food, love, and Eastland.

> **The girls graduate Eastland and open the bakeshop Edna's Edibles.**

The Facts of Life was a *Diff'rent Strokes* spin-off with Mrs. Garrett and that infamous Alan Thicke opening theme. Mrs. G had a bunch of girls, including Molly Ringwald, to care for during the first season of the show.

By the time the second season rolled around, Mrs. G went from house-master to school dietitian and the girls were whittled down to a group of four: rich and spoiled Blair, loud and large Natalie, perky and perky Tootie, and newcomer tough street kid Jo. This famous foursome would grow up and share their journey through the Eastland school for young women.

HIGHER EDUCATION
Fine academic television institutions of learning:
1 Beverly Hills High—*90210*
2 Sunnydale High—*Buffy the Vampire Slayer*
3 Fillmore Junior High—*The Brady Bunch*
4 *Degrassi Junior High*
5 Buchanan High—*Welcome Back, Kotter*
6 Jefferson High—*Happy Days*
7 John Adams High—*Boy Meets World*
8 JFK Junior High—*Saved by the Bell*
9 Riverdale High—*Sabrina*
10 Carver High—*The White Shadow*

To its credit, *The Facts of Life* was not afraid to take on tough issues like abortion, adoption, and Arnold from *Diff'rent Strokes*. It tried to force stardom upon Geri Jewell, a comedienne with cerebral palsy who Blair was ashamed to have as a cousin. Unfortunately, Geri had another problem . . . she just wasn't funny.

The show jumped during its fifth season, when the girls graduated and Mrs. G opened Edna's Edibles. Puberty had run its course and flashback episodes began to appear more regularly. In an effort to jump back, Edna's Edibles was burned to the ground, and George Clooney joined the cast as George the builder, and the bakeshop became a boutique. It didn't help.

The following season, Mrs. Garrett married a doctor and moved to Africa, and her sister Beverly Ann (played by Cloris Leachman) moved in with the girls. Nurse Diesel replacing Mrs. G? We can't make up stuff as good as this.

When did

Family Ties

1982–1989 Thursdays on NBC

jump the shark?

"What would we do, baby, without us?" The Keatons kept us cozy during the eighties, but boy did they know how to jump the shark.

Andrew Keaton is born.

Family Ties revolved around the household of sixties children Steven, who ran a public TV station, and his architect wife Elyse. Their Reaganite son Alex P., ditzy/artsy daughter Mallory, and offensive tackle Jennifer rounded out the brood.

The family humorously debated the generation gap, with next door neighbor Skippy stopping by to add his two cents and hit on Mallory. *Family Ties* took heavy issues dead on as Alex got hooked on diet pills, mourned the accidental death of a friend, and lost Tracy Pollan for Courteney Cox. Any relative who stopped by the Keatons' typically turned out to be a molester, felon, drunk, or addict of some sort. Who could forget Tom Hanks as Uncle Ned the embezzler, and later the serious drunk?

We spotted the fin as puberty began to do its damage to all the children, especially Jennifer. By this point, Skippy had learned he was adopted, Steven and Elyse were propositioned, and Alex was graduating high school. Following a camping trip at the start of the third season, Elyse announced she was pregnant, and we were close to the fatal jump.

Once Andrew Keaton was born, the show was never the same. The next season started with *Family Ties Vacation,* a two-hour disaster of a trip to England. Soon thereafter, Mallory's new boyfriend arrived on the scene (Yo, Nick), Alex hooked up with Ellen, and we heard Billy Vera's "At This Moment" played during the next thirty-seven shows. Andrew replaced Jennifer as the cute Keaton, so she decided to become a musician (a real-life quest she pursues to this day).

Ellen left Alex who later met Lauren, portrayed by Courteney Cox. At this point, Debbie Allen was directing episodes and the shark was well on its way to its next victim. Sit, Ubu, sit. Good dog.

The Flintstones

1960–1966 Fridays on ABC

jump the shark?

"Yabba dabba doo!" We always have a dabba-doo time with this fun-loving, modern stone-age family.

The Flintstones was a successful prime-time animated take on *The Honeymooners,* substituting the prehistoric town of Bedrock for the prehistoric town of Brooklyn.

> **The Great Gazoo moves into the town of Bedrock.**

Fred Flintstone worked in Mr. Slate's quarry pit and was married to Wilma. Fred's best buddy was Barney Rubble, who was betrothed to Betty. Fred had a pet dinosaur, Dino, and a happy rock pile in the town of Bedrock.

> **ANIMATED FAMILIES**
>
> Our favorite cartoon clans:
> 1 The Simpsons
> 2 The Jetsons
> 3 The Hills
> 4 The Olies
> 5 The Marshes

The Flintstones spoofed everything and everyone, from Hollyrock to high society, buffalo conventions to bowling ballet. Three seasons into its run, Fred and Wilma had baby Pebbles, and the Rubbles followed suit by adopting (bet you didn't know that!) Bamm Bamm. The shark alert was sounded.

Spoofs of guest stars such as Ann-Margrock and the Gruesomes began to occur. Pebbles and Bamm Bamm had a hit record with their version of "Let the Sun Shine In." The voice of Betty had changed, and Fred had begun to surf. Mr. Slate became more of a regular, reminding us of Mel Cooley from *The Dick Van Dyke Show.*

> **MOVE OVER, JESSICA RABBIT**
>
> Hot cartoon chicks:
> 1 Daphne
> 2 Wonder Woman
> 3 Trixie
> 4 Josie (and the Pussycats)
> 5 The Teen Angels (not Captain Caveman)

The inevitable jump occurred during the sixth season when a tiny, green, flying outer space creature called the Great Gazoo made an appearance. Gazoo was obnoxious and unfunny, and he affectionately referred to Fred as dumb-dumb. Although the great Harvey Korman provided the voice, Gazoo stuck around Bedrock and the show went sailing right over the shark. Too bad, we had a gay old time.

Frasier

1993– Thursdays on NBC

jump the shark?

Dr. Frasier Crane went from being a married psychiatrist who frequented a Boston bar called *Cheers* to a divorced radio talk-show host in his hometown of Seattle—and that was before this show even started.

> **Niles and Daphne finally get together.**

Frasier revolved around Dr. Crane's day-to-day doings. At home, there was his ornery father, Martin,

HOW NOT TO BE SEEN

Often heard, never seen:

1 Carlton, your doorman (*Rhoda*)

2 Vera, Norm's wife (*Cheers*)

3 Charlie (*Charlie's Angels*)

4 Wilson (*Home Improvement*)

5 Orson (*Mork & Mindy*)

English physical therapist Daphne, and Martin's dog, Eddie. Frasier's brother, Niles, obsessed with Daphne, often stopped by and was more pompous and insecure than Frasier. Niles's wife, Maris, was often mentioned, but never seen. At work, Frasier dealt with his producer, Roz, and the resident sportscaster, Bulldog.

Early on, *Frasier* had the best writing on television and held up very well. Cameos from *Cheers* alums such as his ex-wife Lilith, former love Diane, and bartenders Sam and Woody could have been cheesy, but were expertly handled. Special Guest callers to the talk show were even done with class.

The fin was spotted when Roz became pregnant during the fourth season. At the same time, Niles and Maris decided to separate, and all signs pointed to the inevitable relationship with Daphne. Frasier and the rest of the staff lost their jobs when the station switched formats, and the show began its drift into *Three's Company* territory. What wacky hijinks will ensue on the next *Frasier*?

Daphne was set to wed at the end of the seventh season, when Niles declared his love for her, swept her away on her wedding day, and they ended up in each others' arms. The sexual tension was gone, and the show vaulted right over the shark and became just another sitcom.

MOVING

Changing jobs cross-country style:

1 *Laverne & Shirley*

2 *The Ellen Show*

3 *Benson*

4 *Rhoda*

5 *Northern Exposure*

When did

Friends

1994– Thursdays on NBC

jump the shark?

"I'll be there for you . . ." especially if you're one of six good-looking single people who have a great apartment, very little income, and the ability to hang out all day. The nineties belonged to these *Friends.*

> **Ross and Rachel. Again. And again. And . . .**

Monica, chef of the future, shares a huge New York City apartment with her pampered high school pal, Rachel. Across the hall live Chandler, an office geek, and Joey, a not-too-swift wannabe actor. Hanging around are Monica's brother, Ross, whose ex cares for their baby with her lesbian partner, and her former ditzy roommate Phoebe who plays a mean guitar.

These six *Friends* lounge on couches in each other's apartments and/or at the local coffee shop, Central Perk. Occasionally they have jobs, but for the most part they live lives of leisure. Ross obsesses over Rachel, but plays with a monkey. Joey auditions, Phoebe sings, Monica cooks, and Chandler gains weight as quickly as the girls lose it.

Over the years, *Friends* has been besieged by a plethora of A-list Special Guest Stars, a strong indication that a jump is looming. Elle McPherson, Brooke Shields, George Clooney, Susan Sarandon, and Gary Oldman are but a few who have been there for us.

But it was the romantic saga of Ross and Rachel that would finally cause *Friends* to jump. During the second season, when Ross and Rachel got together for the first time, the show still worked. Smelly Cat, Chandler and Janice, Special Guest Tom Selleck as Richard, and other good stuff was going on. But the next season,

DE-LUXE APARTMENTS

Not necessarily on the East Side, but:

1 *Seinfeld*
2 *Mary Tyler Moore*
3 *The Jeffersons*
4 *The Honeymooners*
5 *Three's Company*
6 *Good Times*
7 *I Love Lucy*
8 *The Bob Newhart Show*
9 *Mad About You*
10 *Laverne & Shirley*

FAMILY OF FAME

Meet these parents:

1 Morgan Fairchild (Chandler's mom)
2 Kathleen Turner (Chandler's dad)
3 Elliot Gould (Monica's dad)
4 Teri Garr (Phoebe's "mom")
5 Brenda Vaccaro (Joey's mom)

MONKEY BUSINESS

Marcel reminds us of our favorite chimp stars:

1 Bear on *B.J. and the Bear*

2 Gleek from *Superfriends*

3 *Lancelot Link, Secret Chimp*

4 Magilla Gorilla on *Magilla Gorilla*

5 Grape Ape on *Scooby's All-Star Laff-a-Lympics*

while Ross constantly reminded us that he and Rachel "were on a break," the show began its downhill slide. Every time Ross and Rachel (surprise!) got back together again, we cared less. The other storylines followed suit—Phoebe gave birth to triplets and searched for her mom, Joey tried for his big break, everyone vacationed in London, and Monica and Chandler ended up getting married.

Despite being long over the shark, *Friends* is still as popular as ever. Surprise, surprise, Rachel is a mommy and Ross is the father. But the shark doesn't care . . . it's on to its next victim, and *we* are on a break.

When did

Full House

1987–1995 Fridays on ABC

jump the shark?

One of the anchors of the infamous ABC TGIF lineup, a.k.a. "My Three Dads," *Full House* combined stand-up-comics-turned-actors with nauseatingly cute kids, manufacturing a comedy hit.

Nicky and Alex Katsopolis meant too many twins.

Danny, whose wife died in a car accident, cared for his three daughters—D.J., Stephanie, and Michele. His best buddy Joey and brother-in-law Jesse moved in to help take care of the kids and create . . . you guessed it . . . a *Full House*!

DOUBLE FEATURE

These shows tried to win with twins:

1 *Sister, Sister*

2 *B.J. and the Bear*

3 *The Cosby Show*

4 *Get Smart*

5 *Superfriends*

We spotted the shark early on as Jesse pursued his rock musician dreams (which John Stamos still does), Joey played a former stand-up comedian (which Dave Coulier still is), and Danny was a talk show host (which Bob Saget really was).

There was never a dull moment in the Tanner household, but any problems, no matter how Very Special they were, could always be resolved in twenty-two minutes.

Jesse was the true shark bait on *Full House*. He dated, then married Danny's co-anchor, Rebecca. They went on to change their last name from Cochran to Katsopolis following a visit from their Greek grandparents.

But the jump finally occurred when the show needed a "cute boost" and Rebecca gave birth to . . . twins! Take that, Mary Kate and Ashley, who together played just one character on this show. (They've made up for that with a vengeance.)

By the end of the show's run, Jesse had inherited and renovated a run-down local hangout, the Smash-Club; Michele was growing up too fast as Danny started seeing double; and the twins just couldn't stay out of trouble. No one ever worked, no child was ever disciplined, and everyone ended up just fine . . . provided you were quick enough to change the channel.

When did
Gilligan's Island
1964–1967 Thursdays on CBS

jump the shark?

The first time someone came to the island and gave them chance to get off.

"Just sit right back and you'll hear a tale . . ." of the seven most infamous castaways ever to grace the small screen.

The S.S. *Minnow* was shipwrecked during its three-hour tour, and Gilligan, the Skipper too, the millionaire and his wife, the movie star, the Professor, and Mary Ann were stranded on a tiny island.

Armed with an endless supply of clothing and a variety of man-made products of unexplained origin, our stranded castaways battled for survival by creating stage shows, playing with monkeys, and neglecting to notice that their ingenious professor could never figure out how to build a boat.

Early on, Gilligan survived the transition from black and white to color, and even a change in its popular theme from "and the rest" to "the Professor and Mary Ann." Each episode we tried to understand why Ginger and Mary Ann fawned over Gilligan, how the skipper kept that gut, and why Lovey and Mr. Magoo had all those different outfits packed for a three-hour tour.

The show would jump the shark when different people began to appear on the island, yet the castaways were never rescued. Special Guest Stars included Kurt Russell, Zsa Zsa Gabor, Phil Silvers, and Don Rickles. Gilligan reaffirmed the jump by choosing to bond with a monkey over Ginger and Mary Ann and was repeatedly on the wrong end of the Skipper's hat as a result.

The castaways were finally rescued in the extremely popular 1978 TV movie, "Rescue from Gilligan's Island," but naturally they ended up right back on the island. The shark was nowhere to be seen by the time the Harlem Globetrotters showed up on the island. Somewhere in the deep Pacific, a fish is laughing its ass off.

GINGER OR MARY ANN?

The debates will rage on . . .

1 Jennifer or Bailey on *WKRP in Cincinnati?*
2 Ponch or Jon on *CHiPs?*
3 Jill, Kris, or Kelly on *Charlie's Angels?*
4 Sarah or Jackie on *Too Close for Comfort?*
5 Bo, Luke, Daisy, or Boss Hogg on *The Dukes of Hazzard?*

When did Happy Days

1974–1984 Tuesdays on ABC

jump the shark?

Close this book and read the title aloud. Now read it again.

TED MCGINLEY

Our patron saint. Ted's curse extends (but is not limited) to:

1 *Sports Night*
2 *Married . . . with Children*
3 *Dynasty*
4 *The Love Boat*
5 *Welcome Back, Kotter* (Beau looked like him)

When did The Honeymooners

1955–1956 Saturdays on CBS

jump the shark?

"The Lost Episodes" were discovered.

"Bang, zoom . . ." A classic comedy with superb acting that took place in a small apartment in Brooklyn.

The Honeymooners opened with fireworks, a full moon, and obscenely loud theme music and narration. The show revolved around Ralph Kramden, a portly "dus briver," and his wife, Alice. Ralph's best friend was Ed Norton, who conveniently lived upstairs with his wife, Trixie.

Ralph was always coming up with some crazy scheme to strike it rich, and Norton was his not-so-swift but willing accomplice. Alice brought Ralph back to Earth, and in retaliation Ralph was constantly threatening her with classic lines like "One of these days . . . Pow! right in the kisser!" or "To the moon, Alice!"

The show was filmed live, and Jackie Gleason, Art Carney, Audrey Meadows, and Joyce Randolph were expert at playing to both the camera and the crowd. Ralph's $99,000 Answer to the composer of "Swannee River" (Ed Norton), the chef of the future, and Ralph's "Man from Space" costume are just a few of the gems from *The Honeymooners*.

The show only jumped the shark when sixty-eight "lost episodes" were found long after the show finished its run. In fact, these were only sketches that had aired as parts of an earlier Jackie Gleason show and were edited to create "new" *Honeymooners* episodes. Upon viewing these programs, we quickly realized that they should have stayed lost, and that the shark had been leaped.

I Dream of Jeannie

1965–1970 Mondays on NBC

A great opening theme. A dimwitted astronaut. Fantastic abs. Put 'em together and you have *I Dream of Jeannie,* more than just a message-in-a-bottle comedy from the late sixties.

> **Jeannie and Tony Nelson tie the knot.**

Captain Tony Nelson found himself on an island after aborting a NASA mission. He stumbled across a bottle, popped it open, and out steamed Jeannie, who deemed Tony her master . . . fulfilling every male's fantasy at the time.

Tony was rescued and returned to Florida, where no one would believe his story, especially the ageless resident shrink Dr. Bellows. Only fellow astronaut Major Healey, whose charms we're still searching for, knew of Jeannie's existence, and his ineptitude constantly put Tony in situations that would result in Master begging for Jeannie's forgiveness.

BOO

Our favorite apparition-themed programs:

1 *Bewitched*
2 *The Ghost and Mrs. Muir*
3 *Topper*
4 *Ghost Story*
5 *Twilight Zone*

Tony didn't exactly have a way with women, and we wondered how this guy could be so blind to Jeannie's love for him. She had that great pink outfit, was indebted to him for life, and wanted nothing more than to serve him in that swanky, pillow-filled bottle. What more could anyone ask?

Unfortunately, Tony eventually wised up. Soon there were evil twin episodes, and Dr. Bellows, Major Healey, and the space program became more of the show's focus. Master finally gave up the fight, and the shark began to circle. Toward the end of the fourth season, Jeannie convinced Master to fall in love with her, and the show went sailing over the shark with a classic wedding episode.

UNVEILED

Our favorite body parts:

1 Sherilyn Fenn's tongue
2 Redd Foxx's beard
3 Jennifer Aniston's hair
4 Pamela Anderson's (your favorite body part here)
5 Max Headroom's head

Although the final season featured Farrah Fawcett as Major Healey's girlfriend, Tina, the sexual tension was now gone. We were left with little more to ponder than whether Tony, Jeannie and their dog Djinn-Djinn would stay in the house or move into the bottle for good.

I Love Lucy

1951–1957 Mondays on CBS

jump the shark?

"Lucy, I'm home!" The country fell in love with this Desilu production that followed the life of the wacky Ricardos.

I Love Lucy was an instant hit and a true comic original. Cuban bandleader Ricky Ricardo was married to Lucy MacGillicuddy, who desperately wanted to be in show business. Their landlord neighbors, Fred and Ethel Mertz, were their best friends and partners in crime. Ricky wanted Lucy to be a stay-at-home housewife, but Lucy had the acting bug and constantly tried wacky schemes to prove something to Ricky and the rest of us.

> **Ricky, Lucy, and Little Ricky move up to Connecticut.**

The program truly set the standard for situation comedies. With its live studio audience, quality filmmaking, and the now traditional camera setup, *I Love Lucy* continues to be emulated by other sitcoms to this day. They just forget the laughs.

During the show's early years, Lucy and Ethel often found themselves in memorable, hysterically funny situations. Ricky's eventual discovery of the problem and completely unintelligible Spanish rants kept us in stitches. The health-tonic ad, clown impersonation, fight in the grape vat, and candy incident are all classic Lucy.

PRODUCTION CREDITS

We remember Desilu and:

1 Sit, Ubu, sit. Good dog. Woof.
2 A Mark Goodson/Bill Todman Production
3 Worldwide Pants
4 Good night, Mr. Walters
5 Meow

Shark warning sings emerged during the third season when Little Ricky was born, coinciding with the real birth of Lucille Ball's second child. The next season, the Ricardos and the Mertzes took the often-fatal car trip to California. They also traveled to Europe, and Ricky opened his own club upon their return. The shark was fast approaching.

Ricky's success enabled the Ricardos to buy a home in Connecticut, and the show took the final leap. The dynamic of their New York

GREAT NEIGHBORS

Fred Mertz next door, or:

1 Kramer
2 Ed Norton
3 Chandler and Joey
4 Rhoda Morgenstern
5 Mr. Bentley

City apartment was gone and Little Ricky was now a full-time cast member. If you happen to catch an episode set in Connecticut, you instinctively change the channel. As Lucy and Ricky's real-life marriage fell apart, *I Love Lucy* followed suit, and the shark swam on to its next victim.

When did

The Jeffersons

1975–1985 Sundays on CBS

jump the shark?

Mike Evans replaces his replacement, Damon Evans (no relation) as Lionel.

The Jeffersons was an *All in the Family* spin-off that had no problem standing on its own. But don't be switching Lionels on me.

George and Louise Jefferson moved on up to a deluxe apartment on the East Side with their sassy maid, Florence. George was as bigoted as Archie Bunker and rich from the success of his dry cleaning business. Neighbors Tom (white) and Helen (black) Willis stopped by often, as did quirky Englishman Mr. Bentley. Our favorite visitor was Mother Jefferson, who didn't hesitate to put everyone in his or her place.

When their son, Lionel, went off to college, he returned as a different actor. Despite coincidentally sharing the same last name (Evans), the two actors were completely unrelated. Lionel had a white girlfriend, the Willis's daughter, Jenny, whom he would marry during the second season of the show. The mixed marriages would torment George for years to come.

The Jeffersons had a bad habit of introducing characters that would disappear for a while, and then return as if nothing had happened. Mr. Bentley, Mother Jefferson, and the

BUNKER SPIN-OFFS

These programs got their start at 704 Hauser Street:

1 *The Jeffersons*
2 *Maude*
3 *Archie Bunker's Place*
4 *Gloria*
5 *704 Hauser Street*

WEEZIE

Great nicknames:

1 Dummy
2 Iggy
3 Fez
4 Cockroach
5 Fonzie

Willises were often on hiatus, though Weezie was always on hand to set George straight with a pillow to the head.

Lionel took the longest hiatus of all. He was noticeably absent for a while, only to reappear with Mike Evans, the original Lionel, in the role once again. Lionel and Jenny had a baby girl, Jessica, but their marriage didn't last and they eventually separated. Apparently, it was difficult to keep anyone whose last name was Evans on the show.

The Jeffersons continued to emulate *All in the Family,* with George and Tom partnering up to buy a bar. Jenny would make occasional appearances on the show, and Florence was off to a different apartment: *227.* Although George and Weezie would resurface—ski jumping in Old Navy commercials—if they paid attention they'd realize they had long ago moved on up . . . and over the shark.

When did

Jeopardy!
1964–1975, 1984– Syndicated

jump the shark?

"This . . . is . . . *Jeopardy!*" From Art Fleming to Alex Trebek, *Jeopardy!* has proven to be not only one of the smartest game shows of all time, but also one of the most successful.

What is "dumbing it down"?

It first aired in 1964 with Art Fleming as host and Don Pardo as the announcer. The unique hook was that contestants were given the answer, and had to phrase their response in the form of a question. This complex conceit ruled out ninety-eight percent of prospective contestants (and winners).

DAILY DOUBLES

Great gamblin' game shows:

1 *High Rollers*
2 *Gambit*
3 *The Joker's Wild*
4 *Card Sharks*
5 *Win Ben Stein's Money*

The show ran for ten years, took a hiatus, and was brought back full-force in 1984 with a video board, Johnny Gilbert as the announcer, and Mr. Hooked on Phonics himself, Alex Trebek, as host. Before *Jeopardy!*, Alex's claim to fame was hosting *High Rollers,* the game show with the big dice and Nanette Fabray and Suzanne Somers ("Who is Chrissy Snow?") assisting.

Video and audio enhancements were integrated into the infamous Daily Double. Alex made sure that the answer was presented in the form of a question, and answers rarely had to go to the judges.

The shark was circling as Alex became more pompous and was capable of speaking every language known to mankind through his eloquent responses. ("What is overenuciation?") Tournaments of Champions, celebrity editions, and teen editions were further warning signs. But as scores around homes across the country increased and the answers became easier to solve, we knew *Jeopardy!* had jumped the shark. The show is still smart, but when we could nail Final Jeopardy! for a week straight, the shark had been leaped and it was time to switch to *Wheel of Fortune*. Oh, Vanna!

When did
The Late Show with David Letterman

jump the shark?

1993– Weeknights on CBS

Dave becomes the establishment, and wears only double-breasted suits.

Let's start by saying that *Late Night with David Letterman* jumped the shark when Dave left NBC. That groundbreaking late-night program kept surprising us every night—there was never a dull moment with Dave. Television at its finest.

After getting screwed out of *The Tonight Show* by NBC, Dave created *The Late Show* for CBS and brought his best material with him. Paul headed up the band, viewer mail and the home office carried on, and the Top Ten list was intact.

Dave opened in the Ed Sullivan Theater with Bill Murray as his inaugural guest and Paul Newman in the audience searching for singing cats. It was a great start, and the only question was whether the *Late Night* bits would work an hour earlier on a different network.

Early on the battle with Leno created a situation that was classic Dave. He got to know his new neighborhood, used 53rd Street as his own personal bowling alley, and took shots at NBC whenever possible.

The fin was spotted during the third season, and it didn't even happen on the show. Dave hosted the Oscars, and for the first time in his late-night television career, he came up short. Back at *The Late Show,* his shtick started to feel recycled.

The jump occurred when we noticed Dave had begun wearing double-breasted suits and buddying up with his guests rather than chastising them. We'd always been able to count on Dave to cleverly stick it to the stars, but suddenly he felt like one of *them*. This, coupled with the loss of freshness, sent Dave over the shark.

Following Dave's heart surgery, he seemed to relocate that fun-loving sarcasm that made *Late Night* work so well. The show got a much-needed boost, but even as the suits and Top Ten lists continued, the shark was searching for fresh blood.

Laverne & Shirley

1976–1983 Tuesdays on ABC

jump the shark?

"One, two, three, four, five, six, seven, eight, Schlemiel, schlamazel. Hasenpfeffer Incorporated." Laverne and Shirley spun off from *Happy Days,* did it their way, and made all their dreams come true in Wisconsin.

Laverne De Fazio and Shirley Feeney worked on the assembly line at Shotz Brewery in Milwaukee

> **The girls leave the Shotz brewery behind and move to California.**

and shared a basement apartment. Visitors included the landlady, Edna Babish; Carmine "The Big Ragoo" Ragusa, Shirley's fantasy "tough" guy who loved to sing and dance; and wacky neighbors Lenny and Squiggy. The crew frequented the Pizza Bowl, which was owned by Laverne's father, Frank De Fazio.

Laverne & Shirley was an instant hit and had plenty of memorable moments. The glove atop a beer bottle on the line, Laverne's signature *L,* Lenny and the Squigtones, and any awful song or dance from Carmine were unforgettable. Richie and Fonzie were spotted double dating with Laverne and Shirley as well. It was well known that several of the stars couldn't stand each other, but it didn't stop the success of the show.

During the third season, the shark fin protruded as Frank began to fall for Mrs. Babish, and they were subsequently married. The visits from Lenny and Squiggy began to get stale and Carmine still couldn't carry a tune. It was time to shake things up, and boy did they ever.

The entire cast packed up and headed to California for no apparent reason. New, completely forgettable neighbors Rhonda Lee and

> **PERFORMANCE ART**
>
> Can't sing, can't dance, what do you do?
>
> **1** Carmine
> **2** Potsie
> **3** Alice
> **4** Rerun
> **5** Hal Linden

Sonny were introduced. Frank and Edna opened a new western-themed restaurant. All members of the cast tried to become movie stars. Cindy Williams, who portrayed Shirley, became pregnant and sat out a season; the show was still billed as *Laverne & Shirley,* though it featured only Laverne in the opening credits.

You could see the shark smiling out there in the ocean all the way from Milwaukee. *Laverne & Shirley* jumped the shark, did it their way, and made all our dreams come true. For me and you.

When did

Law & Order

1990– Wednesdays on NBC

jump the shark?

The police who investigate crime and the District Attorneys who prosecute the offenders make *Law & Order* the best cop show of the nineties . . . if you can keep track of them.

> **Angie Harmon joins the cast and they all become Giants fans.**

Its cold, Dragnet-esque opening and bass-slapping theme combined with on-location New York City filming give *Law & Order* its distinct feel.

The first season opened with Sergeant Greevey and Detective Logan (George Dzundza and Chris Noth) and Captain Cragen (Dann Florek) as "Law," and F.A.D.A. Stone, D.A. Robinette, and D.A. Schiff (Michael Moriarty, Richard Brooks, and Steven Hill) as "Order." Great acting. Great storylines. Great show.

By its second season, *L&O* set its precedent of ever-changing cast members with Detective Cerreta (Paul Sorvino) replacing Sergeant Grevey. The precinct has featured two sergeants, a captain, four detectives, and a

SHUFFLING COPS
Memorable swaps of the boys in blue:

1 Jimmy Smits replaces David Caruso—
NYPD Blue

2 Robert Prosky replaces Michael Conrad—
Hill Street Blues

3 Cheryl Ladd replaces Farrah Fawcett Majors—
Charlie's Angels

4 Rick Schroder replaces Jimmy Smits—
NYPD Blue

5 Josh Hopkins replaces Michael De Lorenzo—
New York Undercover

lieutenant, while the court has highlighted two F.A.D.A.s, five A.D.A.s, and three DAs. Results have been mixed.

The first sign that *L&O* might be jumping came in the fourth season when Michael Moriarty was replaced by Sam Waterston as F.A.D.A. McCoy. The next season, Chris Noth went searching the city for sex instead of perps, and Benjamin Bratt as Detective Curtis was teamed with Jerry Orbach. NBC then began sensationalizing the episodes and promoting them as being "ripped from the headlines."

The fatal jump occurred at the start of the eighth season when Angie Harmon left *Baywatch Nights* and joined the cast as A.D.A. Abbie Carmichael. Although *L&O* had withstood major casting changes, this one put it over the edge. When Jesse Martin, Dianne Wiest, and Elisabeth (don't call me Barbie) Rohm followed, the deed was done.

The following seasons our fears were confirmed as spin-offs *L&O: Special Victims Unit* and *L&O: Criminal Intent* debuted. We anticipate *L&O: Maritime Patrol* to rear its head soon. First case: the search for the shark this classic show leapt a few years back.

THE
MAGNIFICIENT
AMPERSANDS

& the winners are . . .

1 *Rowan & Martin's Laugh-In*

2 *Will & Grace*

3 *Hardcastle & McCormick*

4 *Laverne & Shirley*

5 *Kate & Allie*

6 *Mork & Mindy*

7 *George & Leo*

8 *Live with Regis & Kelly*

9 *Siskel & Ebert*

10 *Lois & Clark*

Little House on the Prairie

1974–1983 Mondays on NBC

jump the shark?

> **Ma and Pa decide to adopt Albert.**

Little House on the Prairie chronicled the life and times of the Ingalls family out on the American frontier.

There was never a dull moment in Walnut Grove with Ma, Pa, and their three daughters, Mary, Laura, and Carrie. During the series run, Michael Landon and crew would give new meaning to the term "extended family."

The series was loosely based on Laura Ingalls Wilder's *Little House* books. Approximately three details from the books made it into the show. Her name was Laura, they actually had a dog, and Pa really did sell that fiddle. Weddings, fires, adoption, rape, morphine addiction . . . *Little House* tackled every conceivable domestic farm issue to strike a tight-knit frontier family.

PERIOD PIECES

They'll go down in history:

1 *F Troop*
2 *The Lone Ranger*
3 *Maverick*
4 *The Secret Diary of Desmond Pfeiffer*
5 *The Flintstones*

During the second season, the first fictional characters (the Sandersons) were introduced, clearing the way for major storyline changes over the next few years. A two-parter meant a Very Special *Little House* episode, typically dealing with young love, racism, a birth, or a death.

We sounded the shark alert at the end of the fourth season when Mary went blind, headed off to the "special" school, and fell in love with her teacher, Adam. The next season, the Ingalls family left Walnut Grove and moved to Winoka (the big city), which might have been more aptly located by the ocean considering what was coming next.

Laura and Charles became good friends with Albert Quinn and decide to bring him back to Walnut Grove. Pa adopted Albert, scoring the son Ma never gave him. Albert then proceeded to become a morphine addict, burn down the

FATHER MURPHY

Football stars that got the acting bug:

1 Alex Karras in *Webster*
2 O. J. Simpson in *The Naked Gun*
3 Fred Dryer in *Hunter*
4 Brian Bosworth in *Stone Cold*
5 Joe Namath in *The Waverly Wonders*

school for the blind, and kill Mary's baby (and Alice Garvey as well). The only redeeming thing he ever did was die.

After that point, the adoptions kept on coming, Adam miraculously regained his sight, Laura lost her pigtails and wed Almanzo, the Olesons wreaked havoc, and Michael Landon went gray. Albert has the unique distinction of causing all the characters and the show itself to jump the shark. Way to go!

When did

The Love Boat

1977–1986 Saturdays on ABC

jump the shark?

> **The captain's daughter, Vicki, permanently boards the *Pacific Princess*.**

"Love . . . exciting and new . . ." *The Love Boat* was the ultimate cheesy destination in the late seventies and early eighties as we set sail with Dennis Cole, Charo, and the Pacific Princess crew.

The Love Boat launched with its crew of Captain Merrill Stubing, Cruise Director Julie McCoy, Purser Burl "Gopher" Smith, ship's doctor Adam Bricker, and bartender Isaac ("Two-handed Snap and Point") Washington. Passengers on its maiden voyage included Meredith Baxter Birney, Bonnie Franklin, Suzanne Somers, and Jimmie Walker. The course for adventure was obviously set, and our minds were on a new romance.

The Love Boat never took itself too seriously, presenting three Special Guest Star story lines that took us from the Acapulco Lounge to the Aloha Deck. You could always count on a battle over the ladies who were invited to sit at the Captain's table, clumsily bumped into by Gopher, or seduced by the ship gigolo, Dr. Bricker. Either Isaac or Julie would fall hard for a passenger, and get dumped by the end of the hour.

A fin was spotted off the Promenade Deck when the boat set sail for a two-part special Alaskan cruise, and Julie was proposed to. She didn't end up getting married, but the shark had found its prey. When Charo made her eighty-seventh appearance, things were beginning to get a bit stale on the Pacific Princess.

During the show's third season, Vicki, Captain Stubing's daughter (by a showgirl, no less), was brought into the cast, and this cute new kid vaulted the vessel right over the shark. Vicki was just plain annoying, the quality of guest stars dropped (if that was possible), and lots of really weird stuff started to happen.

Desperate for a ratings boost in the eighties, Dionne Warwick warbled a new theme and the *Love Boat* Mermaids (including Teri Hatcher) were introduced. Cast members from *Happy Days* began to show up, the captain fell for and married Emily (played by Marion Ross, a.k.a. Mrs. C), and—the biggest mistake—Ted McGinley arrived as photographer Ashley Covington Evans (ACE).

Any time you feature Ted, the patron saint of shark jumping, you might as well admit that the show has leapt. Alas, the *Love Boat* won't soon be making another run.

FAVORITE DESTINATIONS

Set sail for:

1 Puerto Vallarta
2 Acapulco
3 Mazatlan
4 The Virgin Islands
5 Alaska

SPECIAL GUEST STARS

Where do we begin?:

1 Jimmy Osmond
2 Reggie Jackson
3 Scatman Crothers
4 The Harlem Globetrotters
5 Tori Spelling
6 Sonny Bono
7 Vince Van Patten
8 Andy Warhol
9 Tina Louise
10 Charo!

Mad About You

1992–1999 Thursdays on NBC

jump the shark?

Mad About You chronicles the life of the Buchmans, a newly married couple who spend way too much time in their lower Manhattan apartment.

> **Mothers Always Bring Extra Love . . . the birth of Mabel.**

Paul, a documentary filmmaker, and Jamie, a public relations worker, were a nineties couple who were continuously adjusting to their life together. Paul's cousin Ira, Jamie's sister Lisa, her best friend Fran, and their dog Murray made the transition all the more difficult—and hilarious. Mad About You was, as Paul Reiser pitched, a shorter, funnier *thirtysomething*.

Early on, Mad About You found its humor in apartment elevators, family reunions, dog issues, and jealousy. Paul and Jamie clicked as a couple, and we could all relate to the situations in which they found themselves. After season one, Paul's buddy Selby was the first of many characters who mysteriously disappeared from the show with no explanation. We grew suspicious.

A blatant warning sign came at the end of the third season, which featured a bunch of flashbacks and a full rendition of the Paul Reiser–penned opening theme "Final Frontier." The next season had Paul and Jamie "trying" for a child, and a season-ending Very Special episode where they almost broke up.

The show finally jumped at the end of the fifth season when Mabel was born. The dynamic was completely altered as the focus shifted to the baby. We didn't want to spend the entire night, much less half an hour, wondering if we should let the baby cry. The birth coupled with the now constant arguing between Paul and

---

YOU GOTTA SEE THE BABY

Sharks can't resist newborns:

1 Little Ricky (*I Love Lucy*)
2 Andrew Keaton (*Family Ties*)
3 Avery (*Murphy Brown*)
4 Mearth (*Mork & Mindy*)
5 Pebbles (*The Flintstones*)

GET UP, STAND UP

Some good . . .

1 *Roseanne*
2 *The Cosby Show*
3 *Seinfeld*
4 *Ellen*
5 *The Rosie O'Donnell Show*

Some not so good:

1 *Chicken Soup*
2 *All-American Girl*
3 *Cleghorne!*
4 *DiResta*
5 *Platypus Man*

Jamie turned them from a hip, lovable duo into a typical married couple. *Mad About You* went from a light, smart comedy to a preachy, true-to-life saga. The talent was always there, but the storylines were dragged into the deep by the shark.

When did

Magnum, P.I.

1980–1988 Thursdays on CBS

jump the shark?

> **Thomas Magnum dies, and then comes back to life when the show gets picked up for another season.**

The combination of Hawaiian beaches, Tom Selleck, a red Ferrari, and a lavish estate made *Magnum, P.I.* one of the best detective shows of the eighties.

Thomas Magnum is head of security for the estate of wealthy (and never seen) novelist Robin Masters. Vietnam vet Magnum lives on the estate with its manager, the stuffy Jonathan Higgins. War buddies Rick and T.C. are usually around to help out when needed.

If you moved *The Rockford Files* to Hawaii, upgraded Jim's car to a Ferrari, and threw a Detroit Tigers hat on him, you'd have *Magnum, P.I.* From its first episode, it was clear that *Magnum* would have the right combination of gorgeous scenery, fast cars, sarcastic wit, and dangerous activity to sustain it for a long run.

A shark was spotted when the sixth season began with a trip to England with Higgins. Although previously Magnum had successfully traveled to Detroit, an overseas venture does not bode well for any series. Later that season, there was a crossover episode with Jessica Fletcher from *Murder, She Wrote*. The next season, Special Guest Star Frank Sinatra played a

THE RIGHT SCRUFF

To shave or not to shave . . .

1 B.J.'s mustache
(*M*A*S*H*)

2 Stephen Keaton's beard
(*Family Ties*)

3 Steve Austin's mustache
(*The Six Million Dollar Man*)

4 John Gage's mustache
(*Emergency*)

5 Cousin It (*The Addams Family*)

HAWAIIAN PUNCH

Taping in paradise:

1 *Hawaii Five-O*

2 *Byrds in Paradise*

3 *McHale's Navy*

4 *Martial Law*

5 *C.P.O. Sharkey*

retired New York cop who traveled to Hawaii to solve a case—arguably ol' Blue Eyes' only appearance as bonafide shark bait.

The jump came at the end of the eighth season, when it looked like the show was going to be cancelled. The final episode had Magnum getting shot and visiting his friends as a ghost. When the show was renewed for the next season, a confused Magnum surfaced from a coma. After a great run, the show began recycling old plot lines in a desperate attempt to hang on. The shark had done its damage.

When did

Married ... with Children

1987–1997 Sundays on FOX

jump the shark?

Married . . . with Children was the anti-eighties and nineties sitcom. We loved the Bundys because they were real people, warts and all, who were worse off than the rest of us.

> **Peg's relatives visit, run off, and leave the Bundys with Seven.**

The Bundys live in Wanker County. Al is a woman's shoe salesman married to Peg, a housewife who does little more than watch *Oprah*. Rounding out the family was Kelly, their gorgeous but slutty daughter, Bud, their perverted young son, and Buck the dog. Neighbors Marcy and Steve Rhoades (and later Jefferson D'Arcy, played by Ted McGinley) stopped by frequently to stir up trouble in the Bundy household.

Early on, the show focused on the pathetic life of the Bundys, their problems with the house, and the similarly pathetic life of their "successful" neighbors. Strippers, poker games, shootings, and sexual innuendo dominated every episode. The show was a farce, and we couldn't get enough of it.

During the show's third season, Terry

HOOTERS

MWC was a breeding ground:

1 Traci Lords
2 Tiffani-Amber Thiessen
3 Pamela Anderson
4 Tia Carrere
5 Joey Lauren Adams
6 Renee Zellweger
7 Kari Wurher
8 Denise Richards
9 Keri Russell
10 Shannon Tweed

Rakolta, founder of "Americans for Responsible Television," started a letter-writing campaign objecting to the lewd humor used in the show and trying to get it off the air. Her fifteen minutes of fame gave *Married . . . with Children* a ratings boost and expanded the audience. In the fifth season, Joseph Bologna and Matt Leblanc showed up as the Verduccis, setting up a failed spin-off for FOX.

We spotted the fin when Marcy and Steve got divorced and Peggy took Marcy to Vegas. Marcy would later remarry Jefferson D'Arcy, played by our patron saint, Ted McGinley, who immediately got to work helping the show over the shark.

During the sixth season, Peg got pregnant but later miscarried; Al wrote it off to a bad dream, á la *Dallas.* But the show finally jumped for good when Seven was left behind to join the Bundy clan. This "new kid in town" just didn't gel with the cast, and the producers were wise enough to make him disappear later in the season. However, the damage had been done, and the show was never the same.

It's always good to admit your mistakes, and *Married . . . with Children* did just that, having Seven appear as "missing" on a milk carton in later episodes. But by adding both a cute new kid *and* Ted McGinley, the bait was just too tempting for the shark to resist.

The Mary Tyler Moore Show

1970–1977 Saturdays on CBS   *jump the shark?*

"Who can turn the world on with a smile?" From the opening three notes of "Love Is All Around" to the MTM meow at the end of each episode, *Mary Tyler Moore* is a true comedy classic.

> **Mary craves a change and moves into a new apartment.**

Mary Richards is the Associate Producer for "The Six O'Clock News" at WJM-TV in Minneapolis. The newsroom is home to gruff news chief Lou Grant, sarcastic writer Murray Slaughter, and ego-driven anchorman Ted Baxter. At home, Mary has her new pal Rhoda Morgenstern and old friend Phyllis Lindstrom helping her make it through.

The main characters were a delight, but the supporting ones were just as critical to the show's success. *MTM* had a knack for replacing characters with even better ones. Weatherman Gordy, Murray's wife Marie, Ted's wife Georgette, Rhoda's mother Ida, and of course, Sue Ann Nivens are just a handful of the classic characters that frequented the show.

Mary was always searching for romance, but seemed to spend most of her time with her friends. There was never a dull moment—who could forget the plight of Chuckles the Clown, the confrontations with station owner Wild Jack Monroe, Lars's affair with Sue Ann, or Mary constantly calling "Mr. Grant!"?

Shark warning signs went up at the start of the fifth season when Rhoda moved to New York, and later that season Phyllis left as well. The show was able to handle those departures, but the next season Mary searched for change and switched apartments, catapulting the show over the shark.

TED KNIGHT

We love Ted. Here's why:

1 *Caddyshack*

2 *Too Close for Comfort*

3 *The Love Boat* (various guest spots)

4 *The Ted Knight Show*

5 *Superfriends* (he was the narrator—"Meanwhile, at the Hall of Justice . . .")

THIS JUST IN

Our favorite news anchors:

1 Jim Dial (*Murphy Brown*)

2 Floyd Robertson and Earl Camembert (*SCTV*)

3 Norm MacDonald (*SNL's Weekend Update*)

4 Bob Charles (*Not Necessarily the News*)

5 Sam Malone, guest anchor on Eye on Sports (*Cheers*)

Following the big move, Ted and Georgette adopted a son (played by Brady cousin Oliver, Robbie Rist) and Mary and Lou shared a kiss before the show's classic finale. So though it jumped the shark, we tip our cap—actually we toss it—to a great show that really did make it after all.

When did

M*A*S*H

1972–1983 Mondays on CBS

jump the shark?

> **Radar announces that Lieutenant Colonel Henry Blake's plane went down on his way back home.**

"Choppers . . ." The Korean War lasted eleven years for the 4077th, and CBS was home to one of the most successful television programs ever created.

M*A*S*H was based on the Oscar-winning film, which in turn was based on the award-winning book, which happened to be based on true stories that occurred during the Korean conflict. But in truth the show paralleled the Vietnam War, often serving up not-so-subtle commentary.

HARDLY MISSED

Most shows can't avoid the shark when a main character is replaced.

These thrived:

1 *Law & Order*
2 *Cheers* (Coach, not Diane)
3 *Charlie's Angels*
4 *The Daily Show*
5 *NYPD Blue*

These didn't:

1 *The Andy Griffith Show*
2 *Northern Exposure*
3 *Designing Women*
4 *Three's Company*
5 *Welcome Back, Kotter*

M*A*S*H picked up where the film left off. The booze and sarcasm flowed out of Hawkeye and Trapper's tent, Frank and Margaret's affair was in full bloom, and Sidney was psychoanalyzing everyone. The tragedy and drama of the O.R. mixed with the dark and sometimes slapstick humor of the tents was a lethal combination.

At the end of the third season, McLean Stevenson had signed a long-term deal with NBC (to create gems like *Hello, Larry*), and Henry Blake met with his fatal plane accident. Although M*A*S*H continued to have a very successful run, it had lost something and jumped the shark. Subsequent events led to B.J. replacing Trapper, Charles replacing Frank, and Margaret marrying Donald Penobscot. The slide had begun.

*M*A*S*H* also seemed to lose some of its humor, and at times might have been mistaken for The Alan Alda Moral Half-Hour. Entire episodes were devoted to Father Mulcahy and the Korean orphans. Klinger lost the dress and eventually married Soon-Lee. Even Hot Lips and Hawkeye actually got together during one episode.

The finale, "Goodbye, Farewell, and Amen," garnered the largest television audience in history. It just aired a few seasons too late.

When did
Monday Night Football

1970– Mondays on ABC

jump the shark?

"Are you ready for some football?" The groundbreaking, three-in-a-booth *Monday Night Football* hasn't exactly been a "Monday Night party" in recent years.

Who would watch a football game on a Monday night? In 1970, the answer was a heck of a lot of folks, as this sports experiment became one of the most popular shows on television.

Hank Williams Jr. belts out the opening theme to get us ready for some football.

The original team of three in the booth featured Keith Jackson doing the play-by-play flanked by analysts "Dandy" Don Meredith and the one, the only: Howard Cosell. The next season, Frank Gifford replaced Keith Jackson and the most famous *MNF* trio was born. The announcers' personalities made even the dullest games interesting as we anticipated the next words out of their big mouths.

During its run, many other former players have stepped in and out of the *MNF* booth and on to successful television acting careers, including Fran Tarkenton (*That's Incredible!*), Alex Karras (*Webster*), and O.J. Simpson (*1st and Ten,* various *Court TV* installments).

We spotted a fin when ABC began to air Special Editions of *Monday Night Football* on different nights. They actually called the show *A Thursday Night Edition of Monday Night Football* instead of *Thursday Night Football*. Trouble.

The thing that made *MNF* so special was its instrumental opening orchestral theme. As Howard Cosell announced the teams over a bone-crunching montage, the music got the blood pumping. It was indeed time for some football.

In the late eighties, the opening theme was replaced with a customized version of Hank Williams, Jr.'s "All My Rowdy Friends," asking if we're ready for some football. To add insult to injury, the montage was replaced with annoying clips of random fans, with only the occasional football shot. Once they started recruiting rock stars to sing the theme on different nights, we knew *MNF* had jumped the shark.

MNF has tried to fix the problem, bringing back the original opening and toning down the "Up with People" montage. Dennis Miller was added to the booth, which reeked of desperation. It's not that the matchups have gotten worse, but just that the entire Monday Night experience now wears thin.

Monty Python's Flying Circus

1969–1974 Sundays on the BBC

jump the shark?

> **John Cleese leaves for a season and they drop the Flying Circus.**

"It's . . ." *Monty Python's Flying Circus* was a brilliant sketch comedy show conceived, written, and starred in by six gentlemen who are very silly.

Once every twenty-five years or so, a show comes along that truly breaks the mold and makes an everlasting imprint on society. *Monty Python's Flying Circus* is not one of these shows. But whether it's showing us how not to be seen or extolling the virtues of Spam, *Flying Circus* has proven itself to be pure comedic genius.

Monty Python is a British comedy troupe that consisted of Graham Chapman, John Cleese, Michael Palin, Eric Idle, Terry Jones, and lone American Terry Gilliam. Gilliam was responsible for the animation and occasionally appeared on screen with the others, becoming more visible during the later seasons.

WHAT'S IN A NAME?

By the way, which one is Monty? Other classics:

1 Jethro Tull
2 Pink Floyd
3 Molly Hatchet
4 Steely Dan
5 Marshall Tucker

Monty Python's Flying Circus opened with the "It's . . ." man and Sousa's "Liberty Bell March" and just got sillier from there. Classic sketches included Joke Warfare, Hell's Grannies, the Pet Shop (Dead Parrot) Sketch, the Ministry of Silly Walks, the Fish Slapping dance, the Spanish Inquisition, and arguably the most brilliant sketch ever written, the Argument Clinic. (No, it's not.)

Warning signs appeared during the third season, when Terry Jones was added to the opening as the nude organist. Episodes started focusing on one sketch and began to drag, as if they'd lost the dead cow they'd always drop to kill an overdone bit. There was still good stuff coming out, but the troupe was not as lively.

SKETCHING

Other TV sketch comedy troupe shows:

1 *The Kids in the Hall*
2 *Upright Citizens Brigade*
3 *Saturday Night Live*
4 *Fridays*
5 *Just Kidding*

The next season, John Cleese left the troupe to pursue other interests (ultimately creating the classic *Fawlty Towers*), the show was retitled *Monty Python,* and it finally jumped the shark. The opening sketch, the Golden Age of Ballooning, was like a *Saturday Night Live* sketch of today—a premise stretched as far as it could be into a sketch that never seems to end. Singing, which used to be an occasional break in the action, became more the focus of the show.

Thankfully, the troupe moved on to the big screen and created the original gems *Holy Grail, Life of Brian,* and *Meaning of Life,* all of which included John Cleese. Although Monty Python eventually jumped the shark on television, they will always be something completely different.

When did

Moonlighting

1985–1989 Tuesdays on ABC

jump the shark?

David and Maddie finally get together.

We always wonder which was the better *Moonlighting* episode . . . the one that aired on Tuesday nights, or the one happening behind the scenes.

Moonlighting was a self-proclaimed hip, romantic comedy that lived up to its billing. It was an "inside" show with characters involving the audience by talking directly to the camera.

Cybill Shepherd was Maddie, a fashion model who fell out of favor in the business (there's a reach) and went broke, except for one tax-deductible asset: an L.A. detective agency. A wisecracking Bruce Willis (what a stretch!) played David, who ran the agency and teamed with Maddie to crack cases . . . lusting after her all the while. Other regulars included Agnes, the rhyming receptionist who chased after Bert (don't call me Booger), a temp turned detective.

Beginning with its Al Jarreau theme,

Moonlighting always maintained a very sharp wit. The sexual tension between David and Maddie was always lurking, á la Sam and Diane on *Cheers*. There were also plenty of dream sequences, including a memorable spoof of *The Taming of the Shrew*.

A shark alert was sounded at the end of the third season when Maddie finally kissed David in a parking garage. The next season, Mark Harmon appeared as Maddie's perfect-fit astronaut boyfriend Sam, and his arrival pushed the show right up the ramp.

It took four episodes, but *Moonlighting* finally took the leap over the shark when David and Maddie had sex. Their relationship, along with that of Agnes and Bert, became the show's primary focus as weird stuff started to happen at the Blue Moon. They seemed to acknowledge how "cool" they were and the show devolved into a smug self-parody. The trip to Chicago, Walter Bishop, the pregnancy and ensuing miscarriage spelled disaster.

Having already jumped, the death knell sounded when producer Glenn Gordon Caron left the show before it had finished its run. More reruns than live episodes were produced as a result of behind-the-scenes ego bruising, and the fourth wall that *Moonlighting* had opened up simply crumbled as the shark swam away, satisfied.

Mork & Mindy

1978–1982 Thursdays on ABC

jump the shark?

"Nanoo, nanoo." Let's cast Robin Williams as an alien, give him rainbow suspenders, stick him with a woman in Colorado, and see what happens!

The birth of Mearth.

Yet another spin-off of *Happy Days* (don't ask), *Mork & Mindy* chronicled the experiences of a visiting alien—Mork from the planet Ork—and his earthling housemate Mindy McConnell.

OUT OF THIS WORLD

Favorite fictional planets:

1 Remulak
2 The Satellite of Love
3 Alderaan
4 Krypton
5 Hollywood

At the end of each episode, Mork would report his findings to his superior, Orson, who was heard but never seen.

Mindy's father, Fred, who owned a music shop, and her wacky grandmother Cora complimented Mork and Mindy during the first two seasons. Mindy had some issues to deal with, but this show was Robin Williams's chance to show America what he could do . . . and he made the most of it. The show became a tremendous hit as Mork learned human emotions and adjusted to the day-to-day life of an earthling.

The shark fin made an appearance as early as the third season, when Mindy's dad and grandma disappeared, and deli owners Remo and Jean DaVinci relocated from New York to Boulder. Shazbot! Mr. Bickley, a grumpy neighbor (Tom Poston, of course), and Exidor, a bizarre "prophet" that Mork befriended, started to appear more regularly. Special Guest Star Raquel Welch appeared as an alien captain who had the hots for

BEFORE THEY WERE STARS

They weren't Special yet, just guest stars on this classic comedy:

1 David Letterman
2 Morgan Fairchild
3 Kim Fields
4 John Larroquette
5 Richard Moll

Mork, and there was even an episode where Mork met Robin Williams.

Mindy's relatives were brought back for the next season, but the shark was circling in for the big kill. The show took an unprecedented leap over the shark when Mork wed Mindy, they honeymooned on Ork, and Mork laid an egg that hatched into Mearth, as portrayed by Jonathan Winters. Please take a moment and read that sentence again.

The shark wasn't hungry for a while after that.

When did
NYPD Blue
1993– Tuesdays on ABC

jump the shark?

Warning—*NYPD Blue* contains shots of ass cracks and breasts and uses words like "asshole" to prove its grittiness. Bottom line . . . this great police drama doesn't need it.

NYPD Blue was created by Stephen Bochco and David Milch and revolves around the lives of the detective squad in the NYPD's 15th Precinct. The

> **As if he wasn't tormented enough, Sipowicz's wife Sylvia Costas dies.**

strength of the show is its true-to-life characters, most of whom speak fluent Milch (NYPD street lingo).

The original partners of the detective squad were control freak John Kelly and the abrasive Andy Sipowicz. Detective Greg Medavoy, Lieutenant Art Fancy, A.D.A. Sylvia Costas, Donna Abandando, and other recurring characters gradually became part of the main cast, along with a host of others. At the end of a riveting first season, David Caruso—who portrayed Kelly—left the show to pursue a film career (he was last seen still looking for it), and the detective-replacement river began to flow.

Kelly was successfully replaced by Bobby Simone (Jimmy Smits) who stuck around for a few seasons, having already experienced a film career comparable to Caruso's. Shortly after marrying Detective Diane Russell (who's since moved to *Philly*), Simone died from heart failure. Shark fins were spotted when Rick (don't call me Ricky) Schroder was chosen to replace him as Danny Sorenson, but surprisingly he pulled it off like a champ.

The cornerstone of *NYPD Blue* is Andy Sipowicz (Dennis Franz). He is a combination of Milch and Bill Clark, a former detective who started as the show's consultant and became its Executive Producer. The torment never ends for this rough on the outside/sweet on the inside

FAILED EXITS STAGE LEFT
They should've stayed home:
1 Gary Burghoff
2 Rob Morrow
3 Shelley Long
4 Delta Burke
5 Richard Grieco

CLASSIC BOCHCO
Sometimes you win . . .
1 *Hill Street Blues*
2 *L.A. Law*
3 *Murder One*
4 *Doogie Howser, M.D.*
5 *Brooklyn South* (critically)

Sometimes you lose . . .
1 *Cop Rock*
2 *Capitol Critters*
3 *Bay City Blues*
4 *Public Morals*
5 *City of Angels*

61

detective. He has battled alcoholism, had a partner resign, a partner die, a partner go missing, and seen his oldest son shot to death by robbers. The only thing that keeps him going is caring for his young son, Theo, who we expect to be tossed out of a window in a future episode.

NYPD Blue jumped the shark at the end of its sixth season when Sipowicz's wife Sylvia was killed by a stray bullet in a courthouse shootout. There is only so much torment that one detective can take. The program had problems finding a time slot on ABC, and co-creator David Milch left the show. Sipowicz lost yet another partner in Sorenson, to be replaced by none other than *Saved By the Bell*'s Mark-Paul Gosselaar. Successfully tapping a second former child star would take a lot of luck, and we all know Sipowicz has had anything but.

When did

The Odd Couple

1970–1975 Fridays on ABC

jump the shark?

"Can two divorced men share an apartment without driving each other crazy?" They can't, but we love watching them try.

The Odd Couple was a stage play written by Neil Simon, which then became a successful movie and an equally successful sitcom. Oscar Madison, a sportswriter and complete slob, takes in childhood friend Felix Unger, a neurotic neat freak who has just been kicked out by his wife.

The sitcom started where the play and film left off. The first season used only one camera and a laugh track, and featured the poker game with Oscar's buddies and visits from their neigh-

> **Felix's daughter, Edna, wants to run off with Paul Williams.**

bors, the Pigeon sisters. Only Murray the cop remained during the second season, and a live studio audience was brought in for the remainder of the show's run.

During its five years on the air, *The Odd Couple* offered countless unforgettable moments. Oscar and Felix made an "ass out of you and me" and appeared on *Password* ("Aristophanes"?). There were the pits in Felix's juice, Oscar's sleepwalking, "Happy, Peppy and Bursting with Love," and of course, "Oscar, Oscar, Oscar" (not to mention "Jesse, Jesse, Jesse").

We spotted a fin when the Special Guest Stars started to show up regularly. Oscar and his girlfriend Nancy the doctor broke up, and Brett Somers (Jack Klugman's ex) began to appear off and on. Oscar's secretary, Myrna, became more visible, and plots involved her and Murray. Tony Randall's passion for opera and cooking and Jack Klugman's love of horse racing also found their way into the mix.

The Odd Couple jumped in the fifth season when the occasional Howard Cosell or Monty Hall appearance morphed into unwelcome visits from Roy Clark, Dick Clark, and Richard Dawson. When Felix's daughter, Edna, wanted to run off with Paul Williams, we knew it was all over. *The Odd Couple* did end on a nice note with Felix and Gloria finally remarrying, but the subsequent "new" *Odd Couples* are shows better left unseen.

OPENING STATEMENTS

The best way to start a show . . .

1 *Twilight Zone*
2 *Law & Order*
3 *Dragnet*
4 *Star Trek*
5 *Jeopardy!*
6 *Naked City*
7 *The Tonight Show*
8 *Saturday Night Live*
9 *The Rockford Files*
10 *The People's Court*

The Price Is Right

1972– Weekdays on CBS

jump the shark?

"Come on down!" For almost thirty years, Bob Barker has been inviting us to be the next contestant on this classic game show.

The Price Is Right featured a variety of different games that involved guessing the retail price of a sponsored item. The game culminated in the "Showcase Showdown," where contestants would bid on different combinations of big ticket prizes.

> **Bob goes gray.**

SHOWCASING SHOWCASES

Our favorite showcase themes with fabulous prizes:

1 Main Street USA
2 Train Depot
3 Any Fairy Tale
4 Department Store
5 April Fool

Bob Barker hosted the action and was flanked by the original "Barker's Beauties," Janice, Anitra, and Dian, who smiled as they showed us how attractive Jiffy Pop could be. Announcer Johnny Olsen opened each show by inviting studio audience contestants to *come on down* to contestants' row.

Bidding is a science on *TPIR*, with savvier contestants often bidding "$1" in the hopes that the other contestants have overbid. Once on stage, the next step was attempting to win at games like Any Number (Car, Prize, or Piggy Bank), 3 Strikes (the X's in the bag), the Grocery Game ($21 on the cash register), and my personal favorite, Cliff Hanger (can't you hear the yodeler now?).

In the mid-eighties, the shark started to circle Bob and crew when the Showcase Showdown Wheel was introduced in the middle of "Hour Power" to select the final contestants. Other warning signs were the introduction of the larger-than-life Plinko, new Barker Beauties, and syndicated and nighttime versions of the show. The great Johnny Olsen died in 1986 and was replaced by Rod Roddy, and Bob asked us all to get our pets spayed or neutered.

The Price Is Right jumped the shark on the day Bob made his typical opening entrance . . .

HAIR CARE

Classic coifs:

1 Keri Russell's crop on *Felicity*
2 Robert Reed's perm on *The Brady Bunch*
3 Julia Louis-Dreyfus's variations on *Seinfeld*
4 Teri Hatcher's crop on *Lois & Clark*
5 Erin Gray stops bleaching on *Buck Rogers in the 25th Century*

but with frosty white hair. Although we respect Bob's pride in revealing his true colors, it was all downhill from there for the show. Dian sued Bob for harassment. (She later dropped the charges.) The new Barker Beauties, including Gena Nolin and Cindy Margolis, lacked the flair of the originals. Bob has since put in a classic performance in *Happy Gilmore,* but when it comes to *TPIR* it feels like we've just overbid.

When did

The Rockford Files

1974–1980 Fridays on NBC

jump the shark?

"This is Jim Rockford . . ." The greeting on that answering machine never grew old as Jim solved unsolvable cases with a sense of humor.

> **Jim returns in the nineties to let us know he still loves L.A.**

The Rockford Files worked so well because Jim Rockford was not your typical P.I. He was an ex-con who didn't trust anyone and had a paunch from drinking beers and eating crap, and the police didn't like him because he made them look bad. He also rarely carried a gun and would freely admit he was scared . . . a rarity for any private dick.

Regularly joining "Rockfish" were his often confused father, Rocky; pal and attorney Beth Davenport; and his former cellmate and resident pain in the ass, Angel. Detective Dennis Becker was the only cop on the LAPD who would tolerate Jim. Richie Brockelman and Lance White (Tom Selleck) were P.I.s who came on the scene toward the end.

HIGH POST

He's no Alan Thicke, but we'll take Mike Post opening themes anyway:

1 *The Greatest American Hero*
2 *Hill Street Blues*
3 *CHiPs*
4 *Law & Order*
5 *The White Shadow*

Rockford always charged $200 per day, plus expenses, but he rarely got paid. He tooled around L.A. in his Firebird with the classic Mike Post theme music playing in the background. He also had the best sport jackets in town.

The show maintained its high level of quality during its run thanks to those bizarre phone messages, stellar recurring characters such as prison buddy Gandolph Fitch, buddy John

Cooper, and hooker Rita Capkovic (played by Isaac Hayes, Bo Hopkins, and Rita Moreno, respectively), and solid plot lines. But we spotted a fin toward the end of the series when James Garner and Mariette Hartley kept showing up in those Polaroid ads.

Unable to leave well enough alone, *The Rockford Files* jumped in 1994 with its first of many TV movies. Although critically acclaimed, Jimbo's mystique just didn't hold up well in the nineties and a great show was reduced to a reunion tour. The show avoided the shark during its run . . . it never should have gone back into the water.

Roseanne

1988–1997 Tuesdays on ABC.

jump the shark?

I can hear that cackle in my sleep. *Roseanne* never took itself too seriously and was one of the top sitcoms of the nineties.

The Conners hit the lottery.

Following in the eighties tradition of giving any stand-up comedian a sitcom, Roseanne Barr scored with *Roseanne*. Roseanne never pulled any punches and was always armed with a biting remark on or off camera. The "I still love you" smile that followed a line was reportedly nowhere to be found when the cameras stopped rolling.

At home with Roseanne was the rest of the Conner clan, including occasionally working husband Dan, boy-crazy daughter Becky, Roseanne-junior daughter Darlene, and son D.J., who was Dan Junior in every sense of the word. Roseanne's younger sister, Jackie, often dropped by, bringing some bizarre situation along with her. These folks weren't your typical sitcom family, and most of America responded to the reality of the Conners.

Early plots on *Roseanne* typically revolved around money—or the lack thereof. But whether Dan was losing his job, Jackie was suffering through yet another failed relationship, Becky was eloping, or Darlene was finding herself, the laughs never stopped coming.

We spotted a fin during the sixth season when Becky's Lecy Goranson was replaced by Sarah Chalke. To her credit, Roseanne had fun with this by later alternating Beckys and making light of the situation. Jackie and Roseanne went on to have babies under atypical circumstances, and when the seventh season rolled around, Roseanne pulled a Cher, dropping her last name (along with Tom) in the opening credits. The show was on its way up the ramp.

Roseanne finally jumped when, following Dan's heart attack, the Conners hit the lottery and became millionaires. This working-class family had gone off the deep end and could now live the life they had always dreamed of. No one seemed to mind that it was completely inconsistent with the premise that made the show work in the first place. *Roseanne* had become a caricature of itself, and we found ourselves laughing at, not with, this once-classic sitcom.

LOSE THAT LAST NAME

Our favorite on-air credit changes:

1 Meredith Baxter dumps the Birney

2 Roseanne dumps the Barr, Arnold, and Thomas

3 Cher dumps Sonny

4 Lucy loses Ricky

5 Felicia Ayers-Allen loses Rashad (and Moore)

Saturday Night Live

1975– Saturdays on NBC

jump the shark?

"Live from New York . . . it's *Saturday Night*!" This 90-minute classic got its start as *Saturday Night* with Lorne Michaels producing, George Carlin hosting, and zero expectations. Who would have thought that Lorne would find himself in the same situation over twenty-five years later?

> **1980 . . . when the not-ready-to-be-replacements for "The Not Ready for Prime Time Players" joined the cast.**

Saturday Night Live was a groundbreaking late-night sketch comedy show that took no prisoners and couldn't be missed. Dan Aykroyd, John Belushi, Chevy Chase, Jane Curtin, Gilda Radner, Garrett Morris, and Laraine Newman (and later Bill Murray) came into our homes every Saturday night with a late-night edge that has never been equaled.

For five years the Not Ready for Prime Time Players entertained us with characters destined to become part of our cultural lexicon. Samurai anything, Emily Litella, the Blues Brothers, the Coneheads, Chico Escuela, Roseanne Roseannadanna are but a few. No politician escaped unscathed (particularly Gerald Ford), guest hosts and musical guests were the tops, and Generalissimo Francisco Franco remained dead.

The brilliant writing staff and the underrated band were the true backbone of the show. Father Guido Sarducci, Mr. Bill, and Andy Kaufman proved that others could contribute even if they weren't part of the main cast. Paul McCartney and John Lennon even considered reuniting when Lorne Michaels gave them a chance to come on down.

We spotted a fin when movie careers beckoned and Belushi and Aykroyd left the show at the end of its fifth season. Bill Murray

UPDATE ANCHORS

I'm anchoring *Weekend Update* and you're not:

1 Norm MacDonald
2 Jane Curtin
3 Dennis Miller
4 Chevy Chase
5 Garrett Morris (News for the hard of hearing)

was a great replacement, but recurring Franken and Davis appearances were starting to get tough to handle.

SNL jumped in 1980 when the original cast and Lorne Michaels exited, only to be replaced by Woody Allen's pal producer Jean Doumanian and a group that wasn't ready for late night, let alone prime-time playing. The show has been on for countless years since, but even with Eddie Murphy, Mike Myers, Phil Hartman, and other great cast members, it has never approached the edge it had when it came on the scene in the mid-seventies. As a great comedian (I think it was Gilbert Gottfried) once said, Saturday Night Live is just an average restaurant in a great location.

When did

Scooby Doo

1968–1994 Saturdays on ABC

jump the shark?

"Scooby Doo, where are you?" Shaggy and the rest of the Mystery Machine gang have been asking this question, and solving local crimes, for over twenty-five years.

Scrappy.

Scooby Doo is a classic cartoon that features Scooby, a cowardly Great Dane who hangs around with four teenagers in search of mystery and adventure. Ascot-clad Fred, red-hot Daphne, bookish Velma, and perpetually hungry Norville "Shaggy" Rogers occupy the seats in the Mystery Machine.

Thanks to this Scooby gang, we have "The Scooby Doo Rule" which can be applied to any mystery program. The first character that you see who is not part of the main cast is the culprit. It works on every episode and leaves the guilty party always muttering about those meddling kids.

Early on, it was fun following the Mystery Machine and uncovering the ghosts and ghouls that haunted different towns. Scooby and Shaggy were often teamed together and both were scared of their own shadow. They always had the munchies and if a Scooby Snack was on the table, Scooby could take on a pit bull with one paw tied behind his back. Velma sometimes tagged along, but more often she was stuck with Fred (don't call me Alan M.) and Daphne tracking down the "real" clues. Now there's a love triangle that makes *Dawson's Creek* look tame.

In the early seventies, Scooby met up with animated versions of real-life actors in *The New Scooby Doo Movies* such as Sandy Duncan ("Randy!") and Don Knotts ("Ron Rotts!"). An animated Sonny and Cher also guest-starred with Scooby in "The Secret of Shark Island." Scooby's brother, Scooby Dumb, also made a few Special Guest Star appearances, and ABC later combined the power of mighty mutts and created *The Scooby Doo/Dynomutt Hour*.

But this shark bait pales in comparison to what came next: an obnoxious nephew named Scrappy Doo was introduced in 1979, and it was all downhill from there. The introduction of a cute new kid is a surefire trigger for jumping the shark on a network series. In animation, it's even worse because it's young minds that are being corrupted. Millions were scarred from "puppy power," and some are still finding their way back to Saturday morning cartoons to this day. "Scooby-Dooby-Doo-oo-oo!!"

When did

Seinfeld

1990–1998 Thursdays on NBC

jump the shark?

Seinfeld was the must-see-TV comedy of the nineties that spawned many a catchphrase . . . not that's there's anything wrong with that.

George's fiancée, Susan, dies from licking her wedding invitation envelopes.

The *Seinfeld Chronicles* began as a quirky half-hour comedy about "nothing" that only Jews from New York supposedly "got." Jerry, George, Elaine, and Kramer didn't know the meaning of the word "share," and we couldn't get enough of them.

MEET THE PARENTS

Your choice: Frank and Estelle Costanza or . . .

1 Archie & Edith Bunker
2 George & Weezie Jefferson
3 Tony & Carmela Soprano
4 Frank & Marie Barone
5 Al & Peg Bundy
6 Steven & Elyse Keaton
7 Homer & Marge Simpson
8 Mike & Carol Brady
9 Roseanne & Dan Conner
10 Cliff & Clair Huxtable

Seinfeld was expert at integrating quirky characters that worked well within the show. Who can ever forget Poppie, Uncle Leo, Jack Klompus, Frank Costanza, Jackie Chiles, Bania, the Soup Nazi, Delores, the Bubble Boy, Kramer's "small" pal Mickey, J. Peterman, Puddy, Jon Voight, Mr. Lippman, Marla the Virgin, George Steinbrenner, and of course, Newman?

Seinfeld was adept at avoiding the shark early in its run. For a stint during the second season, any entrance by Kramer was met with applause from the studio audience. But before Kramer could become the next Fonzie, the producers wisely stifled the claps, and the program ducked the fin. Rather than spelling doom, Special Guest Stars such as Keith Hernandez and Bette Midler provided some of the show's signature moments.

However, when Kramer moved to Hollywood and Elaine started working for Mr. Pitt, we smelled blood. At the end of the fifth season, George and Jerry agreed to propose to their current girlfriends. Jerry wisely backed away, but George went ahead and got engaged to Susan, the NBC network exec.

Seinfeld avoided a surefire leap over the shark the next season by not having a wedding, but Susan's death from licking the wedding invitation envelopes caused the show to jump. This coincided with co-creator Larry David leaving the show, and *Seinfeld* was never the same. The backward episode was gimmicky, George went from whining all the time to just being angry, the catchphrases seemed less natural, yada, yada, yada. . . . Although some gems continued to surface (Kramer's *Merv* talk show), Thursday didn't have the same flavor through the final episode, which could never meet our expectations.

Sesame Street

1969– Weekday mornings on PBS

jump the shark?

"Sunny day, sweeping the clouds away . . ." This famous inner-city block has taught millions of children their ABCs and 123s with a sense of humor that even parents can enjoy.

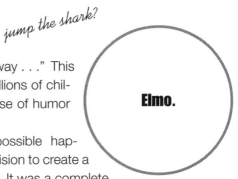

Elmo.

Sesame Street made the impossible happen—it combined education and television to create a program that would change the world. It was a complete departure from any previous children's show, and this gem from the Children's Television Workshop has rightly received more Emmys than any other television program in history.

Sesame Street took place on an inner-city block where real-life folks like Bob, Gordon, Susan, David, Luis, Maria, Linda, and Mr. Hooper coexisted with muppets like Oscar the Grouch, Ernie and Bert, Kermit the Frog, Grover, Cookie Monster, and of course, Big Bird. Mixed in were various animated and quite trippy sequences teaching us the letter or number that the day's episode was "brought to you by."

Early *Sesame Street* episodes had a host of classic recurring scenes including Sesame Street News (with trench-coated reporter Kermit), Super Grover, and Roosevelt Franklin Elementary School. Celebrity cameos were hysterical and stayed with you for a long time. A young, bald James Earl Jones reciting the alphabet still sends shivers down my spine, and who could forget a young Mr. Bentley painting numbers everywhere he went?

Sesame Street withstood the introduction of many different muppets, the departure of David, and the replacement of Gordon by a different actor. We spotted a fin when everyone on

GREATEST HITS

Classic songs from a classic show:

1 Ma-na, Ma-na
2 Sing!
3 C is for Cookie
4 I Love Trash
5 Rubber Duckie
6 Bein' Green
7 The People in Your Neighborhood
8 Dee, Dee, Dee
9 La, La, La
10 Fuzzy and Blue

GROWIN' UP

Do you remember?

1 Don Music composing "Mary Had a Bicycle"
2 Guy Smiley hosting *This Is Your Life* for a tree
3 That red typewriter on wheels that whistled and typed only one letter
4 Hey froggie baby!
5 "We all live in a capital I . . ."

Sesame Street could suddenly see Big Bird's invisible best friend Mr. Snuffle-upagus, and Mr. Hooper passed away.

Sesame Street jumped with the introduction of Elmo in the eighties. It wasn't necessarily the voice or the character itself, but the fact that our favorite PBS show had finally sold out. The early muppets had an edge—Oscar was mean, Bert was anal, and Cookie was a monster. The new muppets were preprogrammed for cuteness and merchandiseability, and the hipness of the show disappeared, along with the classic opening and closing themes.

This entry was brought to you by the letters *R* and *E* and the number *2*.

When did
The Simpsons
1989– Sundays on FOX

jump the shark?

Not yet . . .

"D'oh!" No comedy, animated or otherwise, has generated more belly-laughs over the past decade than this nuclear family from Springfield.

The Simpsons first appeared as a recurring short that aired during *The Tracy Ullman Show*. After about fifty of these vignettes, FOX realized that they had a potential hit on their hands, and wisely gave *The Simpsons* twenty-two minutes of their own on prime time. Creators Matt Groening, James L. Brooks, and Sam Simon have certainly made the most of it.

The Simpsons clan consisted of dopey Homer, supermom Marge, fourth-grade underachiever Bart, wise-beyond-her-eight-years Lisa, and baby Maggie of the surgically affixed pacifier. Dog Santa's Little Helper and cat Snowball II (Snowball I was unceremoniously run over) round out the immediate family, but it is the town of Springfield that made *The Simpsons* so special.

The Simpsons could be found on the

UP WITH PEOPLE

The other voices of Springfield:

1 Harry Shearer
2 Hank Azaria
3 Phil Hartman
4 Kelsey Grammer
5 Marcia Wallace

couch watching *Itchy & Scratchy* (not Poochie!), *Krusty the Klown* (with Sideshow Bob or Sideshow Mel), or a news report from Kent Brockman. There were problems at school with Principal Skinner, Milhouse, Nelson, and Ralph Wiggum. Homer drank Duff with Barney down at Moe's, battled with Flanders and Reverend Lovejoy, or combated town tycoon, Montgomery Burns (and Smithers, of course). It didn't matter . . . every episode was funny and contained more pop-culture references than you'll find in this book.

We got worried at the start of the third season when Special Guest Star Michael Jackson (credited as John Jay Smith) cheesily sang Lisa's birthday song. Right around the corner Krusty reunited with his rabbi father, Barney and Homer battled for snowplow supremacy, and Aerosmith shared the stage with Moe. The seventh season scared us with a "Who Shot Mr. Burns?" cliffhanger, Special Guest Stars Paul and Linda McCartney, and the return of Sideshow Bob. Still, *The Simpsons* persevered.

We finally spotted a fin at the start of the ninth season when Principal Skinner's true identity was revealed as Armin Tamzarian. The show's focus had completely shifted from Bart to Homer—who was charmingly dumb to begin with, but now really, really stupid. The frequency of musical episodes increased and celebrities began to play themselves.

The Simpsons almost jumped the shark during season eleven when Maude Flanders was killed by tossed T-shirts (intended for Homer) that accidentally sent her over the bleachers and down to the concrete below. The show was losing its edge as the "Behind the Laughter" spoof seemed contrived, Sideshow Bob was brought back again, and 'NSync made an appearance. Still *The Simpsons* is bankable for big laughs and, having lasted this long without jumping, is by far the best comedy on television.

The Sopranos

1999– Sundays on HBO

jump the shark?

"Fuggedaboutit . . ." _The Sopranos_ mixes organized crime with psychotherapy to create the best show of its time.

This tale of Tony and his two families gives us a reason to pay for HBO. At the suburban Soprano home, Tony's wife Carmela, daughter Meadow, and son Anthony Jr. lived an upper-middle class New Jersey life. Tony's other family of Paulie, Silvio, and Chris lived an even better life at the Bada Bing, but with great consequences. The problems started when the families mixed. Tony began to worry about his mother, Livia, so much that it drove him to fainting spells. His Uncle Junior felt under appreciated even though he was "officially" in charge of things.

> **Junior sings at Jackie Jr.'s wake.**

MOB TIES

Classic shows that dealt with organized crime:

1 _The Untouchables_
2 _Crime Story_
3 _Wiseguy_
4 _EZ Streets_
5 _Falcone_

When we first met Tony, he was learning to confide in psychiatrist Dr. Melfi—who had her own set of issues. Tony's problems ranged from Meadow having trouble choosing a college to Uncle Junior and his mother putting out a contract on him. The first two seasons followed Chris's journey through the mob, withstood the entrance of Tony's sister, Janice, Carmela's "therapy," and plenty of nights at the Bing.

We spotted a fin when Chris and Adrianna got engaged and Richie and Janice became more of the show's focus. All signs at "work" pointed to Big Pussy being a rat, and at the end of season two, Pussy got whacked and tossed into the ocean . . . literal shark bait.

Tony's mother died the next season, Dr. Melfi was violently raped, and Special Guest Star Annabella Sciorra was always available to chat after the show at hbo.com. This hidden gem had gone mainstream. At the end of season three, Uncle Junior belted out a touching song in Italian, a sad but sure sign that this Emmy winner has indeed jumped the shark.

IT'S NOT TV. IT'S HBO.

These series are almost worth paying for:

1 _Oz_
2 _Sex and the City_
3 _Not Necessarily the News_
4 _The Larry Sanders Show_
5 _Dream On_

When did
South Park
1997– Wednesdays on Comedy Central

jump the shark?

"Come on down to South Park . . ." where foul-mouthed elementary school children in a lovely Colorado town deal with absurd and insanely funny situations in this animated gem.

South Park is the hometown of grade school pals Stan, Kyle, Cartman, and Kenny. Its animation is

> **Bigger, Longer & Uncut—** a great movie, but Matt and Trey forgot about the TV show.

almost as crude as its humor, a winning formula created by Matt Stone and Trey Parker. Wendy, Chef, Big Gay Al, Cartman's mom, and Mr. Garrison are but a few of the distinctive South Park residents. Terrance and Phillip and Mr. Hankey are also memorable recurring Special Guest Stars.

BLACK MOSES

Our favorite feature film contributions by Isaac Hayes (Chef):

1 *Escape from New York*
2 *Shaft*
3 *I'm Gonna Git You Sucka*
4 *Robin Hood—Men in Tights*
5 *Blues Brothers* 2000

The first series episode, entitled "Cartman Gets an Anal Probe," let us know exactly what to expect from South Park. Each show featured Kenny dying in a unique way, including being microwaved, eaten by turkeys, and hanging himself playing tetherball, you bastards.

On April Fools' Day in 1998, Cartman's father was to be revealed, but a Terrance and Phillip episode was aired instead, a sure sign of trouble. Chef was featured in Chef Aid and on a *Behind the Music* spoof, Happy Charlie Manson was introduced, and "Oh my god, they killed Kenny" was left unsaid in some episodes . . . The shark began to circle.

The Oscar-nominated *Bigger, Longer & Uncut* was released the following year. With all the great material in the movie, the show became an afterthought. Mr. Hankey's Christmas Classics and other singing episodes kept coming, Cartman found a note that made everyone literally give a crap, and Timmy joined the gang of four in the fourth grade. South Park had gone to the well one too many times. Although Matt and Trey created a segment with an animated Fonzie failing in his attempt to jump the shark, the same can't be said for their groundbreaking cartoon.

SPECIAL GUEST VOICES

Listen, and you'll hear:

1 George Clooney
2 Jay Leno
3 Jennifer Aniston
4 Rick James
5 Henry Winkler

"Space . . . the final frontier . . ." Final? This journey hasn't ended after thirty-five years of going where no man has gone before.

Gene Roddenberry launched the starship *Enterprise* with the melodramatic Captain James T. Kirk, pointy-eared Vulcan Mr. Spock, Bones "dammit Jim, I'm a doctor" McCoy, Scotty, Chekov, Sulu, Uhura, and a bunch of other expendable guys wearing red shirts. The crew spent their stardates exploring new worlds and dealing with Klingons, Romulans, the Borg, and Ricardo Montalban.

> **Spock sings with the space hippies.**

I'M YOUR CAPTAIN

Our favorites at the helm:

1 James T. Kirk
2 Jean-Luc Picard
3 Kathryn Janeway
4 John Archer
5 Christopher Pike

Star Trek was anything but a big hit when it first aired in the late sixties, but the cult following acquired over the years is absolutely mind-boggling. The quality of an episode often correlated with the kind of shape William Shatner was in. Early classics, with a fit Shatner, included a good Kirk battling an evil Kirk, Kirk fighting a big lizard called the Gorn, and Balok, the freaky-looking blue guy used in the closing credits of each show.

The next season found an oddly behaving Spock killing Kirk and Bones (who were alive, just on tri-ox), Scotty still trying to get more power, and Kirk falling for every woman, alien or otherwise, he could get close to. Our shark phasers were on stun during "The Trouble with Tribbles," when Uhura brought cute little furry creatures with a distaste for Klingons onto the Enterprise.

Shields went up at the start of the third and final season when Spock's brain went missing. *Star Trek* finally jumped with "The Way to Eden," when Spock sang with a rescued musician, Adam—who was traveling with space hippies—and broadcast a concert shipwide to distract the Enterprise crew. Distract us it did.

TIME TRAVEL

Memorable eras visited by the original *Star Trek* crew:

1 Nazi Germany
2 OK Corral
3 Earth, 1994
4 Gangland Chicago
5 Ancient Greece

This classic was followed with a Special Guest Star appearance by former NFL defensive lineman Fred Williamson, and another episode featuring Abraham Lincoln. *Star Trek* had gone where plenty of other shows had gone before . . . straight over the shark.

When did

Survivor

2000– Thursdays on CBS

jump the shark?

"Outwit. Outplay. Outlast." The college psych experiment gone wrong captured the fancy of the nation as we watched to see who would be the sole *Survivor*.

> **Jeff Probst took the world's fastest helicopter ride from Australia to L.A.**

Each season, sixteen strangers are stranded (pay no attention to those TV cameras) in some inhospitable third-world environment, split into two tribes, forced to band together to take part in different challenges and to vote someone off every week. Jeff Probst pops up from time to time to host immunity challenges and the best eight minutes on television, the fatal tribal council. The survivor left standing wins one million dollars plus a feature article in the following week's *People*.

Survivor began on the island of Pulau Tiga and appealed to the voyeur in all of us. It became the anti–*Who Wants To Be A Millionaire*, and we were ready for it. When the remaining members of the Tagi and Pagong tribes merged, sparks started to fly. A fat naked guy dancing (not that there's anything wrong with that), a good ol' Navy SEAL letting go of the pole, the snake and the rat . . . Colleen, Susan, Rudy, Kelly, and Richard became America's guilty pleasure.

SURVIVING AFTER SURVIVOR

Memorable contestants:

1 Colleen
2 Amber
3 Richard
4 Rudy
5 Kentucky Joe

EARLY CASUALTIES

The tribe has spoken.
Ouch.

1 Debb
2 Sonja
3 BB
4 Kel
5 Maralyn

We couldn't miss the huge Target logo when the next season began in the Australian outback; the sponsors made their presence more obvious than a scene in *Wayne's World*. The new contestants seemed like actors, not real people, but their struggle was still somewhat compelling. This second edition didn't have the originality and spontaneity of the first, and the contestants cared more about becoming famous than winning the million. We spotted a fin when Colby cuddled with his mom in the Pontiac Aztec.

In the last episode, Jeff Probst collected the final votes, invited the remaining survivors to join him in L.A. reveal the winner, and took off in a chopper. He must have flown over a shark on his way to the studio, because *Survivor* hasn't been the same since. Back in L.A. all the contestants were smiling and clean when Jeff walked in (still holding the "unread" votes) to reveal that Tina had won the million.

Survivor moved on to Africa and Marquesas, relying on the formula it had created and losing the edge it once had over the aging veteran *Friends*. With talk of a celebrity edition, another sign that the shark has attacked, even Mark Burnett and crew have to admit that reality sometimes bites.

When did

Taxi

1978–1983 Thursdays on ABC

jump the shark?

> **It became the Latka and Simka show.**

The opening notes of Bob James's theme (was that a recorder?) signaled the start of this classic comedy about a bunch of cab drivers searching for a better life.

Based on an article in *The New Yorker*, *Taxi* combined great acting with smart writing to create an exceptional, unique comedy. Imagine *Cheers* taking place in a cab garage, with bad New York accents replacing the Boston ones, and you've got the Sunshine Cab Company.

PLANES, TRAINS, AND AUTOMOBILES

Our favorite modes of transportation:

1 Soul Train
2 Car 54, Where Are You?
3 My Mother the Car
4 Wagon Train
5 Supertrain

Alex was the only lifetime cab driver of the bunch and the oracle of the garage. Bobby was a struggling actor (true-to-life), Elaine and her Nardos dreamed about an art gallery, Tony was a dumb boxer, and Latka was a mechanic that no one could understand. Running things from behind the dispatch cage was the angry, diminutive Louie De Palma.

Typically, someone would have a problem that seemed hopeless, which Louie would make fun of. But after asking Alex's advice, the issue would be resolved and life would go on. *Taxi* got a huge boost when Reverend Jim Ignatowski joined the crew during the second season. Whether pondering what a yellow light means, impersonating a water cooler, or debating Delawarians versus Delawarites, Iggy was the perfect quirk to complete the ensemble.

A shark alert was sounded when Louie got serious with Zena, Latka transformed into alter ego lounge lizard Vic Ferrari, and a two-part fantasy episode with Herve Villechaize featured Elaine in a full-scale Broadway production number. We spotted a fin when Bobby left for California to become an actor (he's still searching) and Latka's girlfriend Simka returned and became part of the cast.

Taxi jumped when most of the plots began to revolve around Latka and Simka, thankyouverymuch. Like Jerry's pals on *Seinfeld*, the Gravases were fantastic supporting players but couldn't be the focal point of the show. *Taxi* moved from ABC to NBC toward the very end and the Sunshine Cab Company closed its doors shortly thereafter. Goodnight, Mr. Walters.

TONY DANZA AS . . . TONY

This master thespian often plays characters named Tony:

1 Tony Banta—*Taxi*
2 Tony Micelli—*Who's the Boss?*
3 Tony Canetti—*Hudson Street*
4 Tony Dimeo—*The Tony Danza Show*
5 Tommy Silva—*The Practice* (hey, it's close enough)

Three's Company

1977–1984 Tuesdays on ABC

jump the shark?

> **Chrissy is replaced by her cute, klutzy cousin, Cindy.**

"Come and knock on our door . . ." The kisses were hers and hers and his on this seventies hit loaded with double entendres, California lifestyles, and Norman Fell.

Three's Company was huge right from the start. The show took place in a Santa Monica two-bedroom condo where the three roommates were the Velma-esque Janet, ditzy blond Chrissy, and the pretending-to-be-gay, although always interested in a bistro, Jack Tripper. The landlords in the apartment downstairs were a horny elderly couple, the Ropers. Swinging neighbor Larry, who had the sex appeal of Quincy, M.E., gave Jack advice that was almost always worth ignoring.

Three's Company never pretended to be anything but a farce. Helen and Stanley Roper were convinced Jack was gay, and so were we, based on his reaction to spilling the water on a sunbathing Chrissy in the opening. Jack kept getting caught in compromising positions and always had a way out.

Chrissy was always stupid. Jack was always goofy. And Janet was always . . . Janet.

At the start of the third season, the Ropers spun off into their own show, only to be replaced by the consummate professional Don Knotts as Mr. Furley. The show never missed a beat. However, as soon as Richard Kline was moved into the opening credits, the shark smelled blood.

The next season, Suzanne Somers held out for a huge raise and a piece of the show, and the producers ignored her. Her role was limited to distant phone calls and she was gone by the end of the season, only to resurface with her Thighmaster years later. Clumsy cousin Cindy was the first of many Chrissy replacements that just didn't work, and the shark had been jumped.

Terri the nurse came next, whose only shortcoming was that she wasn't funny at all. Jack became a professional chef and opened Jack's Bistro, which couldn't compare to the Regal Beagle. The show was eventually cancelled, and then attempted to come back as *Three's a Crowd*, with Janet married and gone and Jack remaining with a live-in girlfriend. No one was watching.

COUNTDOWN

Add 'em up:

1 *One Day at a Time*
2 *My Two Dads*
3 *Three's Company*
4 *Ball Four*
5 *Party of Five*
6 *The Six Million Dollar Man*
7 *7th Heaven*
8 *Eight Is Enough*
9 *Star Trek: Deep Space Nine*
10 *Just the Ten of Us*

When did
What's Happening!!
1976–1979 Thursdays on ABC

jump the shark?

"Hey, hey, hey . . ." It was fun dribbling around this lighthearted inner-city family sitcom with its over-the-top overweight characters and social themes.

What's Happening!! featured an all-black cast and was *Good Times* without the edge. Roger "Raj" Thomas was a high-school geek who lived with divorced big Mama and wise-ass sister, Dee. His pals

Big Earl and Little Earl come to town.

IT'S NOT OVER UNTIL . . .

Mama and Shirley tipped the right side of the scales. Other big favorites:

1 Camryn Manheim
2 Nell Carter
3 Roseanne
4 Delta Burke
5 Kathy Kinney

were the shy, wise-cracking Dwayne and the large wannabe dancer Rerun. The gang would hang out at Rob's place, often waited on by extra-large waitress Shirley, who would stick it to Rerun whenever she could.

What's Happening!! began as a vehicle to make Fred Barry a star, but Rerun did anything but steal this show. Dee and Shirley shined with a host of zingers while Raj, Dwayne, and Mama certainly held their own. Between Rerun's three-minute dancing routines was sharp comedy mixed in with serious themes like Dee running away, Mama's ex trying to return, Shirley getting fired, and the pain of fat jokes.

We spotted a fin toward the end of the second season when Rerun wore a long trench coat and snuck a tape recorder into a special guest star concert of . . . the Doobie Brothers. Although it featured the classic line "Which Doobie you be?" the shark began to circle. Raj the geek became more of a ladies man, Dee and Mama seemed to disappear, and Rerun was still trying to be a star at every turn.

The next season, Raj graduated and moved out of the house into an apartment with Rerun for college. The show went sailing over the shark when we met neighbors Big Earl and his son, Little Earl, whose cuteness was there to combat Dee's puberty.

One of the final episodes of *What's Happening!!* featured Rerun working his final days as a page at ABC and portraying Mork, Jack Tripper, and the Fonz on various sets. It was too late, but we would have loved to see Rerun bust a move in a leather jacket on water skis as he hurdled over the shark.

I'M WITH THE BAND

Memorable musical cameos:

1 Stevie Wonder on *The Cosby Show*
2 R.E.M. on *Sesame Street*
3 Roy Clark on *The Odd Couple*
4 Elton John on *The Late Show*
5 Glenn Frey on *Miami Vice*

When did **Wheel of Fortune**

1975– Weekdays on NBC

jump the shark?

"Oh, Vanna!" Whether it's Chuck, Pat, or a former all-pro kicker named Rolf hosting, we can't get enough of that colorful spinning wheel and Vanna twirling her letters on this classic game show.

> **They give you the S, T, R, N, L, and E for the final round.**

Wheel of Fortune, a Merv Griffin production, features three contestants spinning a wheel with different values, and then choosing a letter to solve a word puzzle à la Hangman. If the spinners can avoid bankruptcy and losing a turn while buying a couple of vowels, they can keep amassing dollars and letters to solve brain teasers like MARY HAD A _ITT_E _AMB.

WHEEL . . . OF . . . FORTUNE!

Our favorite spokes:

1 Bankrupt
2 Free Spin
3 Lose A Turn
4 Trip
5 $5,000

Chuck Woolery was the original host with Susan (Mrs. Dick Ebersol) Stafford spinning the letters. The early years featured post-puzzle shopping as contestants spent their winnings on glamorous prizes, featuring the dalmatian with moveable spots, and putting the remaining dollars on account. Chuck walked after Merv didn't give him a large raise in the show's fifth season. Enter L.A. weatherman Pat Sajak. The next year, Vanna White replaced Susan Stafford, and the show took off in syndication.

Things started to change on *Wheel* when the post-puzzle shopping was eliminated and replaced by cash prizes and a bonus final round. In 1989, Pat tried his luck as a late-night talk-show host and was replaced on the daytime version by former All-Pro San Diego Chargers kicker Rolf Bernischke, and the shark began to circle as NBC dropped the show from its daytime lineup.

The bonus round had the contestant who had amassed the most cash guess five letters and a vowel to determine mind-boggling puzzles like TO_ CRUISE. More often than not, the finalist would choose R, S, T, N, L, and E, and then watch Vanna do her thing. *Wheel of Fortune*

THANK YOU, DON PARDO

The finest off-stage voices:

1 Johnny Olsen on *The Price Is Right*
2 Gary Owens on *Laugh-In*
3 Charlie O'Donnell on *Wheel of Fortune*
4 Colin Quinn on *Remote Control*
5 The judges on any game show, who are related to the parents on any *Peanuts* special.

jumped when those letters were given to the contestant, and they were allocated three additional letters and another vowel.

Shortly after almost half the alphabet was given away Pat returned full-time to *Wheel,* but Vanna now just had to touch the letters, not turn them. Joining "Free spin" on the wheel were more trips, cars, and jewelry, but you could only win the prize if your letter was part of the puzzle.

The puzzles were too easy and the wheel too complex, a telltale sign that *Wheel of Fortune* had jumped the shark.

When did

Who Wants To Be A Millionaire

1999–2002

jump the shark?

The guy from the IRS wins the million.

This British import with Regis at its helm captivated the entire nation (until *Survivor* came along) and resurrected the prime-time quiz show.

Who Wants To Be A Millionaire gave everyone a chance to win (cue Dr. Evil) one million dollars by answering fifteen multiple-choice questions correctly. You needed to have the fastest finger to get into the hot seat with Reege and get a shot at the mil. The single-use lifelines that helped you through your journey included asking the audience, phoning a friend, or 50/50—which eliminated half of the answers.

Millionaire was an instant hit. Its overly dramatic music and lighting created real tension as we watched countless individuals fall short of the grand prize. Questions varied in difficulty, ranging from the $100 "Little Bo Beep lost her what?" to the $32,000 "Female plankton are known as . . . ?" Regis, fully clad in his slick *Millionaire* suit, did a great job of keeping the game moving along without rushing it, all the while yukking it up with the contestants.

As the show's popularity grew, ABC pushed its luck and decided to air it three nights a week. We still couldn't get enough of it, but the shark went on alert. Regis now sped through the first five "moron" questions (although it was classic when a self-proclaimed genius missed one), but the tension remained intense whenever a player approached the million.

Millionaire ironically jumped when someone finally *won*. John Carpenter was so damn snide that we just couldn't root for him, plus he worked for the IRS. Then he used a lifeline to call and tell his father that he just won a million dollars. Jealous? You bet. Although the show remained popular in the ratings, the mystique of *Millionaire* had cracked.

Following the IRS victory, a sports celebrity edition was aired to complement a Super Bowl telecast. Soon after, a contestant used Rosie O'Donnell as a lifeline, a precursor to Celebrity Millionaire where stars played for charity and to show us how smart they think they are. A handful of others have become millionaires since then, but if you're under sixty-five years old, you've moved on to other shows. And that's our final answer.

REGIS

The man is everywhere. He's always been on the small screen, including:

1 *The Joey Bishop Show*
2 *Almost Anything Goes*
3 *The Neighbors*
4 *The Late Show with David Letterman*
5 *Live with Regis & a woman whose first name starts with a K*

MONEY GAMES

It's all about the dollars. Greed is good:

1 *The Price Is Right*
2 *Let's Make a Deal*
3 *The $25,000 Pyramid*
4 *Greed*
5 *Sale of the Century*

When did

Who's the Boss?

1984–1992 Tuesdays on ABC

jump the shark?

> **Tony and Angela finally get together.**

Somewhere in Connecticut, an obsessive career woman took in a laid-back male housekeeper to care for her family in this eighties sitcom.

Who's the Boss? chronicled the lives of the Bower family at home in the high-class Connecticut suburbs. Angela is a Type A+ divorcee living with her young son, Jonathan (not that there's anything wrong with that), and sex-starved mother, Mona. Tony is a former baseball player with an easygoing attitude and a pre-pubescent daughter, Sam. Angela hires Tony to take care of the house, and we're left wondering who's the boss.

Who's the Boss? overcame many obstacles during its eight-year run. It began with Tony Danza playing a former athlete named "Tony." Mix in a "sexy" Katherine Helmond and the sexually-challenged Jonathan and well, at least there was Alyssa Milano to look at. Tony was from the streets, while Angela was president of an ad agency, and this class difference gave the show some tension.

But Tony went back to school and Angela, having been canned by the ad agency, started her own firm, and the differences between them began to fade. When Sam graduated high school, she and her father enrolled at the same college. Jonathan went to high school, so Billy the new cute kid was taken in and the fin was spotted.

The writers, however, were smart enough to keep Tony and Angela from becoming an item for most of the show's run. *Who's the Boss?* finally jumped when the two declared their (surprise) love for each other, but by that time we were only watching to see how much little Sam had grown. Ay. Yo.

ELDERLY VIXENS

If you think Mona is sexy, you'll love:

1 Blanche from *The Golden Girls*
2 Helen from *The Ropers*
3 Lovey from *Gilligan's Island*
4 Mother Jefferson from *The Jeffersons*
5 Dr. Ruth Westheimer

ANGELA'S ASHES

Judith Light has become the poster child for Lifetime. Notice a trend here?

1 *Stamp of a Killer*
2 *Wife, Mother, Murderer*
3 *Betrayal of Trust*
4 *A Strange Affair*
5 *Murder at My Door*

WKRP in Cincinnati

1978–1982 Mondays on CBS

jump the shark?

"I'm living on the air in Cincinnati . . . Cincinnati, WKRP." Cincinnati was the radio home of WKRP, a classic comedy offering more music and Les Nessman.

> **A Very Special episode about the Who concert stampede.**

WKRP in Cincinnati was an unprofitable radio station until new program director Andy Travis came to town and turned it into a Top 40 haven, despite the wishes of owner Mrs. Carlson and her often confused general manger, son Arthur (a.k.a. Big Guy). The WKRP on-air talent included perpetually stoned morning man Dr. Johnny Fever, smooth night jock Venus Flytrap, and the incomparable newsman Les Nessman. The office was staffed with smart, Ginger-esque receptionist Jennifer, Andy's smart Mary Ann–esque assistant Bailey, and the one and only ad salesman, Herb Tarlek.

The acting was tremendous, but the writing was even better on *WKRP*. The show established itself in its first season when the Big Guy's turkey drop promotion produced the classic "As god is my witness, I thought turkeys could fly." Whether it was Herb hitting on Jennifer or Les pronouncing Chi Chi Rodriguez, these scenes were not to be missed.

We spotted a fin when Special Guest Star Sparky Anderson hosted a sports talk show during the second season. It was a sign that *WKRP* was no longer a hidden gem but had hit the mainstream. Our fears were confirmed when a Very Special episode covered the fatal real-life stampede that took place at a 1979 Who concert in Cincinnati, killing eleven people. *WKRP* got preachy, and vaulted over the shark in the process.

WHAT'S WRONG WITH THE OLD?

Can't think of a new show? Just bring back an old one:

1 *The New WKRP in Cincinnati*
2 *The New Twilight Zone*
3 *The New Odd Couple*
4 *The New Mickey Mouse Club*
5 *The New Addams Family*
6 *The New Munsters*
7 *The New Monkees*
8 *The New Hollywood Squares*
9 *The New Dick Van Dyke Show*
10 *The New Avengers*

ON THE RADIO

WKRP was the best of any shows taking place in a radio setting. Other favorites include:

1 *Frasier*
2 *NewsRadio*
3 *Howard Stern*
4 *Rhythm & Blues*
5 *The George Wendt Show*

A decade after its four-year run on CBS, *WKRP* came back with new episodes in syndication for two more years. Only the Big Guy, Herb, and Les returned, with occasional appearances by the great Edie McClurg as Lucille, Herb's wife. Unfortunately, Lucille was the only reason to tune in. When the original *WKRP* now airs in syndication, much of the classic rock played by Johnny is replaced with cheesy generic music. They can replace the music, but not the writing on this memorable program.

When did
The Wonder Years
1988–1993 Wednesdays on ABC

jump the shark?

Daniel Stern's voice guided us through Kevin Arnold's childhood exploits during the turbulent 1960s and touched a nerve in all of us.

Kevin Arnold finally hits puberty.

We all could relate to the growing-up experiences chronicled in *The Wonder Years.* At the Arnold house, Jack, the hard-working blue-collar dad, was married to warm, spunky Norma. Hippie big sister Karen, abusive big brother Wayne, and young wide-eyed Kevin rounded out the clan. Kevin's best friends were the geeky Paul Pfeiffer and dream girl Winnie Cooper. The show's narration, provided by a reflective adult Kevin Arnold, was the glue that held *The Wonder Years* together.

The show premiered after the 1988 Super Bowl and began to interweave the events of the sixties with Kevin's junior-high-school life. *The Wonder Years* was poignant and expertly written, dealing with Winnie's brother dying in one episode, and discussing Paul's basketball ability with Coach Cutlip the next. At home, the Arnolds tried to deal with each other, especially the rebellious Karen and the perpetually screwed-up Wayne.

OPENING COVERS

Joe Cocker's rendition of "With a Little Help from My Friends" set the tone for *The Wonder Years.* Other covers:

1 "Ob-La-Di, Ob-La-Da" from *Life Goes On*

2 "Who Are You?" from *C.S.I.*

3 "My Life" from *Bosom Buddies*

4 "Bad Boys" from *COPS*

5 "Rock Around the Clock" from *Happy Days*

Winnie soon moved to a nearby town and left an opening for other women in Kevin's life, such as Becky Slater, Madeline, Wayne's girlfriend Sandy, and Cara, the hot townie he met at the lake one summer. We all knew Winnie was still on Kevin's mind because Daniel Stern told us. Kevin started to hang out with Doug, Randy, Craig, and classmates other than a maturing Paul (often mistaken for Marilyn Manson), who shockingly lost his virginity before anyone else. The shark was circling.

The Wonder Years jumped when Kevin hit puberty and the show entered the 1970s. The innocence of the kid who wore that New York Jets jacket was gone. Shortly after Kevin's voice cracked, Karen hooked up with Michael (David Schwimmer), got married in a hippie ceremony, and moved to Alaska. Jack started a furniture-making business, Norma became a comptroller, and even Wayne went to work and finally got along with his little brother, who was now a "man."

WHEN IT'S TIME TO CHANGE

Puberty has not been kind to many an actor, including:

1 Urkel on *Family Matters*
2 Jennifer on *Family Ties*
3 Peter on *The Brady Bunch*
4 Screech on *Saved by the Bell*
5 Tommy on *Alice*
6 Rudy on *The Cosby Show*
7 Jonathan on *Who's the Boss?*
8 Tootie on *The Facts of Life*
9 Joanie and Chachi on *Happy Days*
10 Any kid on *Home Improvement*

The finale revealed everyone's fate after the passing of *The Wonder Years*, including Jack's dying from a heart attack and Kevin marrying someone other than Winnie. But as the older Kevin went to play with his son and fireworks exploded, the cheese factor reminded us that this great show had jumped . . . with a little help from its friends.

When did

The X-Files

1993–2002 Sundays on FOX

jump the shark?

"The truth is out there" and we've spent too many years trying to find it on this mysterious cult hit.

The X-Files were unsolvable FBI cases involving situations that defy normal explanation. Agents Fox Mulder and Dana Scully investigated and began to uncover "the truth" of a government conspiracy that would make JFK theorists and Roswell residents drool.

Mulder and Scully Fight the Future on the big screen.

Mulder, whose sister had been abducted by aliens, firmly believed in this conspiracy and would stop at nothing to uncover it. Scully, the medical maven, was skeptical; but after spending time with Mulder, she had no choice but to believe. Skinner, Krycek, and Pendrell were FBI coworkers who helped and hurt at the same time. The only help Mulder could always count on came from the Lone Gunmen, three geeky conspiracy buffs.

Things were never as they seemed when

Mulder and Scully were investigating the X-Files. Early on, hints from Deep Throat and Mr. X brought them closer to the truth, and both were naturally gunned down. In the third season Scully was abducted by aliens and returned seemingly unharmed, but was later revealed to have cancer. Through it all the Cigarette Smoking Man (CSM) seemed to know everything that was going on and revealed that he was indeed involved with the JFK and MLK assassinations.

We spotted a fin when the filming location was switched from the spooky forests of Vancouver to the boring soundstages of L.A. Shortly after Scully's cancer went into remission, CSM was shot (not fatally) and Mulder's files were torched by FBI agents. The show began its climb up the ramp.

The X-Files finally jumped when the feature film *Fight the Future* was released. Chris Carter and crew seemingly put all their work into the flick, which brought us no closer to the "truth." Although successful at the box office, the series became an afterthought. A Roswell explanation of Rebels and the Consortium did little to save the show. The sexual tension between Mulder and Scully was also addressed with a less than memorable millennium kiss.

As Mulder faded away from *The X-Files* so David Duchovny could pursue a film career, Robert *Terminator 2* Patrick was brought in as Agent Doggett. Scully had a baby, whose father was Mulder, but the truth was still out there . . . somewhere. Problem is, we all got sick of looking for it.

ALIEN RACES

Our favorite visitors from outer space:

1 The Newcomers from *Alien Nation*
2 The aliens from *V*
3 Gordon Schumway from *ALF*
4 The Coneheads from *Saturday Night Live* (or France)
5 The Kanamits from the *Twilight Zone* ("It's a cookbook!")

Music

"I hope I die before I get old."

—*The Who* circa 1965

Another Greatest Hits record. A metal band records a sappy ballad. The lead singer leaves the band. A really bad video.

Jumping the shark isn't limited solely to television. Our favorite musicians make similarly fatal mistakes, warning us that something is off.

The categories for music differ a bit from TV, but they're just as potent. Here's a sampling:

Acting—Jon Bon Jovi hits the silver screen

Classical—Joe Jackson wants to be Bach

Death—Any seventies star whose name starts with *J* (Janis, Jimi, Jim . . .)

Double Album—Fleetwood Mac's *Tusk,* Guns N' Roses' *Use Your Illusion I* and *II*

Drugs—Brian Wilson feels those good vibrations

Going Solo—Ozzy leaves Sabbath

Greatest Hits—Did Steve Miller have any other albums?

I Do—John and Yoko, James and Carly, Kurt and Courtney . . .

Noble Causes—Sting battles for the rainforest

One Bad Song—Foreigner wants to know what love is

Puberty—New Kids on the Block, Menudo, Hanson . . .

Pussy Rock Ballads—"More Than Words" from metal band Extreme

Religion—Dylan serves somebody

Reunited—The Eagles, the Sex Pistols, Blondie . . . and it doesn't feel so good

Senility—The Who forgets to die before they get old

Sobriety—Aerosmith actually gets some rehab

Soundtracks—Bryan Adams becomes Kenny Loggins

Video Kills the Radio Star—Olivia Newton-John tries to get "Physical"

Hall of Fame—Music Wing

The most blatant shark jumps in music history (excluding Yoko) are:

10. Styx's stage play of Mr. Roboto

9. Phil Collins is Buster!

8. Any group involved in the film *Sgt. Pepper's Lonely Hearts Club Band*

7. Billy Squier's "Rock Me Tonight" video

6. Stevie Wonder just calls to say I love you

5. Starship builds a city on rock and roll

4. Van Halen goes on without David Lee Roth

3. Cat Stevens is Yusuf Islam

2. KISS takes off their makeup

1. Milli Vanilli live

Aerosmith
1970–

jump the shark?

It's hard to believe that the band seen on MTV today are the same Boston-bred bad boys that were huge in the 1970s. Front man (and former drummer) Steven Tyler, guitarist Joe Perry, and crew have enjoyed a hell of a bumpy ride on and off the wagon.

> **Steven and Joe show Run-D.M.C. how to "Walk This Way."**

Aerosmith first came on the scene in 1972 with "Dream On," but the band was not a big hit initially. Then, like most bands breaking in, they toured and toured and toured. The boys made it big with *Toys in the Attic* and their first Top 40 hit, "Sweet Emotion." "Dream On" was re-released with much success, and "Walk This Way" was another huge hit for the band.

JUST ANOTHER BAND OUT OF BOSTON

These bands found their way from New England:

1 Boston
2 The Cars
3 James Taylor
4 New Kids on the Block
5 New Edition

We spotted a fin a couple of years later when the band appeared in the film flop *Sgt. Pepper's Lonely Hearts Club Band* performing "Come Together." No one, not even George Burns, survived that film unscathed. As the band drifted into solo projects, a Greatest Hits album was released and they entered the abyss of the 1980s.

There was plenty of drug and alcohol abuse to go around, including Steven collapsing onstage during a show (he wasn't just tired). The boys did their obligatory time in rehab, and then three guys from Hollis restarted the band's career.

Run-D.M.C. was at the height of its popularity when it covered "Walk This Way" in the mid-eighties. The ultimate MTV crossover featured Steven and Joe teamed with Run, D.M.C. and Jam Master Jay. The kings of rock (there is none higher) literally showed Steven Tyler how to walk this way, the precise moment that sent all of them hurdling over the shark. The song was a huge hit, but neither band would ever be

KIDS

You can play the guitar? Who's your daddy?

1 Liv Tyler
2 Sean Lennon
3 Carnie Wilson
4 Jakob Dylan
5 Chynna Phillips

the same. Run-D.M.C. faded away, and Aerosmith became MTV darlings.

An unprecedented pop comeback for Aerosmith ensued, with Bruce Fairburn producing the multiplatinum *Permanent Vacation, Pump,* and *Get a Grip.* "Dude (Looks Like a Lady)," "Love in an Elevator," "Cryin'," and other hits were buoyed mostly by videos featuring pre-*Clueless* star Alicia Silverstone.

This formerly hard-rocking Boston band were now pop stars—no longer livin' on the edge. At Disney-MGM Studios, you can ride the "Rock 'n' Roller Coaster Starring Aerosmith." The 2001 Super Bowl halftime show replaced the "Up with People" contingent with today's pop elite: 'NSync, Britney Spears, and . . . Aerosmith. They got their MTV.

When did The Beatles
1964–1972

jump the shark?

John, Paul, George, and Ringo. Need I say more? Okay, try this . . . name twenty Beatles songs. "Yesterday," "Hey Jude," "Revolution" . . . pretty easy, right? Now try to do it for *any* other band. Unless you listen to Abba 24/7, you simply cannot complete this task. If you can, you frighten me.

Yoko.

When the Fab Four made their infamous sojourn across the Atlantic, they embarked upon the small task of changing music forever. Seven of the top ten singles in one week. The *Ed Sullivan* appearance. The classic film *A Hard Days' Night.* Gear!

Nothing could bring down The Beatles. Drugs? *Revolver* and *Rubber Soul* proved that they only made the band better. Fashion? Any way they decided to wear their hair and dress was a trend to be mimicked. Religion? The Beatles were bigger than Jesus. You think the Maharishi is a sham, and they come out of that with

THE OTHER WOMAN
What's she doing here?
1 Yoko Ono
2 Linda Eastman
3 Patty Boyd
4 Patty Scialfa
5 Jeanine Pettibone (girlfriend of Spinal Tap's David St. Hubbins)

Sgt. Pepper . . . even George's "Within You, Without You" couldn't harm that timeless classic.

Then one fateful night, John decided to take a stroll into an exhibition at an art gallery and met his soul mate, Yoko Ono, whose constant presence would send The Beatles sailing over the shark. *Magical Mystery Tour, Yellow Submarine,* Linda Eastman, Apple Records, and the death of Brian Epstein soon followed the union of these free spirits. The foursome were no longer as fab.

It was sad to hear about the battles that ensued in the studio, and even worse to listen to some of the music that came out of it (e.g., the Phil Spector–ized "*Let It Be*"). But The Beatles rallied to close with *Abbey Road* before embarking on their successful solo careers and lives. That made "Free as a Bird" and the other recent *Anthology* stuff all the more painful.

There will never be another band like The Beatles. There will never be another Yoko. The Beatles personified the sixties. Isn't it amazing that a band that broke up over twenty-five years ago had the best-selling CD of the new millennium? Truly number *1*.

When did

The Bee Gees

1958–

jump the shark?

The Brothers Gibb are not just disco. They had unprecedented success in that genre, made the most of it, and then paid the ultimate price.

The Bee Gees are comprised of the Gibb brothers—Barry and twins Maurice and Robin. The trio brought harmonies from Australia to England in the mid-sixties and were Beatles-esque with their sound.

> **Starring in *Sgt. Pepper's Lonely Hearts Club Band.***

They had hits with "Massachusetts" and "Gotta Get a Message to You," and after briefly breaking up, they reformed and scored their first big U.S. hit with the somewhat trippy "Lonely Days."

The next single, "How Can You Mend a Broken Heart?" gave us an inkling of the infamous falsettos we would come to know and dread. The Bee Gees morphed from pop ballads into dance and funk, and had another smash with "Jive Talkin'." The next two singles, "Nights on Broadway" and "You Should Be Dancing," set the stage for the soundtrack that hatched the disco era.

Saturday Night Fever was beyond huge. We all owned the soundtrack (admit it) and attempted to dance to it. "Stayin' Alive," "Night Fever," and "How Deep Is Your Love?" were huge hits and the Bee Gees, for better or for worse, were disco defined. We spotted a fin when brother Andy got into the mix with his solo "Shadow Dancing." There was only so much Gibb to go around.

In 1979, the acting bug bit the Bee Gees. Hard. Not only did they star in the colossal flop *Sgt. Pepper's Lonely Hearts Club Band,* they

FALSETTO

Is there a clamp down there?

1 Leo Sayer

2 Brad Delp—Boston

3 Russell Thompkins, Jr.— The Stylistics

4 Herb—Peaches & Herb

5 Aaron Neville

helped finance the film as well. The flick is in the Jump the Shark Hall of Fame for destroying countless careers, and the Brothers Gibb went right down with it.

The Bee Gees had some post-*Pepper* hits with "Tragedy" and "Too Much Heaven," but the damage had been done. Barry Gibb dueted with various divas and the brothers wrote and produced hits like "Islands in the Stream" for other artists, but the Bee Gees will forever be associated with the disco era, and unable to truly stay alive.

When did

Black Sabbath
1969–

jump the shark?

Black Sabbath transformed rock into metal with its heavy guitar and lyrics of horror, paving the road for countless bands to follow.

Ozzy departs and Ronnie James Dio fronts the band.

Black Sabbath's current incarnation, which also happens to be the original foursome, consists of drummer Bill Ward, bassist Geezer Butler, vocalist Ozzy Osbourne, and guitarist Tony Iommi. Sabbath arrived in 1970 with a sound that the rock world was ready to hear—harder, louder, and edgier.

Paranoid, the second Sabbath album, put the band on the map with classics like the title track and "Iron Man." The band never deviated from this winning formula and followed up with three platinum albums—*Master of Reality, Black Sabbath, Volume 4,* and *Sabbath Bloody Sabbath*.

We spotted a fin when the double album greatest hits compilation *We Sold Our Soul for Rock 'n' Roll* was released. Tony Iommi wanted to shake things up and add new sound elements, but Ozzy wasn't biting. Shortly after *Technical Ecstasy,* Ozzy quit and vaulted Sab-

WHAT'S IN A NAME?

You know you've made it if you can go by one name:

1 Ozzy
2 Slash
3 The Edge
4 Prince
5 Madonna

bath over the shark. In the process, he started the carousel of lead vocalists that was to continue for the rest of the band's days (the current total stands at eight).

In 1980, Ronnie James Dio stepped in front for the commercially successful *Heaven and Hell*. But it wasn't Sabbath without Ozzy. Dio lasted three years, eventually quitting over creative differences with Iommi, and was replaced by Deep Purple's Ian Gillan for *Born Again*. Gillan later reunited with DP, and Ozzy returned for a Black Sabbath performance at Live Aid in 1985. After Geezer Butler left and Ozzy was still away, the band was rechristened Black Sabbath featuring Tony Iommi with (insert Deep Purple vocalist here) fronting the band, a sure sign that the shark had been jumped.

Sabbath has continued to break up and reunite over the past decade and is cashing in on the reunion craze in music. It will never possess the power it once had in the metal world, but after a hell of a ride, it's good to see the original four together again. For now.

When did

Boston
1971–

jump the shark?

Third Stage.

Boston had a problem that any other band would kill for . . . how do you follow up the best debut album of all time?

Boston was led by Tom Scholz, an MIT geek gone mad in a recording studio, who had a truly distinctive guitar sound. Lead vocalist Brad Delp, bassist Fran Sheehan, guitarist Barry Goudreau, and drummers Sib Hashian and Jim Masdea rounded out the original incarnation of a band on the road just trying to make ends meet.

In the mid-seventies, Tom and crew recorded some demo tapes in his basement studio that, with a bit of polishing, resulted in the best-selling debut

GEOGRAPHICALLY
CORRECT

Other bands named after
their favorite points of
reference:

1 Chicago

2 Kansas

3 Alabama

4 Asia

5 Europe

album of all-time, *Boston*. At the height of the disco age, the A side of "More Than a Feeling," "Peace of Mind," "Foreplay/Long Time," and "Rock and Roll Band" was met with open arms. "Smokin'," "Hitch a Ride," "Something About You," and "Let Me Take You Home Tonight" composed the equally stellar flip side. It's as close to a perfect album as you can find, and it was only their first.

Naturally, expectations for the second release were equivalent to those for the *Seinfeld* finale . . . the band could never live up to them. So they did the next best thing: waited two years, cloned their first album and called it *Don't Look Back*. The title track could very well be the ninth song on *Boston*. They even used the same cheesy guitar/spaceship on the album cover. The shark was circling.

Scholz, who is as anal as Felix Unger, never felt that the follow-up was ready for release. It took eight years until *Third Stage* debuted, and only two of the original band members were left. Suffice it to say that the album wasn't worth the wait. Boston's third release catapulted them over the shark. Yes, the album has that distinctive and now recycled Boston sound, but the songs fit the description of most eighties hit music . . . empty and repetitive.

TELESCOPE
REQUIRED

Our favorite album covers
dealing with outer space:

1 *Boston*—Boston

2 *Esc4p3*—Journey

3 *Fragile*—Yes

4 *Point of Know Return*—
Kansas

5 *2112*—Rush

Whitney Houston eventually outsold Boston with her debut album, but the masterpiece is still a rock and roll legend. As Orson Welles discovered with *Citizen Kane,* it's not as easy to produce a classic the second time around. For Boston, the third time was anything but a charm.

David Bowie

1947–

jump the shark?

The chameleon of rock 'n' roll, David Bowie has reinvented himself and his music so many times that we've lost count.

> **He fell to Earth.**

David Jones was a young English sax player with bizarre eyes, a knack for songwriting, and a love for the mod scene. Not wanting to be mistaken for a Monkee, he changed his last name to Bowie and pursued art while playing some gigs on the side.

MASTER THESPIANS

What makes these Brits want to act so badly?

1 Phil Collins
2 Sade
3 Mick Jagger
4 John Lennon
5 Sting

In 1969, Bowie recorded *Space Oddity,* a hit that persuaded him to try music full-time. His next big album was *Hunky Dory* featuring one of his best songs, "Changes," and other singer/songwriter stuff. No one was prepared for Bowie's transformation into Ziggy Stardust, a glam bisexual rock star with a band called the Spiders from Mars.

Bowie's new image didn't stop him from writing other classics, including Mott the Hoople's "All the Young Dudes." We did spot a fin with the release of *Diamond Dogs,* which marked the end of Ziggy's playing guitar, but Bowie followed with *Young Americans* and his biggest hit, "Fame."

He moved to L.A. and finally committed the shark-jumping sin of trying to be a serious actor in *The Man Who Fell to Earth*. Bowie's golden years were over and his acting performances were on par with Davy Jones's turn on *The Brady Bunch*. He returned to England strung out on coke, and after giving the crowd a Nazi salute he went to Germany to work with Brian Eno.

Bowie then morphed into an electronic musician ("Heroes," "Fashion") as he continued to pursue acting, starring in *The Elephant Man* on Broadway. The eighties brought the hits "Under Pressure" and "Let's Dance," and Bowie

BOWIE COLLABORATORS

His musical partners are some of the best:

1 Lou Reed
2 John Lennon
3 Stevie Ray Vaughn
4 Mick Jagger
5 Bing Crosby

suddenly found himself an MTV pop darling. That run ended with his "Dancin' in the Streets" duet with Mick Jagger and "Absolute Beginners" with Sade. Tin Machine was next, but the shark had swum so far away that no one was paying attention anymore.

When did

Garth Brooks

1962–

jump the shark?

For better or worse, the man in the Stetson brought country music into the mainstream and became one of the biggest recording artists of all time. Party on, Garth.

Evil twin Chris Gaines.

In the late eighties, Garth Brooks, like many others before him, moved to Nashville with the hopes of becoming a successful country singer. It took him just a couple of years to become a big hit with the ability to crossover from country to pop music.

Garth's self-titled debut featured the hit "Much Too Young" and put him on the pop and country map. His second album, *No Fences,* sold millions of copies and featured the hits "Friends in Low Places" and "The Thunder Rolls." Such sales numbers were unheard of in country music, and Garth didn't stop there.

Armed with a headset mic, Garth put on country music concerts that were the equivalent of KISS (sans blood and tongue). Fans couldn't get enough. His next album, *Ropin' the Wind*, simultaneously topped both the pop and country charts. It seemed that Garth could do no wrong. Until of course, he released *The Chase,* with the gospel anthem "We Shall Be Free."

Garth was suddenly selling half of what he used to. He pulled off a Central Park concert, but

NO COKE, PEPSI

Pop music and soft drinks, a powerful combination. Pepsi pitch people include:

1 Britney Spears
2 Michael Jackson
3 Ray Charles
4 Madonna
5 Aretha Franklin

we spotted a fin when Garth decided to try out for the San Diego Padres and went to spring training, only to eventually be cut. The shark was circling.

Garth shifted his focus to acting, and won the role of Chris Gaines in the still yet-to-be-released film, *The Lamb*. A method actor, Garth *became* Chris Gaines, growing long hair and losing the coordinated country outfits. He created a persona with a full history and even a TV special, and basically strapped on water skis and went sailing over the shark—not to mention his confused fans.

Following the Chris Gaines disaster, Garth sang on *Sesame Street*, tried out for the Mets (didn't make it), and finalized his divorce. Perhaps it's time to put that Stetson back on and visit those friends in low places.

When did

Jimmy Buffett
1946–

jump the shark?

Wasting away in Margaritaville? Try building an industry.

Jimmy Buffett is a Mississippi boy who made good. He originally moved to Nashville to make it as a country singer, but things just didn't work out. So he moved to Key West, and found his calling on Dog Beach.

He turned Margaritaville into a brand.

The singer/songwriter cultivated a beach-bum persona that appealed to many fans early on with classics like "Why Don't We Get Drunk (and Screw)?" and "Come Monday." But pop stardom came with the hammock hit "Margaritaville" and everyone suddenly wanted a piece of this easygoing conch sensation.

Over time, Buffett developed a cult following on the road with a legion of fans who call themselves "Parrotheads." You know exactly what to expect at any Jimmy Buffett show—a good ol' time. It's quite a sight to see tens of thousands of screaming fans making like sharks and singing "Fins" with the Coral Reefer Band (we're not making this up).

We spotted a fin when this son of a sailor became a fiction writer and sold quite a few books. The jump occurred in his adopted hometown of Key West when a Margaritaville clothing line took off and a Buffett-themed nightclub made its debut on Duval Street. Jimmy continues to play sold-out shows and author best-selling books, and has since released retrospective box-sets and greatest hits compilations. He's a brilliant businessman, but he doesn't need to look out for those sharks off Cuba anymore.

When did

The Cars

1976–1988

jump the shark?

Ben Orr drove us home.

Few bands were more aptly named than The Cars. Their slick singles came out one after another as if they were rolling off a Detroit production line.

The Cars were assembled in Boston as a new wave band without much personality. Front man/luckiest male on the planet Ric Ocasek, bassist Ben Orr, keyboardist Greg Hawkes, drummer Dave Robinson, and lefty guitarist Elliot Easton were the B-52's without the quirkiness, Blondie without the sex, or Talking Heads without the art.

Yet, their basic rocking formula—if a bit mechanical—worked. Starting in the late seventies with their debut LP, *The Cars,* hits like "My Best Friend's

Girl," "Let's Go," "Shake It Up," and "Just What I Needed" delivered, and their albums regularly went platinum.

Their unquestioned leader was songwriter Ric Ocasek. Tall, thin, and dorky (Czech hunk qualities, according to Paulina), he was the public face of the band. And his high-pitched, hiccupy voice was the lead on almost all of The Cars' biggest hits. Almost.

Which brings us to "Drive." The sappy ballad from 1984 was one of the band's biggest hits, yet all across the nation, fans were asking: Is this a bad Foreigner outtake? Or maybe an Air Supply "lost classic"? The band had jumped the shark.

"Drive" is a series of questions from a wimpy guy concerned about the happiness of his annoying girl. He wants to know "who'll tell you when things aren't so great?" If only someone had told The Cars. Another line mentions the singer plugging his ears, a dangerous suggestion on a single like this.

Perhaps recognizing that this song was different—or perhaps simply embarrassed—Ocasek had bassist Ben Orr sing lead. Orr had sung before, but he'd always seemed to do it in the patented Cars' style. For this one, however, he reached deep inside and channeled the soul of Wayne Newton.

The Cars drove down the wrong road and could never recover their quirky magic after *Heartbeat City*. They opted to take the path that leads down that long pier, up the ramp, and straight over the shark.

Chicago

1967–

jump the shark?

Despite XXI original studio albums, a tragic death, and a handful of lead singers, Chicago and its horn arrangements have persevered over the past thirty years.

> **Terry Kath dies and the band forgets about the numbers.**

The band debuted as Chicago Transit Authority and quickly got into the habit of naming its albums after itself. The original lineup is too long to list here, but the mix of horns with the distinctive lead vocals of Terry Kath, Robert Lamm, and Peter Cetera truly set the band apart from the sound of the late sixties.

Their first self-titled recording featured "Beginnings" and "Does Anybody Really Know What Time It Is?," both still FM standards today. They dropped the Transit Authority, kept the script "Chicago" logo, and added a roman numeral to each successive album release. Each album would typically include a tight funky horn-driven tune ("25 or 6 to 4"), a guaranteed pop hit ("Saturday in the Park"), and a really sappy ballad ("Color My World"). The formula worked and their greatest hits album, *Chicago IX*, is one of the best-selling recordings of all time.

> **YOU KNOW MY NAME . . .**
>
> Look up these album numbers:
>
> 1 *IV*—Led Zeppelin
> 2 *1984*—Van Halen
> 3 *90125*—Yes
> 4 *2112*—Rush
> 5 *33 & ⅓*— George Harrison

In 1978, guitarist and vocalist Terry Kath died and a huge part of Chicago went with him—ultimately sending the band over the shark. *Hot Streets* was released following Kath's death, the first album without a number and one that also involved new producer, Phil Ramone. They followed that with disco disaster *Chicago 13* and the totally forgettable *Chicago XIV*.

The band realized its mistakes and enlisted David Foster, king of the power ballad, for *Chicago 16* and *17*. "Hard to Say I'm Sorry," "You're the Inspiration," and "Hard Habit to Break" were huge mid-eighties hits and the

> **HORNS UP**
>
> A great horn section can make a band. Our favorites:
>
> 1 Earth, Wind & Fire
> 2 Kool and the Gang
> 3 James Brown
> 4 Blood, Sweat & Tears
> 5 Average White Band

band had great sales, but Chicago was now little more than the home of the Peter Cetera ballad. When he left the band, a clone (Jason Scheff) was brought in to stop the hurting along with a new version of "25 or 6 to 4." They've been paying the price ever since.

When did
Eric Clapton
1945–

jump the shark?

It's in the way that you use it, and Clapton has used his guitar better than anyone else over the past thirty years.

> **The soundtrack for *The Color of Money*.**

Eric Clapton hails from England and is often described as the finest guitar player that ever lived. He played in practically every supergroup in England during the late sixties, including The Yardbirds, Cream, Blind Faith, and Derek and the Dominoes. His guest spots are legendary as well, soloing for The Beatles and The Allman Brothers, among others.

Clapton was not a tremendously successful solo artist during the seventies. In 1970, he released a self-titled solo effort that included "After Midnight" and "Let It Rain." Heroin took him out of the limelight for a few years, but he returned with *461 Ocean Boulevard* and a cover of Bob Marley's "I Shot the Sheriff." After recording three other lame albums and ending up with good friend George Harrison's wife, *Slowhand* brought Clapton back to the top with the hits "Cocaine," "Lay Down Sally," and "Wonderful Tonight."

THAT'S MY PIE

These ladies seem to get around in the world of music:

1 Patti Boyd
2 Pamela De Barres
3 Jade Barrymore
4 Heather Locklear
5 Pamela Anderson

Clapton always had the ability, but never had a ready supply of material. His eighties records were solid, but nothing spectacular (save a live appearance or two). We spotted a fin when Phil Collins produced *Behind the Sun*, and Clapton shifted toward becoming a force in pop and abandoning his traditional roots.

He inevitably jumped two years later with "It's in the Way That You Use It," the featured track off the *The Color of Money* soundtrack. This marked the official start of Clapton's sellout.

It became even more evident that this god had jumped with the box-set collection *Crossroads*, which chronicles both his group and solo efforts. Once again in the limelight, Clapton became a regular at any blues or rock 'n' roll tributes. If there was a huge crowd of musicians on stage, Clapton would be there taking a solo before once again shrinking back into the shadows.

MTV got a hold of Clapton for *Unplugged*, which won every Grammy in sight and featured the heartfelt tribute to his son's plunge out of an apartment window, "Tears in Heaven." He followed with an all blues album *From the Cradle,* which brought him back to his guitar roots and away from his newfound audience. But the shark had moved on to its next victim.

When did
Phil Collins
1951–

jump the shark?

Buster!

If he hadn't done some good stuff early in his career, Phil Collins would join Ted McGinley as a patron saint of shark jumping.

Phil was raised in London as a child actor. Despite all the musical success that was to come, the acting bug never left and would eventually return to bite him. An art band, Genesis, was looking for a replacement drummer and Phil joined up. Acting could wait for a couple of decades as Phil backed Peter Gabriel and crew.

When Gabriel left in 1974, the band auditioned singers but ultimately decided to give Phil a shot. This began the transformation of Genesis from art rock band to commercial pop success. On the heels of *Abacab,* Phil recorded his first solo album, *Face Value,* which contained the hit "In the Air Tonight" and a huge shot of his face on the cover. Backed by the horns of Earth, Wind & Fire, Phil had great solo success. More impressively, he managed to balance his solo and Genesis careers over the next few years.

But Phil made the mistake of trying to do too much. He produced albums for Eric Clapton and Adam Ant, flew across the Atlantic to appear at both Live Aid concerts, and started recording more soundtrack tunes. The shark was circling.

After a Special Guest Star appearance on *Miami Vice,* Phil was ready to pursue acting once again.

He starred in (and naturally did the soundtrack for) *Buster,* a film about a train robbery that vaulted Phil right over the shark. Even Spielberg wasn't immune to Phil, giving him a small part in the flop *Hook.* But Phil's effect wasn't limited to his acting on the big screen.

The next Genesis album was *We Can't Dance,* a pop throwaway that sounded more like a bad Phil solo record. It should have been, because Phil's next solo effort, *Both Sides,* was a major disappointment and failed to chart at all. Phil left Genesis in 1995, and tried the solo gig one more time with *Dance into the Light.* No luck.

Though he couldn't act in movies, he could create soundtracks—and Phil hit it big with Disney's *Tarzan.* He finally got his Oscar, just not in the category that he expected.

DRUM ROLL, PLEASE

Singing drummers are a rarity. Our faves:

1 Don Henley (The Eagles)
2 Karen Carpenter (The Carpenters)
3 Jimmy Marinos (The Romantics)
4 Levon Helm (The Band)
5 Ringo Starr (You'd better know this one)

When did

The Doors

1965–1973

jump the shark?

Take an annoying organ, mix in some trippy lyrics, don't bother with a bass player, and add lots of drugs. What you get is one of the most influential bands of the late sixties and early seventies . . . plus a bad Oliver Stone film.

Jim dies.

The Doors, who took their name from an Aldous Huxley book (there are others besides *Brave New World*) about mescaline, were a direct reflection of the psychedelic times they lived in. The band consisted of bespectacled organist Ray Manzarek, low-key drummer John Densmore, and young guitarist Robby Kreiger. But essentially, the eclectic Jim Morrison *was* The Doors.

> **POETS**
>
> *American Prayer* showed us the "poetry" of Jim Morrison. Other notable poets:
> 1 Bob Dylan
> 2 Robert Frost
> 3 Rod McKuen
> 4 Maya Angelou
> 5 Muhammad Ali

"Light My Fire" brought the band to national prominence and instilled that organ into everyone's consciousness. "Break on Through (To the Other Side)" and "The End" are other classic cuts off the band's self-titled debut album. If Francis Ford Coppola and Jose Feliciano are using your stuff, you know you've done something right. Jim was stirring things up on *The Ed Sullivan Show* and at live concert performances, always keeping the band in the public eye, for better or worse.

The Doors quickly followed up with *Strange Days,* a continuation of their first album, and *Waiting for the Sun.* "Love Me Two Times," "People Are Strange," and "Hello, I Love You" were solid singles, but "When the Music's Over" was utter self-indulgence. The band was never interested in a bass player, but they thought a horn section might be a good idea for "The Soft Parade" and their Vegas lounge hit "Touch Me." It wasn't. This was around the time that Jim got arrested for indecent exposure at a Miami concert, and shark warning signs were on the wall.

> **OPEN UP**
>
> Doors have been involved in a varied group of tunes:
> 1 "Knock Three Times"— Tony Orlando and Dawn
> 2 "Who's Behind the Door?"—Zebra
> 3 "Knockin' on Heaven's Door"—Eric Clapton
> 4 "Knock on Wood"— King Curtis
> 5 "Let 'Em In"—Wings

113

The Doors proved to be stronger than dirt for a bit longer with the bluesy *Morrison Hotel* and *L.A. Woman,* the last album with a living Jim. "Riders on the Storm" still has people looking over their shoulders on rainy nights. When Jim died from an overdose in Paris later that year, the band vowed to carry on without him and proceeded to carry itself straight over the shark.

The Doors continue to have an effect on music today, and were even commemorated (along with JFK and professional football) by an Oliver Stone film released well after Oliver himself had jumped. These days, you can pick up *Best of The Doors, The Best of The Doors,* or *The Very Best of The Doors* . . . no small feat for a band with only six brief studio albums.

When did
Bob Dylan
1941–

jump the shark?

Bob got religion and had to serve somebody.

The Band to The Beatles . . . the Velvet Underground to 10,000 Maniacs . . . these bands, and countless others, wouldn't be the same without the guy with that annoying nasal voice.

Robert Zimmerman hailed from Minnesota and changed his last name to Dylan as a tribute to the poet Dylan Thomas. He was a folk musician who played guitar and harmonica and eventually wrote his own songs. He ended up in New York in the early sixties, playing many a coffeehouse and becoming a staple of the Village music scene.

In 1962, Dylan crossed over from folk to pop with *The Freewheelin' Bob Dylan,* which included "Blowin' in the Wind" and "A Hard Rain's A-Gonna Fall." Peter, Paul, and Mary covered "Blowin' in the Wind" the next year, while Dylan hooked up in more ways than one with Joan Baez and for the first time gained national recognition for his music.

Soon thereafter, Dylan plugged in and went electric with *Bringing It all Back Home,* avoiding the shark with the hits "Subterranean Homesick Blues" and "Maggie's Farm," and leaving it in the distance with *Highway 61*

Revisited. Blonde on Blonde was a double album with surreal songwriting classics like "Just Like a Woman" and "Rainy Day Women #12 & 35," and found Dylan now being backed by The Band.

We finally spotted a fin when Dylan had that mystery motorcycle accident and ended up at Big Pink for a while. This was a precursor to "Lay Lady Lay" (who *is* singing that?) and other late sixties cuts that just weren't up to par. But Dylan soon rebounded with *Blood on the Tracks* and *Desire,* and seemed to be headed back to prominence.

In 1979, Dylan announced that he had become a born-again Christian and released *Slow Train Coming*. Can you say "Yusuf Islam?" The album was comprised completely of religious songs, and the prolific Dylan had finally jumped the shark.

In the wake of the shark, Dylan stopped writing for a while, touring with the Grateful Dead and Tom Petty, and even becoming a Wilbury. His song "Hurricane" was the basis for an Oscar-winning film, and Dylan himself won an Oscar for "Things Have Changed" off the *Wonder Boys* soundtrack. Dylan doing soundtracks? The past twenty years have proven that the times are indeed a-changing.

The Eagles
1971–1982, 1994

jump the shark?

The rumor was that the members of this ego-driven SoCal band couldn't stand each other . . . until they saw how much money they could make if they reunited.

Tim B. joins the band.

The Eagles got their start as four guys who were hired to back up Linda Rondstadt in the early seventies. Don Henley, Glenn Frey, Randy Meisner, and Bernie Leadon debuted with a self-titled album that featured "Take It Easy," "Witchy Woman," and "Peaceful Easy Feeling." The hits just kept on coming.

Desperado, a personal favorite of an Elaine Benes ex, was an old West–themed LP that also included "Tequila Sunrise." Don Felder joined the band for *On the Border*, which included the sappy "The Best of My Love" and positioned the band for superstardom. *One of These Nights* was the album that took them to the top, featuring the title cut, "Lyin' Eyes," and "Take It to the Limit." The Eagles won every Grammy in sight and soared to the top of the charts.

We spotted a fin when Bernie Leadon left the band and was replaced by Joe Walsh. However, the band took a break and released *Their Greatest Hits: 1971–1975,* which became one of the best-selling albums of all time. They followed that success with *Hotel California*, featuring a title track that's considered to be one of the best songs ever recorded. The band was on an incredible roll, but it abruptly jumped when Randy Meisner left and was replaced by falsetto bassist Timothy B. Schmit.

It took almost three years to produce *The Long Run,* and "The Disco Strangler" reminded us that the Eagles were on the decline. The band broke up shortly after as all five members released their own albums. Don Henley had solo success, Glenn Frey was spotted on *Miami*

GREATEST GREATEST HITS

Most of these types of compilations are a joke. These are actually worth owning:

1 *Greatest Hits*—Elton John
2 *Greatest Hits*—Queen
3 *Greatest Hits 1974–1978*— Steve Miller
4 *Legend*—Bob Marley
5 *10 From 6*— Bad Company

BALD AMERICANS

I coulda been an Eagle:

1 Jackson Browne
2 J.D. Souther
3 Garth Brooks
4 John Denver
5 Harold Carmichael

Vice, and Joe Walsh just kept on being Joe Walsh. More than a decade later, they put the band back together for the colossal Hell Freezes Over tour that produced yet another hit in "Love Will Keep Us Alive." They've been busy counting the money ever since.

Fleetwood Mac
1967–

jump the shark?

How does an underground British blues band turn into the featured performer at Bill Clinton's inauguration? Ask the really tall drummer.

Tusk.

Mick Fleetwood and John McVie spun out of John Mayall's Bluesbreakers to create Fleetwood Mac along with Peter Green and Jeremy Spencer in 1967. Five years and many drugs and lawsuits later, Christine McVie was in with Mick and John, and they were off to California where they met up with recording duo Lindsey Buckingham and Stevie Nicks. The chain was now complete.

MAC ATTACK
Other Macs we enjoy:
1 Big Mac
2 MacGyver
3 Mack the Knife
4 John McEnroe
5 Apple Macintosh

Fleetwood Mac's self-titled U.S. debut was tremendously successful, featuring hits like "Say You Love Me," "Rhiannon," and "Over My Head." Their record sales were the antithesis of their personal lives, as the McVies divorced and Buckingham and Nicks broke up. This set the stage for *Rumours,* which turned out to be the second best-selling album of all-time with hits like "Dreams," "Go Your Own Way," and the future Clinton inaugural anthem "Don't Stop."

Things could not possibly get any better for Fleetwood Mac, and of course, they didn't. Two years later, the band followed *Rumours* with the double album *Tusk,* which featured a video with the USC Marching Band that sent Fleetwood Mac straight over the shark.

The next step was for everyone in Fleetwood Mac to release a solo album, but only Stevie Nicks became a star in her own right. The band would get back together for mediocre albums like *Mirage* and *Tango in the Night*, but Lindsey Buckingham was the first to officially leave the band for a critically acclaimed but seldom listened to solo career. Sadly, none of the band members was able to make it on his or her own without incurring some sort of weight, drug, or lack of audience problem. And who could forget Mick Fleetwood's pivotal acting with Arnold Schwarzenegger in *The Running Man*?

The inevitable reunion took place in 1997 with *The Dance,* which mixed classic hits with new tracks. The original American five were back together, proving that you could bend it a little, but never break the chain.

When did
Aretha Franklin
1942–

jump the shark?

If you need one word to define soul, it would be *Aretha.* There are plenty of powerful pipes in music, but no one can sing a song like Lady Soul.

Aretha, a reverend's daughter who could play a mean piano, originally debuted as a young gospel singer in the 1950s. She eventually found her way to

She exploded onto the Freeway of Love in her pink Cadillac.

Atlantic Records, who realized that they had a diva on their lucky hands. Her first big hit in the sixties was the title track off *I Never Loved a Man (the Way That I Love You)*, an album that also produced "Do Right Woman, Do Right Man" and "Respect."

After finding out what respect meant to her, she followed with "(You Make Me Feel Like)

a Natural Woman" and "Chain of Fools" off the legendary *Lady Soul*. Whether it was a Beatles cover or steady rocking, the late sixties and early seventies belonged to Aretha.

In *The Blues Brothers* movie (the good one) in 1980, Aretha shined as the waitress who reminded Matt "Guitar" Murphy to really think about what he was trying to do to her. However, we spotted a fin as Aretha began to grow not only in popularity, but in size as well. The first lady of soul was beginning to drift into pop music and sway from her roots.

When she left Atlantic Records in the eighties, a literally larger than life Aretha came on the scene with equally huge Clarence Clemons on sax for "Freeway of Love." This classic soul singer was now positioned as a pop act, a crossover later to be matched by Tina "Private Dancer" Turner. Aretha followed up her travels in a pink Caddy with "Who's Zoomin' Who?" a question we ask ourselves to this very day. Thankfully, this pop portion of her otherwise stellar career was short-lived.

These days, Aretha is called upon to perform from her sixties trove of classics and is rightfully acknowledged as one of the finest soul singers of all time. Her tribute albums and gospel records are as moving today as they were thirty years ago, and Aretha has landed on her feet after her jump in the eighties.

UNDER THE COVERS

Aretha has a knack of taking others songs to a different level. The originals:

1 "A Natural Woman"— Carole King

2 "Respect"— Otis Redding

3 "Bridge over Troubled Water"—Simon & Garfunkel

4 "Spanish Harlem"— The Drifters

5 "Eleanor Rigby"— The Beatles

When did
The Grateful Dead
1965–1995

jump the shark?

This psychedelic band took a long strange trip from being sixties cult favorites to nineties pop stars with plenty of miracles along the way.

I saw a deadhead sticker on a BMW driven by an 18-year-old preppie son of a Woodstock survivor.

The Dead, named after a Middle Eastern prayer, got its start on Ashbury Street in San Francisco during the mid-sixties. Singer/songwriter Jerry Garcia, a great guitarist and eventual ice cream flavor, hooked up with bassist Phil Lesh, guitarist Bob Weir, keyboardist Pigpen, and drummers Bill Kreutzmann and Mickey Hart. Studio albums never really worked for the band, but their live performances were not to be missed.

Workingman's Dead, bookended by "Uncle John's Band" and "Casey Jones," was the first studio album to show the band was making inroads. *American Beauty,* released at the same time, is the Dead's best studio work and features "Box of Rain," "Friend of the Devil," "Truckin'," "Sugar Magnolia," and other classics. But the best Dead compilations come from bootleg tapes of the live performances, a practice that the band aided and encouraged.

FAN CLUBS

There are devoted fans, and then there are the insane ones that have their own titles:

1 Deadheads
2 The KISS Army
3 Parrotheads (Jimmy Buffett)
4 The Children (Korn)
5 Toriphiles (Tori Amos)

Deadheads followed the band coast to coast and supported themselves selling tie-dyes and other psychedelic paraphernalia. It was hard to tell what was more entertaining at a Dead show— the Deadhead scene or the music itself. Pigpen died in '73 and was replaced by Keith Godchaux, the first of many keyboard substitutions.

The Dead had absolutely zero success in studio album sales for the next fifteen years, but they continued to sell out on the road and keep the music going. Dying keyboardists and Jerry's battles with drugs, gray hair, his health, and his weight were warning signs that the shark was circling fast.

MERRY PRANKSTERS

Ashbury and Haight in the sixties churned out many San Francisco treats:

1 Jefferson Airplane
2 Big Brother and the Holding Company
3 Sly and the Family Stone
4 Santana
5 Journey

In 1987, the Dead released their first studio album in seven years, *In the Dark*, which included the hit "Touch of Grey." Suddenly the band was all over MTV and tickets to the live shows were snapped up by bandwagon-hopping yuppies. Although the Dead tried to remain true to their core fans, their pop success had vaulted them over the shark.

Jerry continued to pop in and out of the hospital, and Bruce Hornsby became the oddest keyboard replacement yet. Dead T-shirts, compilations, and other marketing items were everywhere, and the sell-out was virtually complete. Jerry finally died of a heart attack in '95, and although the boys have continued to play together, the Dead are gone . . . but not forgotten.

When did

Guns N' Roses

1985–

jump the shark?

G N' R brought hard rock back into the mainstream and is primarily responsible for the shift in Top 40 music that occurred in the mid-1980s.

> **Axl gets caught in the "November Rain."**

Guns N' Roses is a prototypical metal band that hailed from L.A., consisting of guitarists Slash (don't call me Saul) and Izzy Stradlin, Duff McKagan on bass, Steven Adler on drums, and front man Axl Rose. These boys flat-out rocked—practicing and preaching the value of sex, drugs, and rock 'n' roll. They pissed people off, and that was a good thing.

SKULLS

Skulls are always nice for a cover shot:

1 *Appetite for Destruction—* Guns N' Roses

2 *American Beauty—* Grateful Dead

3 *Iron Maiden—* Iron Maiden

4 *Rust in Peace—*Megadeth

5 *Brain Salad Surgery—* Emerson, Lake & Palmer

Their first album, *Appetite for Destruction,* was a memorable debut that features "Welcome to the Jungle," "Paradise City," and "Sweet Child o' Mine." The outfits, screaming fans, over-the-top live shows, and hair (save Slash's hat) were stereotypical metal band excess, and it worked to perfection. It didn't hurt that Izzy and Slash's guitar playing was the best stuff heard in a long time.

The band wasn't ready with a follow-up, so they released *G N' R Lies*, which mixed live and acoustic stuff. "Patience" was a huge hit, but also their first sappy ballad—a sign of things to come. Still, "Used to Love Her (But I Had to Kill Her)" showed that the band hadn't lost its dark edge . . . yet.

G N' R dumped Steven Adler, whose drug use hampered his drumming, and added keyboardist Dizzy Reed to the mix. They eventually released not a double album, but two separate records. *Use Your Illusion I* and *II,* which included covers of "Live and Let Die" and "Knockin' on Heaven's Door"—pretentious shark bait.

The jump occurred with "November Rain," a song penned by Axl as a touching power ballad that ranks up there with "Every Rose Has Its Thorn" and "Without You." Guns N' Roses had tried to become "recording artists" and would never be the same (Axl's angst in the video was well-deserved).

The Spaghetti Incident? came next and brought a return to rock, but the damage had been done. The band seemed desperate for the publicity now being given to Seattle grunge. Axl and Slash had creative differences, prompting Slash to eventually leave the band. G N' R was spotted playing a New Year's show in Vegas . . . need we say more?

When did

George Harrison
1943–2001

jump the shark?

My sweet lord, doo-lang doo-lang doo-lang.

This quiet Beatle and underrated guitarist had quite a career after leaving Liverpool as a lad.

George Harrison learned how to play the guitar thanks to the urging of an older classmate, Paul McCartney. By the age of sixteen, George was a Beatle, and his life would never be the same. *Revolver* was George's breakout Beatles record, featuring the

CHARITY CONCERTS

The concert for Bangladesh started it all. Here are the most memorable:

1 Live Aid
2 Farm Aid
3 We Are the World
4 Hands Across America
5 A Salute to Heroes

catchy "Taxman" and sitar-driven "Love to You." You could always count on George for a quality sitar number.

But let's give George Harrison his due. It doesn't get much better than "While My Guitar Gently Weeps," "Here Comes the Sun," and "Something." Then again, the low point of *Sgt. Pepper* is "Within You, Without You." We spotted a fin when George got a little too much Maharishi going on in his music.

When The Beatles parted ways, it was George who initially had the most solo success with producer Phil Spector's wall of sound on the triple album *All Things Must Pass.* His benefit for Bangladesh was the first large rock/charity event ever held, and the Madison Square Garden concert was a huge success. George was also the first Beatle to record a number one song as a solo artist.

Problem is, if you listen to Harrison's "My Sweet Lord" and the Chiffons' "He's So Fine," it is obvious that the former is derivative of the latter. Intentional or not, George vaulted right over the shark when he was successfully sued—although he eventually bought the Chiffons' recording and owned both songs in the end.

He basically disappeared for the nineties until ELO's Jeff Lynne brought George back into the mainstream with *Cloud Nine* and the number one single "Got My Mind Set on You," a song with a chorus that repeats itself roughly 104 times. George soon became a Traveling Wilbury with Lynne, Bob Dylan, Tom Petty, and Roy Orbison, but listening to him during these years felt like watching Old Timer's Day. We prefer to remember George when he was fab, and sometimes even find ourselves clamoring for the sitar.

AND THE OSCAR GOES TO . . .

Maybe he didn't win an Oscar, but George produced some memorable films including:

1 *Monty Python's Life of Brian*
2 *Time Bandits*
3 *Mona Lisa*
4 *The Missionary*
5 *Nuns on the Run*

Jimi Hendrix

1942–1970

jump the shark?

He released more albums posthumously than when he was alive.

Everyone can hear Jimi.

Jimi Hendrix hailed from Seattle, where he taught himself how to play guitar left-handed. In the four years of his life that followed his first album release, he revolutionized the way the electric guitar would be played.

It's impossible to categorize Jimi's style, as he truly invented his own. R&B, blues, jazz, rock, and classical were all meshed together with plenty of feedback and distortion. However, during the early sixties Jimi was a sideman to many other successful R&B acts. Chas Chandler of The Animals convinced Jimi to go to London and put the Jimi Hendrix Experience together with bassist Noel Redding and drummer Mitch Mitchell, and the rest is history.

Jimi only recorded three studio albums. The first, *Are You Experienced?*, includes "Hey Joe," "The Wind Cries Mary," "Purple Haze," "Foxy Lady," and countless other rock classics. He followed with *Axis: Bold as Love*, which contains "Castles Made of Sand" and "Little Wing," and then the double album *Electric Ladyland*, which took the recording studio to new heights and featured his rendition of "All Along the Watchtower" and the frequently covered "Voodoo Child (Slight Return)."

But it was the live performances that made Hendrix a legend. If he wasn't setting fire to his guitar, he'd be playing it with any available body part. His 1967 Monterey Pop performance put him on the map. He closed a disappointing performance at Woodstock (on par with Jimmy Page's appearance at Live Aid) with his infamous rendition of "The Star Spangled Banner."

An underrated key to Hendrix's success was the Experience, Mitch Mitchell and Noel Redding. When Jimi dumped the boys in 1969 in the pursuit of funk, we spotted a fin. Confu-

LEFTIES

Jimi played a guitar strung for a right-hander with his left hand. Other famous southpaws:

1 Paul McCartney
2 Elliot Easton
3 Phil Collins
4 David Bowie
5 Rocky Balboa

R.I.P.

Drugs helped 'em, then destroyed 'em:

1 Janis Joplin
2 Elvis Presley
3 Jim Morrison
4 Kurt Cobain
5 John Bonham

sion reigned in Jimi's life, which tragically ended in 1970 from excessive drug use.

Hendrix had recorded a ton of stuff, and almost all of it has been released posthumously. There's been overdubbing, the addition of new parts, and a bastardization of many of the recordings—all of which infuriates Hendrix fans to no end. Jimi's father eventually regained the rights to the estate, but we're happy Jimi's not around to see what's been done to his legacy and how it has vaulted his career over the shark.

When did

Whitney Houston

1963–

jump the shark?

Whitney Houston was born musical royalty. Her mother Cissy was a great gospel singer and her cousin was Dionne Warwick. With her beautiful voice and supermodel looks, Whitney made becoming a pop star look like the most natural thing in the world.

> **Whitney weds Bobby.**

Her first single "You Give Good Love," went to number three in 1985. After that, she had a stunning string of seven consecutive number one hits, including "Saving All My Love for You," "Greatest Love of All," and "I Wanna Dance with Somebody (Who Loves Me)." Her first album, *Whitney Houston,* was one of the best-selling debuts ever, and the follow-up, *Whitney,* fared well, too.

She sang a memorable rendition of "The Star Spangled Banner" at the Super Bowl in 1991 in Tampa. In 1992, she starred in the box-office smash *The Bodyguard* with Kevin Costner. It featured the enormous hit and Dolly Parton cover, "I Will Always Love You." Whitney was on top of her game.

Around the same time, Whitney wed new jack musical star and former New Edition member Bobby Brown. Their marriage was the meet-

DIVAS

Whitney's got the pipes. So do:

1 Celine Dion
2 Aretha Franklin
3 Ella Fitzgerald
4 Barbra Streisand
5 Bette Midler

ing of the pop peerage. Little did she know that when she said "I do," the sharks began to circle.

First, Bobby's career went south while his wife's was still big, which may have caused some marital tension. In 1996, he crashed a Porsche and broke some ribs (his own). Turns out his blood alcohol content was more than double the legal limit. He was convicted of drunk driving and got some jail time. Later, he was arrested for (and cleared of) sexual battery.

Whitney wasn't used to this tabloid world, and she and Bobby separated for a while. They got back together and Brown tested positive for cocaine—he wasn't charged, however. Then Whitney's name was dragged down as well. In September of 2000, a half-ounce of marijuana was found in her bag at a Hawaiian airport. Though she didn't stick around long enough to be arrested, next thing we knew rumors started spreading that the super-skinny superstar had an eating disorder.

Her life had been a wondrous pop opera. Once she married, it became a soap opera. She was canceling performances and looking more and more like an *Ally McBeal* reject. Her music and film career has taken a backseat to gossip. Perhaps Whitney needs to take some time to rediscover the greatest love of all—herself.

I Do?

Musical marriages often prove to be fatal for bands in a variety of ways. Memorable nuptials:

1 John Lennon–Yoko Ono
2 Michael Jackson–Lisa Marie Presley
3 Kurt Cobain–Courtney Love
4 Bruce Springsteen–Patti Scialfa
5 John McVie–Christine Perfect
6 Chris Frantz–Tina Weymouth
7 Elvis Costello–Caitlin O'Riordan
8 James Taylor–Carly Simon
9 John Phillips–Holly Michelle Gilliam
10 Sonny–Cher

When did
Janet Jackson
1966–

jump the shark?

One of the most popular, and certainly the best looking of the bunch, Janet (Ms. Jackson, if you're nasty) has grown from young TV star to gorgeous pop diva right before our eyes.

> **We became members of *Rhythm Nation 1814*.**

The youngest of the nine Jackson children (you're familiar with five of her brothers) it's safe to say Janet was destined for a career in showbiz. Then again, so was LaToya—look how she ended up.

Unlike most singers who aspire to have acting careers, Janet started on the acting side before branching into music, making her mark as Penny on *Good Times,* Willis's girlfriend Charlene on *Diff'rent Strokes,* and Cleo on *Fame*—who ironically couldn't dance to save her career.

> **JACKSON ACTION**
>
> It's a tough choice, but here are our five favorite Jacksons:
> 1 Randy
> 2 Tito
> 3 LaToya
> 4 Reggie
> 5 The two snakes in the cartoon

Boosted by her *Fame,* Janet released a couple of forgettable albums that yielded one minor hit, "You Don't Stand Another Chance." Janet was looking for a distinctive style and sound to set her apart from her "cute" acting career and her big brother who was in the process of dominating the pop world. Enter Jimmy Jam and Terry Lewis.

Janet needed to take control of her career, and Jimmy Jam and Terry Lewis enabled her to do just that. *Control* was a blockbuster with hits like "What Have You Done for Me Lately?," "Nasty," and "When I Think of You." Almost every cut was released as a single, and they all charted. This took Janet's career to a new level and her physical appearance began to follow suit.

Janet didn't jump with the political themes in her next Jimmy Jam/Terry Lewis production, *Rhythm Nation 1814.* She jumped when we learned the meaning of "1814": *R* is the eighteenth letter of the alphabet, *N* the fourteenth. Pretty deep. The title track, "Black Cat," and "Miss You Much" were hits, but the shark had moved on to its next victim.

> **JIMMY AND TERRY**
>
> Every thing these producers touch turns to gold:
> 1 S.O.S. Band
> 2 Vanessa Williams
> 3 Herb Alpert
> 4 Human League
> 5 Boyz II Men

127

The album *janet* was next, with the big hit "That's the Way Love Goes," but this record fell short of her previous work. She followed with the sexually provocative *The Velvet Rope*, which includes a cover of Rod Stewart's "Tonight's the Night," and many members of the *RN* fled.

These days, Janet has eclipsed her brother as a successful pop performer. Then again, so has Kid Rock. Her concerts feature tons of dancers, and enough energy to practically force you out of your seat. Penny sure has come a long way.

When did
Michael Jackson
1958–

jump the shark?

Michael Jackson defies description. In 1984, he was the King of Pop. These days, who knows what he is?

Michael shows Wesley Snipes who's "Bad."

Michael was born and raised in Gary, Indiana, with his now famous brothers and sisters. By the time he was eleven, he was the lead singer of the Jackson Five, with huge hits like "ABC" and "I Want You Back." Motown attempted to launch a solo career for Michael, but it didn't take off. Other than "Dancing Machine," all of the Jacksons disappeared for the remainder of the seventies.

In 1979, a seemingly mature Michael appeared on the scene with *Off the Wall* and the dance hits "Don't Stop 'Til You Get Enough" and "Rock with You." The album was enormously popular, but barely hinted at what was to come.

The timing was perfect for *Thriller*. MTV was gaining in popularity. Michael brought in some help from Eddie Van Halen, and the obligatory cheesy duet with Paul McCartney. "Beat It" was the first single, but "Billie Jean," buoyed by Michael's moonwalk on the Motown Anniversary special, was the first megahit. Seven of the nine tracks were top-ten smashes, and the album charted for over two years. The video for the title track (starring

SIGNIFICANT OTHERS

Michael has been married twice, but these were our favorite partners:

1 Brooke Shields
2 Emmanuel Lewis
3 Elizabeth Taylor
4 Macauley Culkin
5 Bubbles the Chimp

Ola Ray) is the best ever to air on MTV. *Thriller* was beyond huge, and Michael was anointed the King of Pop.

There was nowhere to go but down as Michael reunited with his brothers for *Victory,* leaving us all in a state of shock. A flame got hold of Michael's hair during a Pepsi ad shoot. Francis Ford Coppola directed him in the short film *Captain Eo,* which featured Angelica Huston and aired at Disney World. Michael then teamed with recording artists to create USA for Africa and "We Are the World," where he lobbied to insert a foreign echo into the chorus. It was summarily rejected by Quincy Jones. The shark was champing at the bit.

The stage was set for Michael's next solo release, which featured an hour-long CBS special presentation of the first video, "Bad." It was directed by Martin Scorcese, featured plenty of wild screaming, and a physically changed Michael getting the best of a pre–Nino Brown Wesley Snipes on a subway platform. Weird Al's "Fat" parody was more entertaining, and *Bad* sent the gloved one straight over the shark. The album contained the obligatory hits like "The Way You Make Me Feel" and "Man in the Mirror," but the music simply lacked the power of *Thriller.*

JACKSONIAN POSSESSIONS

There's only one Michael. Some of his properties:

1 The Lennon/McCartney catalog
2 The Elephant Man
3 The Neverland Ranch
4 The oxygen machine
5 The white glove

Four years and even more plastic surgery later, *Dangerous* was released to a large but shrinking fan base. Michael wed Lisa Marie Presley (they divorced two years later) and was later accused of sexual abuse by a teenager he had befriended as a child—an accusation he vehemently denied. *HIStory* came next, half greatest hits and half forgettable new material. He married Debbie Rowe and had a son named Prince. In 2001, Michael released *Invincible,* proving only that he is anything but. The heralded King of Pop lost his crown when he showed us who was really, really "Bad."

Jefferson Airplane

1965–1990

jump the shark?

This sixties child made its mark on music with many hits, many members, and many different band names.

> **As Starship, they built that city on rock n' roll.**

Jefferson Airplane launched out of San Francisco in 1965 with more members than can possibly be listed on this page. Marty Balin was the dominant force on their first album, but that all changed when Grace Slick joined the band the following year.

Surrealistic Pillow was not only a great album title, but the first record out of Haight-Ashbury to have a national impact. "Somebody to Love" and "White Rabbit" can still be heard in any Vietnam film made these days. The summer of love belonged to Jefferson Airplane.

Grace Slick's arrival was part of a pattern of change that never seemed to end, but the band continued to thrive. As everyone left to create solo albums, Paul Kantner credited the friends backing him as Jefferson Starship. When Marty Balin returned four years later, Airplane had departed and *Red Octopus*—which included the hit "Miracles"—brought Jefferson Starship into the pop world.

Mickey Thomas joined whatever was left of the band in the late seven-

GOING SOFT

Starship wasn't the only former rock band building cities:

1 "These Dreams"—Heart
2 "Open Arms"—Journey
3 "I Want To Know What Love Is"—Foreigner
4 "Hard To Say I'm Sorry"—Chicago
5 "The Search Is Over"—Survivor

ties and "Jane" and "Find Your Way Back" became hits. Grace had quit and come back by now, but Paul Kantner finally left the band and the remains re-dubbed itself Starship. Still with us? The bait had been set.

Starship wasted no time, jumping the shark with their first album *Knee Deep in the Hoopla* and the single "We Built This City." Not only was it a slap in the face of any Jefferson (insert name here) fan, but in its lyrics this pop song prided itself on "Rock and Roll."

The next album, *No Protection,* included the pop smash "Nothing's Gonna Stop Us Now." Grace Slick had gone from "White Rabbit" to the theme for *Mannequin.* Airplane and Starship have reunited in different forms, but no one has seemed to notice. We're busy digging ourselves out of the rubble of the city they built on rock 'n' roll.

When did

Jethro Tull

1967–

jump the shark?

> **They defeat Metallica for the inaugural best metal performance Grammy.**

That flute. That damn flute.

Jethro Tull, named after an eighteenth-century inventor, was an innovative British band that meshed folk and hard rock into its own unique sound. However, many thought Tull was the name of the crazed flautist and driving force of the band, Ian Anderson.

Jethro Tull got its start as a blues band, and its sound evolved with the growing prominence of Anderson's flute. Although much of Tull's music and lyrical themes were perceived as being too highbrow, *Aqualung* proved that notion wrong with its title track and "Locomotive Breath."

Tull's follow-up, *Thick As a Brick,* was a full-length concept album in which one song stretched over the entire record, with classical folk and var-

ORCHESTRAL MANUEVERS

It's not often a flute is your featured instrument in a hard rock band. Other quirks:

1 Violin—John Mellencamp
2 Gong—Queen
3 Violin bow—Led Zeppelin
4 Banjo—Doobie Brothers
5 Harmonica—Bob Dylan

ious other influences mixed in, and it worked. The edited title track was one of Tull's most popular records in the U.S., and they quickly followed with a best of their earlier releases titled *Living in the Past*.

But Ian Anderson pushed the Tull concept album too far with the next one, *A Passion Play*, incorporating religious themes and an A.A. Milne story (not *Winnie the Pooh*). *Warchild* followed with the hits "Bungle in the Jungle" and "Skating Away on the Thin Ice of a New Day," but the band was losing its momentum as Anderson drifted from concept to concept and overproduced each record.

The late seventies and early eighties featured greatest hits compilations and new records that not many folks chose to hear. When *Original Masters,* essentially another greatest hits album, was released, the shark tightened its circle. But not even Ian Anderson and his flute could prepare for what was coming next.

ACROSS THE ATLANTIC

Other distinctive British-sounding bands that don't change their accents:

1 Yes
2 King Crimson
3 Fairport Convention
4 Marillion
5 The Moody Blues

In 1987, Tull released *Crest of a Knave,* which had a harder sound than past records, but was by no means a metal record. Later that year, the Grammy winner in the Heavy Metal category was . . . Jethro Tull, their reward for a great career. Only Milli Vanilli's victory could compare to this injustice, but at least those boys gave the Grammy back. Tull's latest release was *J-Tull.com.* Say no more.

Billy Joel
1949–

jump the shark?

If you're in the mood for a melody, chances are this masterful singer/songwriter at one time or another has made you feel all right.

> **He met his uptown girl, Christie Brinkley.**

Billy Joel learned to play piano in Hicksville, just south of a town known as Oyster Bay, Long Island. In the early seventies, he entered into the first of many bad business deals when he unknowingly signed for life with a small record label, and then released *Cold Spring Harbor* (a town east of Oyster Bay, Long Island). Two years and one trip to L.A. later, his next album *Piano Man* was a modest hit, and Billy was on his way to becoming the entertainer we now know.

MODEL MARRIAGES

Singers and supermodels . . . a potent combination:

1 Ric Ocasek and Paulina
2 Rod Stewart and Rachel Hunter
3 Richie Sambura and Heather Locklear (she counts)
4 Any member of Mötley Crüe and (insert name of model here)
5 David Bowie and Iman

His breakout record was the multiplatinum *The Stranger,* which contained megahits such as "Scenes from an Italian Restaurant" and "Just the Way You Are." He followed up this smash with *52nd Street,* which features *Bosom Buddies'* theme "My Life," "Big Shot," and other classics. You didn't have to be from Long Island to know the words to a Billy Joel tune anymore.

We spotted a fin with the release of *Glass Houses* with hits "It's Still Rock and Roll to Me" and "Sometimes a Fantasy" (woah oh oh oh). Billy had a nasty motorcycle accident where he broke his wrist, and also decided he didn't love his wife/manager just the way she was.

The critically acclaimed/listener-boycotted *The Nylon Curtain* soon followed before Billy sweated to the oldies with *An Innocent Man.* It was around this time that he met Christie Brinkley, and the piano man would never be the same. Although the album went multiplatinum, his new "Uptown Girl" brought Billy to MTV (with the unforgettable Joe Piscopo in "Keeping the Faith").

HERE COMES THE BRIDE

He didn't intend it, but Billy is a nuptial standard:

1 "Just the Way You Are"
2 "She's Got a Way"
3 "Honesty"
4 "She's Always a Woman"
5 "Movin' Out"

The obligatory *Greatest Hits* double album soon followed, another sign that Billy had indeed jumped the shark. *The Bridge* had him fronting his band and playing guitar (!), on "A Matter of Trust." His next big hit, "We Didn't Start the Fire," was a laundry list of various moments in history. Billy proceeded to dump his band (except for drummer Liberty Devito, of course) and long-time producer Phil Ramone.

Billy has since divorced Christie, grown a beard, put on a few pounds, and shifted his focus to classical music. It's nice to see him back at the piano again and telling tales on *Inside the Actor's Studio.* There is no one better at sitting behind a piano, playing songs and cracking jokes than Billy Joel.

When did
Elton John
1947–

jump the shark?

Elton is the most successful pop singer of all time. Need proof? He has had at least one hit song almost every year for the past thirty years. Whoa.

Reg still standing on the beach after all this time.

Elton John, born Reginald Dwight, was a piano prodigy who had begun playing in bands by the time he was fourteen years old. A few years later, he met lyricist Bernie Taupin, and the pair started writing songs together. In 1970, *Elton John* was released and "Your Song" became the first of his countless hits to chart.

The string-heavy *Tumbleweed Connection* and *Madman Across the Water* were conceptual albums that hold up well over time, but Elton began to slowly drift into the world of pop with *Honky Chateau* and its hits "Honky Cat" and "Rocket Man." When the double album *Goodbye Yellow Brick Road* was released, Elton the songwriter started to take a backseat to Elton the glitzy performer.

You could feel the cheese beginning to spread with "Crocodile Rock," "The Bitch Is

BIG PIANISTS

Which piano man would you rather see tickling the ivories?

1 Billy Joel
2 Ray Charles
3 Fats Domino
4 Rick Wakeman
5 Stevie Wonder

Back," "Philadelphia Freedom," and "Island Girl."
Right after this run of pop hits, Elton revealed to
Rolling Stone that he was bisexual, trying to
throw us off the trail of the fact that he was actually homosexual. It was around this time that
Elton declared a short-lived retirement from performing live, and his relationship with Bernie
Taupin began to fade. No longer did every record
he touched turn to gold. The shark was circling.

"Little Jeannie," "Empty Garden," and "Blue Eyes" were hits, but they
couldn't save him. Elton sailed over the shark with the aptly titled *Too Low for
Zero,* and the hit single "I'm Still Standing." Instead of "Tiny Dancer" and
"Mona Lisas and Mad Hatters," we got "Nikita" and "Sad Songs." Elton also
got married to a woman for four years despite the fact that everyone knew he
was gay. Alcohol and drugs were a staple of his life, and Elton auctioned off
all his concert costumes and any reminders of his earlier musical existence.

Elton resurfaced with *The Lion King* soundtrack and the death of
Princess Di, which forced us to listen to "Candle in the Wind" every ten minutes for months. Seeing as how it took an animated Disney movie to bring
this pop icon back, the shark clearly did its damage.

When did

Journey
1973–1987, 1996–

jump the shark?

Journey traveled from hard rock to cheesy pop
and created many a memorable tune, for better or
worse, along the way.

In the early seventies, former Santana guitarist Neil Schon put together this jazz-rock band
that was named in a radio contest. Like most other
Frisco bands, Journey had a strong live following, but they
realized they needed a stronger front man to really put them on the map.
Enter Steve Perry.

The band goes its "Separate Ways."

GOING SOLO

You're only as good as your
lead singer:

1 Van Halen

2 The Go-Go's

3 Genesis

4 Pink Floyd

5 The Commodores

In 1978, Journey cut the jazz and went straight to platinum with *Infinity*, as "Lights" and "Wheel in the Sky" hooked mainstream listeners. The follow up was *Evolution*, with the huge hit "Lovin', Touchin', Squeezin'," and constant touring ensured that Journey would be a fixture on the pop charts for a long time. "Anyway You Want It" was a highlight of their next release, *Departure,* and gave Rodney something to dance to in *Caddyshack.*

The crossover into Top 40 was complete when *Esc4p3* took Journey from cult band to superstar. "Who's Crying Now" and "Don't Stop Believin'" were huge hits, although there's no such place as South Detroit. But we spotted a fin when the first of many Steve Perry cheesy ballads, "Open Arms," became a major hit in suburbs everywhere.

Journey tried to clone *Esc4p3* with its next album, *Frontiers.* "Faithfully," "Send Her My Love," and "After the Fall" had plenty of synthesizer and sap. But it was "Separate Ways (Worlds Apart)" that vaulted the band over the shark. The memorable video featured the band running around a warehouse in full eighties gear as they reminded us of the different ways love can find us. Journey was a band raised and bred solely for the radio.

The next year, Steve Perry released the solo album *Street Talk* with pop ballads "Oh, Sherrie" and "Foolish Heart." Journey began to fall apart with band members exiting and Perry eventually leaving in 1986. The inevitable reunion happened a decade later, but it was an obvious "we're in it for the money" tour. Without Perry fronting the band, Journey is anything but fantastic.

SOUNDS LIKE

Journey is sometimes confused with:

1 Styx

2 REO Speedwagon

3 Toto

4 Foreigner

5 Survivor

KISS

1973–

When did

jump the shark?

Gene. Paul. Ace. Peter. This made-up fab four of the 1970s made its everlasting mark on fans throughout the world with a live show that was second to none.

They lose the makeup.

Bassist Gene Simmons, who never met a dollar he didn't like, and guitarist Paul Stanley came up with the "KISS Koncept" in the early seventies. Drummer Peter Criss and lead guitarist Ace Frehley were brought into the fold, and the lineup was set. The makeup and the pyrotechnics were there from day one, and the band took off with its first release.

KISS has always gotten a bad rap about being all show and no substance. Although Gene's tongue and the fireworks are integral parts of the band, the early songs are decent rock and roll. "Strutter," "Deuce," and "Rock & Roll All Night" hold their own on early studio albums, but the power of KISS was finally unleashed with *Alive,* a solid live album.

Following *Alive,* every teenager was enlisting in the KISS Army of fans.

They followed up with the studio album *Destroyer*, which featured the hits "Detroit Rock City" and "Shout It Out Loud," and the first KISS cover with cartoon images instead of photos of the foursome. We thought we smelled shark bait with the Peter Criss ballad "Beth," which included strings and plenty of cheese. Were they going soft? Thankfully, "Rock and Roll All Over" and "Love Gun" indicated that this wasn't the case.

During this run, the KISS merchandising arm began to spread its wings. T-shirts and hats, lunch boxes, pinball machines, comic books, TV movies . . . if the product existed, the KISS logo was slapped on to it. Their next album, *Alive II,* featured recent hits on three sides live and one in studio, but it was an indication that the well was starting to run dry. *Dynasty* followed with the disco hit "I Was Made for Loving You," and the next year all four members simultaneously released solo albums (with Gene singing "When You Wish upon a Star" and a duet with Cher, "Living in Sin"). Soon after, Peter Criss got into a nasty car accident and was eventually replaced by Eric Carr, Vinnie Vincent stepped in for Ace Frehley, and the shark began to circle.

In a hall of fame shark jump, KISS removed its makeup for the 1983 release *Lick It Up* and it was all downhill from there. Without their makeup, KISS became just another early eighties pseudo–metal band. The band rotated members for the next decade and hit new lows with "Let's Put The 'X' in Sex." The original four reunited in 1996 and have been on a farewell tour ever since, continuing to rock and roll all night and party every day.

Led Zeppelin
1968-1980

jump the shark?

Presence.

Page. Plant. Jones. Bonham. No rock band had more of an influence on popular culture during the 1970s than Zeppelin. Just ask Damone.

Jimmy Page was the last member of The Yardbirds and held both the rights to the band name and the contractual obligation to keep the balance of the band's tour dates. He formed the New Yardbirds with lead singer Robert Plant, bassist/keyboardist John Paul Jones, and drummer John Bonham to complete the band's remaining shows. After that tour concluded, this new band recorded a debut album in a little less than thirty hours and changed its name to Led Zeppelin.

Beginning with the first album, Zeppelin electrified Southern blues and transformed it into a new brand of rock and roll. *Led Zeppelin I* and *II* contain too many classics to list . . . every song is good. *III* takes a turn toward folk with "Gallows Pole" and "Bron-Y-Aur Stomp"—once you get past the whine of "Immigrant Song"—but it's still a great album.

The band brought it on home with *Led Zeppelin IV.* "Black Dog," "Rock and Roll," and the infamous "Stairway to Heaven" . . . this record holds up as a legendary piece of work. The only confusing thing about this record is Page's use of symbols to represent each band member. The band stopped numbering their albums at this point, but *Houses of the Holy* picked up right where *IV* left off.

Zeppelin tours broke Beatles' records with their stadium shows, and the band established its own recording label, Swan Song. We spotted a fin with the release of a double album, *Physical Graffiti,* after a two-year hiatus. Plant was then injured in a car accident and any touring plans were scrapped. They finally jumped with *Presence,* their most disappointing album release, which comes up empty when compared

CONCERT FILMS
The midnight movie feature this week:
1 *Stop Making Sense*
2 *Rattle and Hum*
3 *Gimme Shelter*
4 *Truth or Dare*
5 *Woodstock*

POST ZEP
These singles were far from Stairway, but still . . .
1 "Sea of Love"
2 "Radioactive"
3 "Big Log"
4 "Yallah"
5 "Rockin' at Midnight"

to its predecessors. The band followed by releasing a film of a three-year old Madison Square Garden concert appearance, *The Song Remains the Same.* Zeppelin finally toured again the following year, but stopped when Plant's six-year-old son died from a stomach illness.

Two years later, they released *In Through the Out Door* with hits "All My Love" and "Fool in the Rain" and prepared to tour, but tragedy struck when John Bonham died choking on his own vomit after a hard day of drinking. Zeppelin was done.

Page went on to assemble some outtakes to create *Coda* and he and Plant reunited from time to time, but Led Zeppelin was buried with John Bonham. They have been the classic rock standard for the past twenty years, and the six albums they released over a six-year period are simply unparalleled.

When did

John Lennon
1940–1980

jump the shark?

Imagine.

We know there's a certain amount of sacrilege in suggesting that rock and roll's greatest martyr ever jumped the shark. But then again, he didn't believe in Jesus, anyway.

John Lennon emerged from a Dickensian childhood into the pop spotlight in the early 1960s and stayed there until his assassination in 1980. He has now been a dead legend longer than he was a live one, and his influence is still extraordinary and shows no sign of waning. That's good news.

The front man and brains behind The Beatles, Lennon created the most important and apparently immortal band in rock history. His marriage to Yoko might have pushed The Beatles over the shark, but it was a different story when it came to solo works. Lennon's output

BEFORE THEIR TIME

Don't any rock and rollers die of natural causes?

1 Buddy Holly
2 Janis Joplin
3 Mama Cass
4 Brian Jones
5 Keith Moon

paled in comparison to McCartney's in terms of commercial success, but was much more important artistically—to Paul's never-ending irritation. Just compare greatest hits albums. Lennon's stuff still sounds fresh and contemporary, while McCartney's work feels uneven and dated.

In the early seventies, John put out two masterpieces, *Plastic Ono Band* and *Imagine.* The latter would be his last great album, and marks the point when he jumped the shark. Though *Mind Games* two years later was nearly as good, *Sometimes in New York City* and *Walls and Bridges* lacked real oomph. Dr. Winston O'Boogie made some appearances with Elton John and David Bowie, but laid low for a few years raising his son Sean in New York City.

Five years out of the game, Lennon returned in 1980 with the wonderful comeback *Double Fantasy.* Half the record was great stuff, and the other half was Yoko. God deliver us from "Kiss Kiss Kiss." Lennon's death robbed us of a chance to ever know the artist as a mature man. We bet he would have jumped back. I guess we'll just have to imagine . . .

When did
Madonna
1958–

jump the shark?

Madonna redefined the pop star of today by constantly reinventing her image yet never failing to forget to keep her music on top of the charts. My childhood friend Todd Anderman said it best back in 1984 . . . "She's so hot."

She writes about sex.

Madonna Louise Ciccone hails from the great state of Michigan and is a fellow U of M alum (there's a shrine in her former dorm room). She came to New York to be a ballerina,

THE BIG SCREEN

Madonna has conquered pop music and fashion, but she just can't do the same in movies. Here's why:

1 *Shanghai Surprise*
2 *Who's That Girl?*
3 *Body of Evidence*
4 *Bloodhounds of Broadway*
5 *The Next Best Thing*

but ended up as a drummer for the pop/disco band The Breakfast Club. She soon became the lead singer, and then went out on her own penning catchy club tunes.

Madonna debuted with a self-titled album that brought dance music to the forefront of pop. "Holiday," "Borderline," "Lucky Star," "Everybody," "Physical Attraction," "Burning Up" . . . nearly every cut was a bonafide hit. Her boy-toy sex appeal helped sell records, but Madonna's dance music (she wrote the songs) was what put her on the map.

A superstar was born with her follow-up album, *Like a Virgin,* which featured the title track, "Into the Groove," and "Material Girl." The music fell short of her first release, but her image was cranked up several notches by the videos that built up her sexy profile. She soon launched her acting career by playing herself in *Desperately Seeking Susan,* which is critically acclaimed for reasons that elude me to this day.

Old *Playboy* and *Penthouse* nude photos soon emerged as she began her rocky marriage with Sean Penn, but nothing could hinder Madonna's celebrity. Her next release, *True Blue*, featured the title track, "Open Your Heart," "Live to Tell," and a cropped blond haircut. It also included the preachy "Papa Don't Preach," a horrible "Thriller"-length video chronicling Madonna's struggle with abortion and featuring Danny Aiello as her father. Later that year the film *Shanghai Surprise,* which co-starred hubby Sean, was released. The shark couldn't even circle, so repelled was it by this garbage.

ACCENTUATE THE POSITIVE

I went to Michigan, and folks there don't speak like Madonna does. Other mysterious accents:

1 Alex Trebek
2 Jackie Onassis
3 Marvin Hagler
4 Dr. Ruth
5 Howard Cosell

Who's That Girl? came next with typical results—number one single, horrendous film. After divorcing Penn, Madonna got back to basics and released *Like a Prayer,* which featured many hits including "Vogue" and "Express Yourself." Not willing to give up the big screen, Madonna starred in *Dick Tracy* and a concert tour film, *Truth or Dare,* which were moderately successful at the box office, and followed with an appearance in the chick flick *A League of Their Own.*

In 1992, it was time for another image makeover, so Madonna released *Erotica,* which was not as successful as her other albums. She sailed over the shark with her book, *Sex,* a steel-bound, soft-core collection of photographs of herself, Vanilla Ice, and other "models." Madonna hasn't been the same since.

Bedtime Stories was moderately successful with "Take a Bow," but Madonna was losing her trend-setting impact. She took yet another crack at movies with a critically acclaimed, hardly seen performance as *Evita,* and also had her first child, Lourdes. Madonna the mom. *Ray of Light* and *Music* became popular techno albums, but the Material Girl has fallen in with the pack instead of brazenly leading it as she once did.

When did

Paul McCartney
1942–

jump the shark?

Paul McCartney is arguably the most influential songwriter of our time—not to mention an under-rated bass player—who made his mark (and money) in music.

His first duet with the gloved one.

Some have dismissed McCartney's music as nothing but silly love songs, but look around and you'll see it isn't so. The "cute" Beatle hailed from Liverpool, England, and had always wanted to be a musician. Growing up, he met some guys named John, George, and Ringo, and the rest was history.

Paul officially broke up The Beatles. He wed Linda Eastman in 1969, and shortly thereafter began recording his first solo album, *McCartney,* which was released weeks before *Let It Be.* Paul was not making friends. He followed the next year with *Ram,* another self-produced album that Linda appeared on and that featured the single "Uncle Albert/Admiral Halsey." It was a success, and Paul and Linda were ready to put a band together and tour.

For the next decade, Paul fronted Wings and had many hits including "Band on the Run," "Jet," and "Live and Let Die," plus cheese like

BANDS ON THE RUN

Paul has always fared better playing with or as a member of a band:

1 The Beatles
2 Wings
3 Badfinger
4 James Taylor
5 Elvis Costello

"Silly Love Songs" and "Let 'Em In." At the end of the decade, Linda and Paul were busted for pot possession in Japan and imprisoned for ten days before being released.

McCartney II in 1980 was another solo release that signaled the end of a band. Paul didn't want to tour in the wake of John Lennon's death, and Wings was no more. Two years later, Paul reunited with George Martin to create *Tug of War,* which featured the hits "Take It Away" (with Ringo on drums), and a duet with Stevie Wonder, "Ebony and Ivory." The cheesy duets with Motown artists had begun, and the shark started to circle.

The next year, Paul dueted with Michael Jackson on *Thriller* with "The Girl Is Mine," and Michael returned the favor on *Pipes of Peace* with "Say, Say, Say." These two music legends were a hit, but McCartney had finally jumped the shark.

The next year, he directed his first film, the flop *Give My Regards to Broad Street*. Shortly after, his singing pal Michael purchased the publishing rights to all of The Beatles' songs. Nice friend. Paul's next hit was the theme from *Spies Like Us,* another flop. Paul toured successfully during the nineties, but his albums have been disappointments that left Paul believing in yesterday.

When did

John Mellencamp

1951–

jump the shark?

He finally dropped the Cougar from his name and ironically became a "pop singer."

The journey from Johnny Cougar to John Cougar to John Cougar Mellencamp to John Mellencamp is fraught with Midwestern rock anthems, pop singles, and cheesy covers from this Indiana boy raised in a small town.

If you know his music, you pretty much know the story of John Mellencamp and his rebellious Indiana childhood. After moving to New York to make it as a musician, a manager signed him, recorded a cover album, and then billed Mellencamp as "Johnny Cougar." The album tanked, but the name stuck for a while.

Johnny Cougar's first hit was "I Need a Lover," which happens to have the longest instrumental intro of any Top 40 single ever recorded. *American Fool* took John (no longer Johnny) Cougar to the pop charts, with singles like "Hurts So Good" and "Jack and Diane." John Cougar was starting to become something of a singing/songwriting force in music, a Springsteen from the heartland.

In his quest to reclaim his name, the next release, *Uh-Huh,* was credited to John Cougar Mellencamp. The hits kept on coming with "Pink Houses" and "Authority Song," but the lyrics touched on how tough life now was in the heart of the USA in the mid-eighties. Mellencamp was never about the hits . . . he wanted to make music that made a difference and a statement. Then again, he also thought he was a good dancer (as he proclaims in "Crumblin' Down"), but if you've seen the videos, you know the truth.

Soon performing as John Mellencamp and showing a more socially aware side, he released *Scarecrow,* which ranges from the pop hit "Lonely Ol' Night" to the anthem "Small Town." He combined social commentary with catchy tunes in this great album, but the cheesy pop anthem "R.O.C.K. in the U.S.A." was tasty shark bait. When a violin became a permanent part of

Mellencamp's now folksy repertoire on *The Lonesome Jubilee,* the songs that had come naturally began to feel like a reach. "Cougar" was gone, and Johnny sailed over the shark.

"Pop Singer," a single off his next album, *Big Daddy,* cemented the jump. Mellencamp had fought so hard to be taken seriously, but his lifeblood hits were gone and fewer folks were listening. He charted again with a remake of Van Morrison's "Wild Night," and "I Saw You First" recalled the old "Cougar" days. We look forward to the day when John forgets all about that macho shit and simply plays guitar.

jump the shark?

Metallica is a great heavy metal band. Metal by the people, of the people, and for the people. Lars even has a list of them now.

The Black Album.

Metallica was formed in 1981, and its lineup for their first album *Kill 'Em All* featured vocalist/guitarist James Hetfield, lead guitarist Kirk Hammett, drummer Lars Ulrich, and bassist Cliff Burton. They combined metal with punk to create "speed metal" or "thrash," and remain masters of the sound.

> **NO TITLE**
>
> Untitled albums often leave us wondering about not only the title, but the music as well:
>
> 1 *The Beatles*
> 2 *Peter Gabriel*
> 3 *Prince*
> 4 *90125* (Yes didn't pick it, it was the ID number)
> 5 *Led Zeppelin IV*

Early on, Metallica was dismissed as just another punk metal band. But the complexity of their music was evident in their second record, *Ride the Lightning,* which mixed all different styles and set a new standard for metal bands. Their next album, *Master of Puppets,* garnered a tour with Ozzy as Metallica crossed over into the mainstream.

While touring in 1986, their bus skidded out of control in Sweden and Cliff Burton was killed. Jason Newsted stepped in, and two years later the band released . . . *And Justice for All,* which featured their first Top 40 hit and MTV video (which they had sworn they'd never do), "One." We spotted a fin.

Metallica jumped the shark upon the release of its untitled Black Album. Shorter songs, simpler arrangements, and MTV awards all reeked of a commercial sellout, and it was all downhill from there. After four more years, they followed with the disappointing *Load* and *Reload,* and then recorded *S&M,* a live performance with the San Francisco Symphony. This was Metallica?

The band further distanced themselves in 2000 by keeping a high profile in a lawsuit against Napster, the online haven for swapping music. Lars led the charge to kick off a list of

> **FASTEN YOUR SEAT BELT**
>
> Car or motorcycle accidents have done damage to many a band:
>
> 1 Miami Sound Machine
> 2 Def Leppard
> 3 Billy Joel
> 4 Jan and Dean
> 5 Teddy Pendergrass

over a quarter million users arguing that fans shouldn't be downloading their music for free. Metallica has since dropped the lawsuit and cut their hair, Napster has disappeared, and the former band of the people is now searching for the legions of fans it lost.

When did
Milli Vanilli
1989–1991

jump the shark?

A hall-of-fame shark jump not only for the eighties, but for all time.

It was Memorex.

Producer Frank Farian recruited Rob Pilatus and Fab Morvan to form the duo Milli Vanilli, and each played their part perfectly. These good-looking German fellows were masterful at dancing and conducting interviews, but they suffered in one key area: singing. They never sang a note on their multiplatinum record.

LITERALLY UNPLUGGED

Our favorite live lip-synching shows:

1 American Bandstand
2 Solid Gold
3 Soul Train
4 Puttin' on the Hits
5 Dance Fever

Farian had created the perfect Euro-dance album in *Girl, You Know It's True,* but he needed front men. Rob and Fab lip-synched their way to winning the Grammy for Best New Artist, and the album went platinum with huge hits like the title track, "Blame It On the Rain," and "Baby Don't Forget My Number."

After winning the Grammy, the boys were busted at an MTV stage performance, when their "live" music got stuck and kept repeating. The secret was out, and the public was outraged, as if the music wasn't pure cheese to begin with. The boys gave

back their Grammy, but unwilling to let sleeping dogs lie, Rob and Fab tried to prove that they really *could* sing.

Image is everything, especially when you're lip-synching.

When did Mötley Crüe
1981–

jump the shark?

Think of the classic sex and drugs and rock 'n' roll band, mix in some big hair and tattoos, and you've got the Crüe.

"Without You."

Bassist Nikki Sixx, drummer Tommy Lee, guitarist Mick Mars, and vocalist Vince Neil formed Mötley Crüe and were a popular club band in the early eighties. There were never enough women, drugs, or fast cars to go around right from the beginning.

In 1983, the band released *Shout at the Devil,* which contained the hit

OUTRAGEOUS ACCENTS

Gotta love that umlaut. Accents we love:

1 Mötley Crüe
2 Blue Öyster Cult
3 ♀
4 Motörhead
5 Spiñal Tap

"Looks That Kill." The Crüe looked like KISS with its makeup and rocked like Aerosmith (pre-1980)—a lethal and successful combination. Their follow-up was *Theatre of Pain,* featuring their first chart single, a remake of "Smokin' in the Boys Room," and their crossover power ballad "Home Sweet Home."

But the troubles had already started, as Vince Neil was found guilty of vehicular manslaughter and forced to do some minor jail time. Tommy Lee married Heather Locklear right before the Crüe's next release, *Girls, Girls, Girls,* and their commercial success and personal excess continued.

We spotted a fin when Nikki Sixx nearly overdosed during that year's tour and all four members headed in for rehab. A sober Crüe didn't have as much appeal, but somehow they emerged with their best-selling album *Dr. Feelgood*. Although commercially successful, the album featured the sappy ballad, "Without You," that vaulted the band right over the shark.

By the early nineties, the hair brand of metal just wasn't as popular as it used to be, and group infighting reached a new low. Vince Neil was fired from the band and replaced by John Corabi for a disappointing self-titled album. Neil was back for *Generation Swine,* but fewer fans were listening. Tommy was making his own videos with new wife Pamela Anderson, Mick Mars was physically falling apart, and Nikki Sixx drifted in and out of rehab.

Without the sex and drugs, there's not much rock and roll or reason to listen to Mötley Crüe.

When did
Nirvana
1987–1994

jump the shark?

Nirvana epitomized the Seattle grunge movement of the early nineties and brought alternative rock into the mainstream.

Kurt says nevermind.

Punk met pop in this Seattle cult band that college radio couldn't get enough of in the late eighties. Drummer Dave Grohl, bassist Chris Novoselic, and guitarist/vocalist Kurt Cobain stepped into the limelight with a new brand of angst rock.

In 1991, Nirvana released *Nevermind* and was totally unprepared for its sudden success. "Smells Like Teen Spirit" quickly became an MTV staple as grunge replaced hair bands in the main video rotation. Nirvana loved to stir things up by destroying their instruments and throwing curves like Grohl and Novoselic's smooch on *Saturday Night Live.* To complicate matters, Kurt wed Hole lead singer Courtney Love and the happy couple were con-

SLEEPLESS IN SEATTLE

Nirvana is the cream of an eclectic Seattle crop:

1 Jimi Hendrix
2 Pearl Jam
3 Heart
4 Soundgarden
5 Alice in Chains

stantly fighting accusations of heroin addiction and battling for custody of their newborn child, Frances Bean.

Nirvana began canceling tour dates and Kurt frequently complained of stomach troubles, which many believed to be heroin-related, and even started attempting suicide. We spotted a fin when these suspicions were confirmed with heroin overdoses over the two years it took to create their next album, *In Utero.* An "Unplugged" appearance boosted the album sales, but early the next year, Kurt attempted suicide again and seemed to be slipping away.

Nirvana jumped the shark when Kurt finally got it right, skipping the overdoses and simply shooting himself in the head in April 1994. He had become a martyr for Generation X and the teenage angst of the mid-nineties. Grohl and Novoselic released *Unplugged in New York* later that year, revealing the softer side of a band whose legend would live on.

SNL

Nirvana's appearance rivaled other classic sets on *Saturday Night Live*:

1 Sinead O'Connor tearing up the Pope
2 Elvis Costello switching songs
3 The Blues Brothers singing "Soul Man"
4 Opera Man
5 Andy Kaufman singing the *Mighty Mouse* theme

Grohl went on to form the Foo Fighters, Novoselic busied himself protesting various causes, and Courtney Love cleaned up somewhat and became a notable actress. Subsequent live and tribute albums keep Cobain's legacy alive, but the fatal gunshot was a painful leap over the shark.

Pink Floyd

1965–

jump the shark?

If you've ever gotten stoned, chances are that this is the band you were listening to the first time you lit up.

The Final Cut.

Pink Floyd, named after two old bluesmen, was created in London and was a psychedelic band from the get-go. Drummer Nick Mason, keyboardist Richard Wright, bassist Roger Waters, and guitarist/vocalist Syd Barrett were the original members. Floyd's early vision started and ended with Syd—who was always in his own world, as is clearly evidenced by their first album, *The Piper at the Gates of Dawn.*

Guitarist David Gilmour was quickly brought on board to give Syd space to do his thing, but the front man balked and took his vision and songwriting off to an institution. A Sydless Floyd focused on the concept album, not the pop single, and honed their sound and form with *Ummagumma, Atom Heart Mother,* and *Meddle.* In 1973, Pink Floyd recorded its masterpiece, *Dark Side of the Moon*, which spent over *fourteen years* on the Billboard album chart. Enough said.

COVER THIS

Dark Side of the Moon has that great prism. Other memorable album covers:

1 *Santana*—Santana

2 *Two Virgins*—John & Yoko

3 *Revolver*—Beatles

4 *Black Moses*—Isaac Hayes

5 *Jazz*—Queen

Roger Waters took more of the conceptual lead as Floyd followed up with *Wish You Were Here* and *Animals.* Their next release, the double album *The Wall,* was another smash with special performances that included building and blowing up a huge wall onstage. However, we spotted a fin right behind that giant flying pig when "Another Brick in the Wall, Part 2" was released as a single. It was tough to accept them as a concept-driven group while Dionne Warwick announced on *Solid Gold* that Floyd had its first number one single.

By the time the eighties rolled around, all was not well for Pink Floyd. We waited four years for their next record, *The Final Cut,* to hear

CLASSIC PICKS

Pick up your air guitar for these Floyd moments:

1 "Comfortably Numb"

2 "Wish You Were Here"

3 "Shine on You Crazy Diamond"

4 "Have a Cigar"

5 "Hey You"

Roger Waters deal with his father's death in World War II. This depressing album was not up to Floyd's standards, and the shark had been jumped. At least its title was appropriate, though, because the band subsequently broke up, and Roger later ended up suing to prevent Pink Floyd from continuing to use the name without him. Unfortunately, he lost.

With a second visionary now out of the picture, Pink Floyd released *A Momentary Lapse of Reason* and later *The Division Bell* with modest commercial success, but those who went to see them live were just waiting to hear the old stuff. Gilmour, Mason, and Wright continue to oblige and the band is still a huge draw on the road. Roger Waters has had success as a solo artist and plays Floyd songs when on tour as well. These days, though, we're all left wondering, Which one is Pink?

When did

The Police
1977–1986

jump the shark?

'86.

This tremendously talented threesome mixed light punk and reggae to create a barrage of hits and some bizarre album titles.

The Police consisted of guitarist/ten years senior Andy Summers, drummer/CIA agent son Stewart Copeland, and bassist/lead singer/songwriter/schoolteacher Sting. The band was designed to be a British new wave/punk outfit but turned out to be anything but.

Their first release, *Outlandos d'Amour,* proved to be popular in the UK with the big hit "Roxanne," which Sting now sings acoustically. They followed up with *Reggatta de Blanc* and the successful single "Message in a Bottle," which follows "Roxanne" on Sting's set list. The Police also recorded great quirky tunes like "On any Other

GORDON SUMMER— THE ACTOR

Sting's acting career headed in the opposite direction of his recording career. His appearances, in chronological order:

1 *Quadrophenia*
2 *Brimstone and Treacle*
3 *Dune*
4 *The Bride*
5 *Plenty*

Day" and "Be My Girl Sally," keeping the band true to its roots.

The Police entered the eighties with a breakthrough album, *Zenyatta Mondatta.* "Don't Stand So Close to Me" and "De Do Do Do, De Da Da Da" climbed the charts, and all the other cuts (particularly the first side) are classics. They soon followed with their most comprehensible title, *Ghost in the Machine*, and the hits "Spirits in the Material World" and "Every Little Thing She Does Is Magic."

After spending a few years apart to let their egos cool off, The Police reconvened to create their biggest selling and final album, *Synchronicity.* "Wrapped Around Your Finger," "King of Pain," and the hugely popular "Every Breath You Take" were hits, but Sting's sappiness and arguably the worst song ever recorded, Andy Summers's "Mother," baited the shark.

Their creative differences couldn't prevent the inevitable reunion, and The Police sailed over the shark with *Every Breath You Take—The Singles* in 1986. They released the single "Don't Stand So Close to Me—'86." Yes, that's the actual title. They should have tried calling it something in French or Latin.

When did

Elvis Presley

1935–1977

jump the shark?

From Sun Records to bad movies, Colonel Tom to Bill "Superfoot" Wallace, Graceland to Vegas . . . Elvis will always be the king of rock 'n' roll.

Elvis Aron Presley grew up in Memphis, Tennessee, and was working as a truck driver before recording those famous demos for Sam Phillips at Sun Records. "That's All Right Mama" and "Blue Moon of Kentucky" proved Elvis was a natural—a good-looking white guy who could

The King becomes a private in the U.S. Army.

sing black R&B tunes. Elvis's popularity grew in the south after Colonel Tom Parker became his manager and Phillips sold the King's contract to RCA.

"Heartbreak Hotel," "Hound Dog," and "Don't Be Cruel" became huge hits, mostly because of Elvis's national TV appearances and controversial gyrating hips. In the mid-fifties, Elvis *was* cutting edge rock 'n' roll, and everyone, including The Beatles, idolized him and his music. His Ed Sullivan appearance is legendary, paving the way for the Fab Four.

The King wanted to be a movie star and held his own in *Love Me Tender* and *Jailhouse Rock,* better known for the title tunes than for the flicks themselves. We spotted a fin when Elvis was backed by the Lawrence Welk precursor Jordanaires, who always seemed to be just over the King's shoulder. Elvis was losing his rockabilly style and starting to belt out some cheesy ballads, an inevitable sign of things to come.

VIVA LAS VEGAS

When you're on the strip, be sure to check out:

1 Tom Jones
2 Cher
3 Tony Bennett
4 Tony Orlando (sans Dawn)
5 Siegfried & Roy

In 1958, Elvis was inducted into the Army for two years, and although his popularity never wavered, he had jumped the shark. His music began to feel recycled, the movies were a transparent way to make money (*Clambake*, anyone?), and four guys from Liverpool had arrived to steal the King's thunder. It wasn't until the '68 comeback special that Elvis once again found himself in the limelight, and "Suspicious Minds" and "In the Ghetto" soon put him back on the charts. But the Vegas shows had begun, and the King was quickly becoming a caricature of himself.

Everything Elvis did was grandiose . . . his weight, failed marriage, prescription drug addiction, rhinestone clothing, and judo lessons were all over the top. He settled into Graceland for the remainder of his life and reportedly died of an overdose. But just like his waistline in the later years, his legacy and legend continue to grow.

When did

Prince

1958–

jump the shark?

He was funk personified in the eighties and nineties, deftly mixing music and sex into a potent combination.

Prince Rogers Nelson grew up in Minneapolis, site of his future film smash. Prince could do it all—a great guitarist, gifted songwriter, intriguing vocalist, and dynamic dancer. He funkily played all instruments and sang in detail about sex. In short, he couldn't miss.

He lost D Revolution.

We wondered if a girl was singing his first hit, "I Wanna Be Your Lover" off his self-titled second album. Prince established his signature on his next two releases, *Dirty Mind* and *Controversy,* playing all instruments and mixing diverse styles of music with sexually explicit lyrics. "Jack U Off" was the first indication of Prince's fascination with rebus.

Prince crossed over to pop with his heavily synthesized double album *1999,* which includes the title track, "Little Red Corvette," and "Delirious." He desired superstar status and brought his backup band the Revolution into the forefront for *Purple Rain*. Prince's acting was solid in the Oscar-nominated movie, and its soundtrack was his best-selling album ever, featuring the hits "When Doves Cry," "Let's Go Crazy," and "I Would Die 4 U."

SYMBOLISM

Prince was one of many acts that featured intriguing uses of the English language. C U L8R:

1 *OU812*—Van Halen
2 "Thank You (Falletimme Be Mice Elf Agin)"— Sly & The Family Stone
3 *Esc4p3*—Journey
4 The Jackson 5ive
5 *Se7en*—Brad Pitt

The success of *Purple Rain* got Prince his own recording label, Paisley Park, and he followed up with the overly psychedelic *Around the World in a Day,* which included the hit "Raspberry Beret." Prince went back to the well for a second film, *Under the Cherry Moon,* and the accompanying soundtrack album *Parade,* which features "Kiss," most notable for the Tom Jones cover. The shark was circling.

Prince dropped the Revolution and finally brought his game of *Concentration* into an album title, *Sign O' the Times*. This double album was a complete mess and a sure sign that Prince had jumped. His *Batman* soundtrack was recycled early-eighties music and the *Purple Rain* sequel *Graffiti Bridge* was a bust. He formed the New Power Generation to back him in the nineties and legally changed his name to a symbol that we can't type since we don't have that font.

Prince has since escaped his recording contract, dumped the symbol for his original name, and done the obligatory remastering of *1999* at the turn of the century. He seems to release three and four disc sets of new and old material routinely now, but sales indicate that fans have told Prince, "we R tired of waiting around 4 U."

Queen
1971–1995

jump the shark?

No band could pull off the diverse range of music and kitsch and also thrive through the punk, disco, and rock eras better than Queen.

All we hear is radio ga ga.

Queen was formed in London in the early seventies when underrated guitarist Brian May and drummer Roger Taylor recruited lead singer Freddie Mercury and bassist John Deacon. The foursome graduated college and then turned their focus to music.

Queen debuted with a hard rocking self-titled album that contained the hit "Keep Yourself Alive," but broke through in England with *Queen II* and the hard-rocking tune "Seven Seas of Rhye." In the States, this album was more widely known for the diamond facial pose of the band on the cover that was later used in the "Bohemian Rhapsody" video and still later beaten to death in Mountain Dew ads.

Sheer Heart Attack was the record that introduced Queen to America with the hit "Killer Queen," but *A Night at the Opera* made the band's indelible, over-the-top mark with the infamous opera-meets-rock classic, "Bohemian Rhapsody." Now superstars with a truly unique style, Queen followed with *A Day at the Races,* which featured "Somebody To Love."

Queen shifted to anthem rock in *News of the World,* which contained the overplayed stadium classics "We Will Rock You" and "We Are the Champions." It's hard to determine whether the best part of their next release *Jazz* was the combination of "Fat Bottomed Girls" and "Bicycle Race" or the photos on the album sleeve insert.

Queen entered the eighties on top of the

disco craze with *The Game* and their most successful singles, "Another One Bites the Dust" and "Crazy Little Thing Called Love." We spotted a fin when the band recorded the soundtrack to the feature film flop, *Flash Gordon.* Their next release, *Hot Space,* was a disappointment except for "Under Pressure" with David Bowie.

Queen tried to recapture anthem rock, but the band jumped the shark with the single "Radio Ga Ga" off their 1984 record, *The Works.* The album isn't terrible, and Queen maintained its superstar status internationally, but their American appeal was gone. They continued to release nondescript albums until Freddie's death from AIDS in 1991. "Bohemian Rhapsody" resurfaced thanks to *Wayne's World,* but for most fans, all we heard was radio ga ga.

When did

R.E.M.
1980–

jump the shark?

Monster rock.

If you visited any college campus during the last twenty years, chances are you'd hear a R.E.M. record blaring out of someone's dorm room.

Down in Athens, Georgia, guitarist Peter Buck and vocalist Michael Stipe met up with drummer Bill Berry and bassist Mike Mills. They chose the name R.E.M. after flipping through a dictionary. Moody folk-rock was their thing and they quickly built a reputation as southern college radio's best garage band.

The critically acclaimed *Murmur* contained their first hit, "Radio Free Europe," and introduced R.E.M. to mainstream campuses across the country. You needed a beret and black turtleneck to appreciate *Reckoning,* but the pop crossover began with their next album *Fables of*

ABRVTD BND NMS

Behold the power of punctuation:

1 AC/DC
2 U2
3 INXS
4 N.W.A.
5 TLC

the Reconstruction, which contained the hit "You Can't Get There From Here." The band was at its depressing best, with a newly blond Stipe leading the charge.

Life's Rich Pageant was a breakthrough with the hit "Superman," and the fact that you could finally understand what Michael Stipe was singing about. But the band made it big in 1987 when *Document* hit the top ten with the joyful "It's the End of the World as We Know It (and I Feel Fine)" and "The One I Love."

The release of *Green* verified that R.E.M. was little more than a pop band with distant alternative roots, evidenced by the radio-ready singles "Stand" and "Orange Crush." After a three-year break—and a Stipe shaved head— *Out of Time* greeted us with "Losing My Religion" and "Shiny Happy People." R.E.M.'s edge was trampled beneath its MTV success. The band was briefly back at its creepy best with

HAIR CARE

The many moods of Michael Stipe often followed his haircuts. Other notably varied coifs:

1 Sinead O'Connor
2 Annie Lennox
3 Cher
4 Cyndi Lauper
5 Red Hot Chili Peppers

Automatic for the People (see the depressing "Everybody Hurts" and "Man on the Moon," two songs that ended up on prominent film soundtracks). Stipe's other creative interests had led him to filmmaking, and a fin had definitely been spotted.

R.E.M. jumped the shark when it released its self-proclaimed rock album, *Monster,* which featured the single "What's the Frequency, Kenneth?" Although commercially successful, the album was a harbinger of bad things to come. The band decided to tour for the first time in years, and Bill Berry suffered an aneurysm on stage that temporarily halted performances. They resumed touring two months later, only to have both Mike Mills and Michael Stipe go under the knife for a stomach tumor and an emergency hernia operation, respectively.

After the tour, their manager was dismissed from the band after a female staffer complained of sexual harassment. Bill Berry announced he was leaving to live on his farm, and R.E.M. was suddenly a trio with a drum machine. After the band leapt over the shark in 1994, everybody hurt.

The Rolling Stones

1963–

jump the shark?

The world's greatest rock and roll band continues to entertain packed stadiums almost forty years after its debut.

Hailing from London, and named for a Muddy Waters tune, the Rolling Stones' initial lineup featured perpetually baked guitarist Keith Richards, smiling bassist Bill Wyman, steady drummer Charlie Watts, eclectic guitarist Brian Jones, and London School of Economics alumnus Mick Jagger on vocals. They were billed as the bad boys of rock— or the anti-Beatles—and easily lived up to their reputation.

> **The South American gangster video for "Undercover of the Night."**

Initially the Stones recorded mostly covers and first hit with "Time Is on My Side." Mick and Keith began to write more and more, and finally broke through in 1965 with "(I Can't Get No) Satisfaction." Over the next few years, the Stones would release "As Tears Go By," "19th Nervous Breakdown," "Get Off of My Cloud" and countless other hits. *Aftermath* was the first entirely original album and featured "Paint It Black" and "Under My Thumb."

To one-up The Beatles, the Stones performed "Let's Spend the Night Together" on *Ed Sullivan*, with Mick incoherently mumbling the title. Jagger, Richards, and Jones were busted for drug possession as well, further enhancing their bad-boy image. The Stones moved away from psychedelics and back to good ol' rock and roll, hitting their stride and producing a stream of memorable hits with *Beggars Banquet*.

While recording *Let It Bleed,* Brian Jones was completely hooked on drugs and left the Stones . . . only to be found dead in a swimming pool shortly thereafter. Jones was soon replaced by Mick Taylor. Mick Jagger got the acting bug around this time and began to appear in feature films. The Stones toured America and on the advice of the Grateful Dead, hired Hell's Angels as security at a free concert at Altamont, where the bikers ended up murdering a black man. The Stones responded to this tragedy with two of their best albums, *Sticky Fingers* and *Exile on Main Street*.

COVER ART

The best part of a new Stones album was seeing what was going to be on the cover. Our favorites:

1 *Sticky Fingers*
2 *Beggar's Banquet*
3 *Exile on Main Street*
4 *Some Girls*
5 *Let It Bleed*

We spotted a fin in the mid-seventies as Mick focused more on acting, Keith focused more on drugs, and albums like *Goat's Head Soup* and *Black & Blue* were released. Ron Wood replaced Mick Taylor, and the band seemed to find its groove with *Some Girls* and *Tattoo You.* The video for "Waiting on a Friend" is an absolute classic.

But the Rolling Stones jumped with their 1983 record *Undercover of the Night* and the concept video that accompanied the title track. Showcasing their acting skills, Mick, Keith, and crew live a dangerous life in South America. Keith wanted to rock, Mick wanted to shine, and the result is as bad as it sounds. The Stones have since followed with various albums and successful tours, but it feels like Old Timer's Day when you see them on the road these days. Mick and Keith have had their differences and probably want to rock on forever, but you can't always get what you want.

When did

Diana Ross

1944–

jump the shark?

These days this Motown legend is best known for "discovering" Michael Jackson and getting soaked during a Central Park concert.

She eased on down the road.

In the 1960s, The Supremes were the most popular girl group in America and their lead singer was Diane Earle from Detroit. "Where Did Our Love Go?" "Stop! In the Name of Love," "Baby Love," and other songs containing the word "love" are modern standards and karaoke favorites. The Hit Factory kept Diana Ross at the top of the charts for over a decade.

WHO NEEDS BACKUP?

Diana reigned supreme over her fellow singers. Other leads that came to the forefront:

1 Michael Jackson
2 Stevie Nicks
3 Jim Morrison
4 Phil Collins
5 Ben E. King

Berry Gordy, the mastermind behind Motown, had tenderly nurtured Diana's career from the beginning. Her talent was not limited to a voice like candy and diamonds—the camera loved her, too. She emoted in a way that other singers couldn't touch. Her beautiful and expressive face, dominated by large, emotional eyes, made her a cinch for the movies.

We spotted a fin when the supergroup officially became known as Diana Ross and the Supremes in 1967. Three years later Diana dumped the Supremes and, under Gordy's guidance, began her film career. Sounds like a classic jump, but the Motown diva repelled the shark by receiving a well-deserved Oscar nomination for her performance as Billie Holiday in *Lady Sings the Blues.*

Her next films did not fare as well. *Mahogany* was painful, but at least the music was good. She then teamed with Michael Jackson, Nipsey Russell (yes, Nipsey!), and others for *The Wiz,* a black adaptation of *The Wizard of Oz.* Diana eased on down the yellow brick road and jumped right over the shark.

SMALL STAGE TO THE BIG SCREEN

Unlike *The Wiz,* some Broadway musicals do work on screen:

1 *West Side Story*
2 *My Fair Lady*
3 *Hair*
4 *The Rocky Horror Picture Show*
5 *Grease*

The early eighties served up disco Diana and her hit "Upside Down," which incidentally, if played at 33⅓ (we're dating ourselves), eerily sounds like a man singing at a slower tempo. But I digress. "Endless Love" was her last cheesy hit before the "Best of" collections started to appear. Someone carts Diana out every few years for a Motown Tribute or a VH-1 special. The ultimate insult was a failed Supremes reunion that left Diana wondering where her love went.

When did

Rush

1968–

jump the shark?

p/g.

Their brilliant musicianship and bizarre lyrics leave you wondering how this Canadian trio generates all that music.

Rush was born in Toronto in the late sixties with guitarist Alex Lifeson, bassist/vocalist/soprano Geddy Lee, and drummer John Rutsey. Rutsey was replaced by drumming god/Ayn Rand fan Neil Peart, who is responsible for the futuristic/sci-fi lyrics that have become the band's staple.

> ### CANADIAN BAKIN'
> Toronto is really clean, but also the birthplace of these classic acts:
> 1 Neil Young
> 2 Robbie Robertson
> 3 Triumph
> 4 Dan Hill
> 5 Saga (who could forget their eighties classic "On the Loose"?)

The band broke through with its third album release *2112* and the self-titled, twenty-minute first side. Rush was seventies album rock at its best, and their uncanny abilities were highlighted like never before. They followed with *A Farewell to Kings,* which introduced synthe-sizers, shortened song times, and included their first hit, "Closer to the Heart." *Hemispheres* came next and contained only four songs, but "The Trees" and "La Villa Strangiato" are two of their all-time best.

Rush began to cross over into the mainstream, incorporating modern sound in *Permanent Waves* and the hit "The Spirit of Radio." Their next album, *Moving Pictures,* was their most commercially successful, with clas-sics "Tom Sawyer," "YYZ," and "Limelight." *Exit . . . Stage Left* tried to cap-ture the magic of a Rush live performance, but you need to see a Peart, Lifeson, or Lee solo to fully appreciate them.

We spotted a fin when synth began to re-place guitars in *Signals.* Even Geddy's classic solo performance on Bob and Doug McKenzie's "Take Off" couldn't keep the shark at bay. Where had By-Tor and the Snow Dog gone?

Rush jumped with its next release, *Grace Under Pressure,* when Geddy's synthesizers began to dominate this classic rock band. We still appreciate their musical talents, but the

> ### THE GREAT WHITE NORTH
> Our favorite Canadian im-ports:
> 1 Mike Myers
> 2 Anyone from *SCTV*
> 3 Molson
> 4 Montreal Canadiens home or away jerseys
> 5 *Hockey Night in Canada*

modern sound of *Power Windows, Hold Your Fire,* and *Presto* are just too much to take. If someone headed up to the Great White North and unplugged Geddy's synth, Rush's vital signs might once again be renewed.

When did Bruce Springsteen

1971–

jump the shark?

If you can only see one rock concert in your life-time, Bruce Springsteen would be an excellent choice. No one can match the Boss when it comes to a live performance.

> **Courteney Cox hops up on stage to dance.**

"Bruuuuuuce" was a working-class hero, Jersey singer/songwriter who first came on the scene with *Greetings from Asbury Park, NJ* and *The Wild, The Innocent and The E Street Shuffle.* A *Soprano paisan*, Conan O'Brien's bandleader, a big black sax player, and three other guys who called themselves the E Street Band backed him.

LIVE

Classic concert albums:

1 *Frampton Comes Alive*
2 *Cheap Trick at Budokan*
3 *Live at the Fillmore East*
4 *Stop Making Sense*
5 *Kiss Alive*

"Born to Run" got Bruce on the cover of *TIME, Newsweek,* and *Tiger Beat* as a new rock and roll savior. However, it was the nonstop hard rocking three-hour live shows that won over Bruce's fans. *Darkness on the Edge of Town* was the last album cover with a photo of Bruce looking smashed, and consequently we started looking for sharks with the double album *The River.*

We spotted a fin when Bruce released a bunch of demo tapes, aptly calling it *Nebraska* as Nils Lofgren replaced little Stevie in the E Street Band. Two years later, *Born in the USA* became an instant smash as new fans who didn't bother with lyrics hopped on the bandwagon interpreting the title track as an anthem of American pride.

"Dancing in the Dark" was the album's first single, and the video featured the Boss pulling a fan—Courteney Cox—onto the stage to dance with him. With that yuppie grab, Bruce had become the antithesis of the working-class guitar playing hero and jumped the shark. This single was followed by the softer side of Bruce (the actor) in the "I'm on Fire" video and an overpriced box set of live performances that capitalized on his massive appeal.

Bruce ended up getting married, dumping his wife for one of his band mates, dumping his band, and simultaneously releasing two albums that no one listened to. Although he won an Oscar for "Streets of Philadelphia" and reunited the E Street Band, the damage was done. You can't start a fire without a shark.

When did
Steely Dan
1972–1981, 1995–

jump the shark?

The studio proficiency of this classic seventies band is unmatched, the lyrics are quirky and entirely cynical, and they won a Grammy for best album . . . in 2001.

Donald Fagen and Walter Becker met at Bard College and played in a variety of bands before deciding to record their originals as Steely Dan, naming themselves after a dildo out of William S. Burroughs's *Naked Lunch.* Fagen and Becker were wise early on to hire the best musicians to play their intricate melodies, and were absolute perfectionists when it came to making music.

Steely Dan's first album, *Can't Buy a Thrill,* yielded the FM standards "Do It Again" and

The perfect seventies studio band reunites to tour in the nineties.

"Reeling in the Years." They followed with the critically acclaimed/hardly purchased *Countdown to Ecstasy,* then brought in future Doobie Brother Michael McDonald for *Pretzel Logic* and the hit "Rikki Don't Lose That Number." After unsuccessful tours, Steely Dan decided

LOCATION, LOCATION, LOCATION

Steely Dan songs were often set in the most interesting places:

1 My Old School up in Annandale
2 Biscayne Bay, where the Cuban gentlemen sleep all day
3 Brooklyn holds the charmer over me
4 The Caves of Altamira, when there wasn't even any Hollywood
5 Aja, under the banyan tree

they'd be best as a studio pop/fusion band and quit the road . . . at least for the next twenty years.

Katy Lied and *The Royal Scam* found the band drifting toward a jazzier sound, which arrived full force in their most popular album, *Aja,* featuring "Peg" and "Josie." The band began the 1980s with *Gaucho,* but Becker and Fagen decided to go their separate ways and Steely Dan exited on a high note. Fagen released his solo masterpiece, *The Nightfly,* in 1981, and then disappeared along with Becker for a decade or so.

But they couldn't stay away. We spotted a fin when Fagen put together a doo-wop-esque tour called the New York Rock and Soul Revue. After unsuccessful solo releases in the early nineties, Becker and Fagen reunited for a Steely Dan tour, a complete 180 for the band, and a jump right over the shark.

Their successful tour led to a concert album, *Alive in America,* and more touring. Was this Steely Dan? The next logical step was *Two Against Nature,* the band's first studio album in two decades. It happens to sound like a watered down Steely Dan album from the seventies, so naturally, it won the Grammy. We shouldn't have been so surprised given Santana's win the previous year. We're banking on the Guess Who to take home the prize next.

Cat Stevens
1947–

jump the shark?

My aunt Marcy had me convinced that his real name was Steven Katz, but this folksy singer of the 1970s gave it all up for Islam at the pinnacle of his career and promptly disappeared from the music scene.

> **He became Yusuf Islam.**

Cat Stevens, born Steven Georgiou, hailed from London and was arguably one of the most influential singer/songwriters of the seventies. A la Carole King, Cat's songs were popular ("Here Comes My Baby," "First Cut Is the Deepest") long before he hit it

big as a singer. It was Jimmy Cliff's version of "Wild World" that brought him into the spotlight.

Tea for the Tillerman was Cat's breakthrough album, containing the hits "Father and Son" and his own version of "Wild World." His sound, as well as his cartoon album covers and bizarre titles, became trademarks that carried through with hits "Moonshadow" and "Peace Train"—both off his next release, *Teaser and the Firecat.* Cat was synonymous with "mellow."

After *Catch Bull at Four* and the less successful *Foreigner,* Cat had another hit single with "Oh Very Young" off *Buddha and the Chocolate Box.* We spotted a fin with its religious implications, but this was just the tip of the iceberg.

In a move that qualifies for the Jump the Shark hall of fame, Cat Stevens jumped when he became a Muslim and officially adopted the name Yusuf Islam. He had some kids, got rid of his material possessions, and dropped out of the pop music world. The Cat Stevens we had known and loved was simply gone.

He eventually resurfaced in the eighties by

PET SOUNDS

Music and animals, an intriguing combination. Zoo names:

1 Phish
2 The Stray Cats
3 Three Dog Night
4 Snoop Dogg
5 Seals & Crofts

publicly supporting the hunt for Salman Rushdie, not exactly the best way to endear yourself to your fan base. Yusuf recently tried to come back with a *Behind the Music* episode and remastered Cat Stevens recordings. He even toured for a bit, but the fans came to hear Cat Stevens (or even Steven Katz) sing and strum, not Yusuf Islam's greatest hits.

When did

Styx

1970–

jump the shark?

Too late for classic rock and too ugly for MTV, Styx was one of the top arena bands of the late seventies and early eighties. They were decent rockers who knew how to write a melody, too. But they had their eyes on grander things, and their fancy arrangements pointed to a progressive rock influence that suggested they had something to say. Always a bad sign.

> **Thank you very much, Mr. Roboto.**

Styx was born in Chicago in 1970 as a stadium rock band with an artistic edge. *The Grand Illusion* was an early breakthrough album featuring the title track and "Come Sail Away," and *Pieces of Eight* was a follow-up hit album in the same vein. Styx's rock image all but disappeared in 1979, and we spotted a fin with the sappy, huge number-one hit "Babe" off *Cornerstone.* A power ballad? Clearly shark bait for Styx. They were once a simple, rockin' band, but now a rock concert wasn't enough—they wanted to be *theatah.*

LET THE RIVER RUN

Our favorite Greek mythological rivers and possible band names:

1 Acheron (woe)
2 Cocytus (lamentation)
3 Lethe (forgetfulness)
4 Phlegethon (fire)
5 Styx (sacred river of oaths)

In fact, *Paradise Theater* was their next release and a concept album of sorts. The rise and fall of the titular theater was a metaphor for America (or whatever). Styx was more popular than ever, but their basic rock was being replaced by Dennis DeYoung's fuzzy grasping toward depth.

If you wondered whether Styx had jumped the shark, *Kilroy Was*

Here—featuring the gold single "Mr. Roboto"—settles the matter. It's all about a world where Japanese robots perform the manual labor and society has suffered for it. To make matters worse, the world's been taken over by fascists who've banned rock and roll! Rock star Kilroy has been framed on a murder rap, and he escapes from prison to team up with rebel Jonathan Chance. Together, they face the evil Dr. Righteous.

POWER BALLADS

The softer side of rock:

1 "Beth"—KISS
2 "Heaven"—Warrant
3 "I Want to Know What Love Is"—Foreigner
4 "Is This Love?"—Whitesnake
5 "Keep on Lovin' You"—REO Speedwagon
6 "Love Bites"—Def Leppard
7 "Love Song"—Tesla
8 "Nobody's Fool"—Cinderella
9 "Sister Christian"—Night Ranger
10 "Something to Believe In"—Poison

This is unpleasant enough on an album, but Styx wanted to *act it out.*

The concert began with a short film to bring the audience up to speed. They were then treated to the spectacle of singer Dennis DeYoung as Kilroy in full, silver-plated robot gear. Bandmate Tommy Shaw played Jonathan Chance, while James Young was Dr. Righteous. Dialogue was included. (Why sing when you can act?)

We were dumbfounded. Some booed, others laughed derisively. We all knew it was over. Even Styx realized they'd gone as far as they could, short of mime. They split up not too long thereafter. Over the years they've reunited occasionally, and these days they know enough to stay away from costumes.

James Taylor

1948–

jump the shark?

The barstool and acoustic guitar were tailor-made for this singer/songwriter and his distinctively smooth voice.

> **Carly Simon says "I do."**

New England born and bred, James Taylor was depressed and drug dependent in his early years. A heroin addict in the late sixties, he moved to London, was signed by The Beatles' label, Apple Records, and recorded *James Taylor.* Unable to kick his habit, he returned to the U.S. and broke both his hands in a motorcycle accident.

Now in California, JT recorded his second album, *Sweet Baby James,* featuring the autobiographical "Fire and Rain." This success got folks interested in his first album, which yielded the hits "Something in the Way She Moves" and "Carolina in My Mind."

BALD IS BEAUTIFUL

J T lost his hair and his songwriting seemed to go with it. Others follicly challenged:

1 Michael Stipe
2 Alex Van Halen
3 Paul Shaffer
4 Mick Hucknall
5 Sinead O'Connor

TIME anointed James Taylor America's singer/songwriter for the seventies. His next release, *Mud Slide Slim and the Blue Horizon,* includes Carole King's "You've Got a Friend," which proved to be JT's most popular single. It took almost two years for the release of *One Man Dog,* which contained a bunch of instrumentals and was a general disappointment. The shark was circling.

While touring in 1972, James Taylor announced to a stadium crowd that he had just gotten engaged to fellow singer/songwriter Carly Simon. The couple duetted on a version of "Mockingbird," and JT jumped the shark. Although he would achieve modest success over the next few years, it was limited and his music would simply never be the same.

His next hit was a remake of "How Sweet It Is," the beginning of a trend in recording oldies for his hits. He later had another hit with his version of "Up on the Roof," but his marriage to

APPLE TREE

Other than The Beatles, JT was the most successful Apple artist. Others:

1 Badfinger
2 Yoko Ono
3 Mary Hopkin
4 Billy Preston
5 Ravi Shankar

Carly Simon soon fell apart. His *Greatest Hits* is well worth the purchase, as it highlights how good JT used to be.

James Taylor had some success with a cover of Buddy Holly's "Everyday" and continues to tour to packed houses. Balding, sober, and showing his age, he's still one of the best at sitting down and strumming, and is worth seeing live any day.

When did
U2
1976–

jump the shark?

U2 formed in Dublin when drummer Larry Mullen Jr. posted a notice at school that he was looking for musicians to form a band. Bassist Adam Clayton (who kept his full name), guitarist David Evans (who became the Edge), and vocalist Paul Hewson (later Bono) answered the call, and together the foursome made musical history.

> **They focus on political causes and forget about their music.**

U2 was always a political band, no question. Their classic early albums, *Boy* and *October,* had something to say, as three of four band members were professed Christians. On their third album, *War,* they got even more politically explicit, raging about Northern Ireland in "Sunday, Bloody Sunday." Nevertheless, the music was postpunk, fresh and nonmechanical, and somehow managed to support even the heaviest lyrics. Each album brought them more popularity and critical attention.

The band broke through with a more atmospheric sound on *The Unforgettable Fire.* They soon hit an artistic peak with their biggest success of all, *The Joshua Tree.* Including "With or Without You" and "I Still Haven't Found What I'm Looking For," the 1987 album is considered to be a classic.

But being huge changed them. They became greater political activists, especially lead singer Bono. Whereas once they were an un-

FOR THE CAUSE
Bands most often rock for these causes:

1 Homelessness
2 The rainforest
3 Abortion rights
4 World hunger
5 Family farms

derdog outfit struggling to get their point across, suddenly they had the world's ear. What was once earnestness turned to lecturing. The change happened gradually, but their causes and their messages starting overshadowing their music.

We spotted a fin when the film *Rattle and Hum* and its double-album soundtrack came up short. It seemed U2 thought they had the weight of the world on their shoulders. Where they'd once been fairly unassuming, the whole *Rattle and Hum* project seemed designed to show how important U2 was.

After briefly considering a breakup, the band bounced back with the adventurous *Achtung Baby,* but it soon became clear that they were stuck in a trap of their own design. They became self-conscious, mocking their own position as rock stars, but it was too late. Their next album and tour, *Zooropa,* was a disappointment that proved they'd crossed over and were never coming back. Bono had morphed from lead singer to oracle, and the shark had been jumped.

Some time later, U2 appeared on *The Simpsons.* Homer was running for sanitation commissioner and when Bono found out, he interrupted a concert to have a discussion of waste management. It was good to see that Bono can laugh at himself, but the shark had swum on to its next victim.

DON'T WASTE LETTERS

Bands with really short names:

1 Abba
2 Asia
3 B-52's
4 Hole
5 KISS
6 Korn
7 Poco
8 Ratt
9 R.E.M.
10 UB40

Van Halen
1974–

jump the shark?

The shortest albums ever recorded didn't stop Van Halen from becoming a rock sensation during the seventies and eighties.

> **Diamond Dave flies solo.**

At their height, this Pasadena rock quartet featured an odd marriage. The eponymous Eddie Van Halen was the greatest guitar god since the heyday of Hendrix. His astonishing technique—fluid and fast—included technical tricks that sent a generation of guitar students down into the basement to figure out just how he made that sound. Meanwhile, singer David Lee Roth almost seemed like a parody of a front man, all shameless posturing. We felt the guy spent hours in front of the mirror to get his hair *just right.* And whereas Eddie was inspired by rock greats, David seemed to be from the school of Louis Prima. Drummer Alex Van Halen and bassist Michael Anthony were the rhythm section along for the ride.

But somehow it worked. From their self-titled debut, Van Halen's peculiar brand of pop-metal went platinum album after album. Their early albums

NAMING THE BAND

Hey, let's use our last names:

1 Hanson
2 The Jacksons
3 The Allman Brothers
4 The Pointer Sisters
5 Santana

rarely exceeded thirty minutes and featured covers like "You Really Got Me" and "(Oh) Pretty Woman" along with popular originals like "Jamie's Cryin'" and "Runnin' with the Devil." And of course, those Eddie solos were not to be missed.

With their sixth release, *1984 (MCMLXXXIV)*, they became bigger than ever. The album included their smash number one hit "Jump," "Panama," and "Hot for Teacher." The videos, with the preening David and the smiling Eddie, cemented their rep as a top act. But we spotted a fin as Eddie began to focus on the synthesizer as much as he worshiped his guitar.

Dave and Eddie were huge stars. Too huge. There was tremendous tension within the band. When Dave delayed the next Van Halen release, he was booted. Sammy "I Can't Drive 55" Hagar replaced him in 1985, and the band sailed over the shark.

Without the lightness and silliness of Diamond Dave, Van Halen, though popular, seemed to plod along. Meanwhile, David Lee Roth fell even further. While he hired fine musicians such as Steve Vai, one of the few guitarists who could match Eddie Van Halen note for note, his music seemed like a parody of hard rock—a lounge act version. Fans eventually rejected it.

When the two went their separate ways, it was a double shark jump. Certain combinations can make magic. Eddie and David didn't know it at the time, but they were a regular Siegfried & Roy.

BOOTED

David Lee Roth is one of many memorable bouncings from bands:

1 Pete Best (The Beatles)
2 Florence Ballard (The Supremes)
3 Al Kooper (Blood, Sweat & Tears)
4 Brian Jones (The Rolling Stones)
5 Dave Mason (Traffic)
6 John Cale (Velvet Underground)
7 Glen Matlock (The Sex Pistols)
8 Bob Stinson (The Replacements)
9 Chad Channing (Nirvana)
10 Tons of teenagers (Menudo)

When did

The Who

1964–

jump the shark?

Love 'em or hate 'em, The Who must be acknowledged as one of the greatest rock and roll bands
of all time.

Formed in London in 1964, madman drummer Keith Moon, spider bassist John Entwistle,
brilliant songwriter/guitarist Pete Townshend, and
wannabe actor/screaming
lead singer Roger Daltrey were a motley crew.
But each member of the quartet added an es-
sential part to the band's indispensable sound.

The Who did more than just smash their
instruments. They also produced a series of
great singles, including "I Can't Explain," "The
Kids Are Alright," "Happy Jack," and "I Can See
For Miles." They performed two Townshend
rock operas, the groundbreaking *Tommy* and
mixed-up mod-fest *Quadrophenia*. In between,
the detritus of the failed rock opera *Lighthouse*
became one of their greatest releases, *Who's
Next,* with album rock staples "Behind Blue
Eyes," "Baba O'Riley," and "Won't Get Fooled
Again." They also found time to put out the classic concert album *Live at Leeds.*

But as The Who entered the mid-
seventies, a simple line from their decade-old
anthem "My Generation" was eating them. Did
they hope to die before they got old? How long
could one of the loudest, most exciting, intense
bands of all time keep it up? We spotted a fin
with *The Who by Numbers,* and *Who Are You*
was their weakest work yet.

Keith Moon, the wild spirit of the band,
died from an overdose in 1978, and The Who
went sailing over the shark. The band soldiered

> **Keith Moon dies and the others get old.**

SIX FEET UNDER

They OD'd with a little
help from their friends:

1 John Bonham
2 Steve Clark
3 Jimi Hendrix
4 James-Honeyman Scott
5 Shannon Hoon
6 Janis Joplin
7 Bon Scott
8 Bob Stinson
9 Sid Vicious
10 Jim Morrison

THE BRITISH ARE COMING?

Some great bands that
invaded U.S. soil in the
sixties

1 The Beatles
2 The Rolling Stones
3 The Who
4 The Kinks
5 The Animals
6 The Yardbirds
7 The Zombies
8 The Hollies
9 The Troggs
10 The Small Faces

on with Kenny Jones on drums, but they were clearly going through the motions. *Face Dances* and *It's Hard* were so far from the glory days that they might as well have been another band. Since then, it's been endless rereleases and greatest hits and repackagings and farewell concerts. *Tommy*, the Broadway Sensation? Who cares?

When did Stevie Wonder
1950–

jump the shark?

It's fascinating how such a masterful, soulful singer/songwriter could become the complete opposite in such a short period of time.

The Woman in Red.

Born blind, Stevland Morris hailed from Saginaw, Michigan, and was making records for Motown by the time he was eleven years old. Little Stevie Wonder had mastered the harmonica and drums and had a huge hit with "Fingertips—Part 2."

Stevie had many Motown hits, including "Uptight" and "My Cherie Amour," but he felt restricted creatively. Stevie took music to an entirely different level once he gained creative control, releasing groundbreaking classic albums such as *Music of My Mind, Talking Book,* and *Innervisions.* Stevie's best work was *Songs in the Key of Life,* and around the same time he displayed a great sense of humor when he acted in a memorable spoof of a Canon commercial with John Newcombe on *Saturday Night Live* ("Here, Stevie, you try it!").

We spotted a fin with *Journey Through the Secret Life of Plants,* and *Hotter than July* had more pop in it than soul. Stevie was always politically and socially active, but "Front Line" and "Livin' for the City" had become "Ebony and

THE MOTOWN SOUND

Motown was the place to be if you had any soul:

1 The Temptations
2 The Supremes
3 Marvin Gaye
4 The Miracles
5 The Jackson Five
6 Three Degrees
7 Gladys Knight and the Pips
8 The Four Tops
9 Martha and the Vandellas
10 Junior Walker

Ivory" and "That's What Friends Are For." He waited four years to record the soundtrack for *The Woman in Red,* a hall of fame jump straight over the shark.

Not only is the cheesy "I Just Called to Say I Love You" featured, but the soundtrack ends with the message song "Don't Drive Drunk." Stevie later appeared on *The Cosby Show* and taught Theo and the Huxtables how to jam on the one. Stevie Wonder has been searching for the soul in his music ever since.

Celebrities

"You like me, you really like me . . ."

—Sally Field winning the Oscar for
Places in the Heart at the 1984 Academy Awards

A sequel. A chance encounter on Sunset Boulevard. An attempt at comedy. An Oscars acceptance speech.

When it comes to jumping the shark, celebrities have the most difficult time of all, since at any moment one can "pull a Travolta" and louse everything up.

John Travolta was coming off *Saturday Night Fever* and *Grease* when he decided his next project should be *Moment by Moment,* a love story costarring Lily Tomlin. That's borderline hall of fame shark jumping, as his next choices included *Staying Alive, Two of a Kind,* and *Perfect.* Ten years later, Travolta got the lead in *Pulp Fiction,* and suddenly he was once again cooler than Vinnie Barbarino.

Actors, directors, producers, and writers all have their ups and downs, but there is a defining moment in each of their careers where you knew they were never going to be the same. Cue the shark. Categories include:

At the Oscars—Rob Lowe dances with Snow White

Directing—Barbra Streisand is *Yentl*

Singing—Eddie Murphy wonders "How Could It Be?"

Hair Care—Meg Ryan crops her hair short

Aging—Robert Redford, Gregory Peck, Liz Taylor . . .

Sequels—*Speed 2, Caddyshack 2, The Sting 2* . . .

I Do—Woody Allen weds his adopted daughter

The Color of Money—This Scorsese film took down Clapton, Newman, Mastrantonio, and more

Flops—*Heaven's Gate, Howard the Duck, Ishtar* . . .

The Other Woman (or Man)—Hugh Grant in L.A.

Comedy Is Hard—Meryl Streep, Sylvester Stallone . . . ouch

The most blatant shark jumps in Hollywood history are (the envelope, please . . .):

10. Billy Crystal is *Mr. Saturday Night.*

9. Francis Ford Coppola gives *One from the Heart*.

8. Sally Field accepts her second Oscar and reminds us how much we really like her.

7. Arnold Schwarzenegger is *The Last Action Hero.*

6. George Lucas executive produces *Howard the Duck.*

5. Richard Gere channels Tibet at the Oscars.

4. Woody Allen marries Soon-Yi.

3. Roseanne grabs her crotch after "singing" the National Anthem.

2. John Travolta in *Battlefield Earth.*

1. Kevin Costner in *Waterworld*.

When did

Woody Allen

1935–

jump the shark?

No filmmaker can make New York look better than Woody Allen.

> **He married his stepdaughter.**

Woody helped set the standard for intelligent comedy as a contributing writer (along with Carl Reiner, Mel Brooks, and Neil Simon) on Sid Caesar's *Your Show of Shows* in the fifties and sixties. He segued into a brilliant stand-up gig and then launched into a prolific, unique, and amazing film career.

Some of the greatest comedies of all time, *Take the Money and Run, Sleeper, Bananas, Everything You Always Wanted to Know About Sex (But Were Afraid to Ask), Love and Death,* and Oscar-winner *Annie Hall,* were all released within an eight-year period. Woody was the thinking person's clown. The neurotic's neurotic. Thanks to him, everyone knows what a "nebbish" is.

Whenever Woody gets serious, that's when you have to keep your eyes peeled for a fin. The man who got caught cheating on his college metaphysics final because he looked into the soul of the boy sitting next to him transitioned into a period of Bergman-inspired yawners, beginning with

the sterile *Interiors.* Fortunately, *Manhattan* soon followed, and the shark was temporarily avoided.

We did spot a fin with the angry *Stardust Memories,* but Woody followed with five solid comedies including *Zelig, The Purple Rose of Cairo,* and the Oscar-winning *Hannah and Her Sisters.* The shark drew closer with the Bergman-esque *September* and *Another Woman,* and the comedies grew less farcical and more edgy in *Crimes and Misdemeanors* and *Alice.* We felt like we were in Woody and Mia's family room watching their relationship fall apart in *Husbands and Wives.* It was shortly after this film that Woody's personal life took over his career.

In 1993, Woody was accused by his live-in love Mia Farrow of incest with her adopted son Dylan and infamy with her seventeen-year-old adopted daughter Soon-Yi Previn. The incest with Dylan was never proven, but Woody jumped the shark and lord knows what else when he ended up marrying his stepdaughter in 1997. As funny as the man is, it just doesn't get much creepier than that (*Scenes from a Mall* is a distant second).

Yes, Woody has every right to keep his private life private. But there isn't a fan who wasn't taken aback by the news of Woody and Soon-Yi. His movies today are hit and miss, but even the best of them pales in comparison to his classic films. Still, his fans will remain loyal and his work will stand the test of time. Woody, we hardly knew Yi.

James Cameron
1954–

jump the shark?

He's the greatest living director of action films, and we wish he would stick with them.

> **"I'm King of the World!"**

This Ontario native got his start in film, like many others, working with Roger Corman as an art director. James Cameron's directorial debut was *Piranha II—The Spawning,* which didn't garner any Oscar nominations, but put the Canadian wunderkind on the map.

Jim thought he'd give writing a try, so he penned *The Terminator, First Blood: Part II,* and *Aliens* in a three-year span. Cameron directed *The Terminator* and gave action/sci-fi a desperately needed shot in the arm. The film also showcased Arnold in his first English-speaking role, since the *Conan* flicks really don't count.

$100 MILLION MEN

Few directors have the power to get big budget films made. Here are a few who do:

1 James Cameron
2 George Lucas
3 Steven Spielberg
4 Chris Columbus
5 Cecil B. DeMille (adjusted for inflation, plus the fact that he's dead)

His directorial follow-up was *Aliens,* a sequel quite different than the spooky original and a great action movie in its own right. Jim tempted the shark with his next film, *The Abyss,* which was technically amazing but not up to par story wise. He entered the nineties with two hits, *Terminator 2—Judgment Day* and *True Lies,* but parted ways with Arnold action flicks to try a different kind of blockbuster.

In 1997, Cameron taunted the shark a second time with another water film, the $200-million chick flick *Titanic.* Legend says that he kept a razor blade taped to his editing machine with a sign reading "Use only if the film sucks." No worries. It would win Best Picture and become the all-time highest-grossing flick.

But Oscar's red carpet is a shark tank in its own right, and in his Oscar glory James Cameron strapped on the skis and jumped the shark when he proclaimed himself "King of the

OSCAR NIGHT

The Academy Awards are a shark's den. Classic jumps:

1 David Letterman's "Uma. Oprah."
2 Rob Lowe dances with Snow White.
3 Sally Field's "You really, really like me."
4 Vanessa Redgrave's PLO speech.
5 Richard Gere channeling to Tibet.

World!" We understand his excitement and his referring to a line from the film, but it came off as arrogant and put off even the biggest *Titanic* fans.

His next project was the FOX series *Dark Angel,* and sequels to *True Lies, The Abyss,* and *The Terminator* are on tap. After the fallout from the *Titanic* speech, we understand his reluctance to jump back in the water once again.

When did **Cher**
1946–

jump the shark?

Trying to pinpoint the moment Cherilyn Sarkisian jumped the shark is like trying to figure out when politicians started lying.

In the 1960s and 1970s, as one half of Sonny and Cher, we thought she was a flash in the pan. Then in the 1980s, when she started acting, we began to take her seriously. By the 1990s, we were over

> *The Witches of Eastwick.*

her again. What will the new millennium do to Cher's respectability?

Sonny and Cher made their breakthrough appearance on *Merv Griffin* in 1962. A husband-and-wife pop team, they worked their marriage banter into an act that was fresh and campy. They were Steve and Eydie for the younger, modder set.

"I Got You Babe" and a great agent got them a TV series in 1971 (*The Sonny and Cher Comedy Hour*). The show was an enormous success, and it gave rise to a new generation of variety shows. In fact, it paved the way for *The Osmonds,* and we're all thankful for that. Waning success, a divorce, a self-named solo series in '75 and a special in '78 followed, but Cher's core audience stuck with her and still does today.

Cher made her major film debut in Robert Altman's 1982 drama *Come Back to the Five and Dime, Jimmy Dean, Jimmy Dean.* She showed a serious side that we had never seen. Not a big hit, it led to more dramatic roles in *Silkwood, Mask,* and *Suspect.* Cher was suddenly a critically acclaimed and popular actress, and she even won an Oscar for her delightful performance in *Moonstruck.*

But the shark was on the prowl, and Cher jumped when she costarred in *The Witches of Eastwick.* It was an adaptation of John Updike's novel about three witches wreaking havoc over a New England town while courting the devil (in the form of Jack Nicholson). Aiming to be serious, the movie just came off as campy. Cher's cred began to deteriorate.

Her jump has been cemented by the lack of film work she has done since. 1990's *Mermaids* was an uninteresting Hollywood single-mom drama. It would be nine years until she would tackle another major part, and she had to go to Italy to do it. *Tea with Mussolini* received good critical notice, but nobody went to see it.

In the meantime, Cher returned to singing as her major vocation and had a number one hit in 1998. She can still pack 'em in for concerts and she sells lots of records. But that brief foray into acting legitimacy in the eighties represents the peak of an odd but interesting career. Believe it.

Francis Ford Coppola

1939–

jump the shark?

No director past or present has taken a steeper nosedive than Francis Ford Coppola.

One from the Heart.

The disparity between phenomenal to god-awful is astounding. In fact, if you remove *The Godfather* and *The Godfather: Part II*, *The Conversation*, and *Apocalypse Now,* he's a decent director at best. Conversely, if you ignore *Gardens of Stone, The Cotton Club, Jack,* and *Dracula,* he's the greatest director of all time.

OTHER HATS

While best known as a director, here are a few other works in which he's had a hand:

1 *THX 1138*—Executive Producer

2 *Patton*—Co-Screenwriter

3 *American Graffiti*— Producer

4 *The Great Gatsby*— Screenwriter

5 *The Rainmaker*— Screenwriter

Hofstra grad Francis Ford Coppola first made it in Hollywood as a writer, helping pen classics like *Is Paris Burning?* and *Patton.* He and George Lucas then formed American Zoetrope and produced *American Graffiti* and other gems. Coppola was succeeding on all fronts, but he hadn't shown us what he could do as a director yet.

He became a worldwide sensation when he returned to his New York Italian roots for *The Godfather* and *The Godfather: Part II.* Well-deserved critical and audience approval put these gems on top of every Best Movies of All Time list. Coppola even managed to do the very rare—make a movie that was better than the book and then make a sequel better than the original. How do you follow this? With *The Conversation* and the screenplay to *The Great Gatsby.* He simply couldn't miss.

A torturously long and expensive shoot for *Apocalypse Now* came several years later and resulted in one of the most astounding explorations of the human soul ever produced on film. In the tradition of *The Deer Hunter* and *Hearts and Minds, Apocalypse Now* gave us a trench-eye glimpse of Vietnam, and it was his last masterpiece.

FAMILY BUSINESS

With a name like Coppola, it has to be good! Or Francis, or Ford . . .

1 Nicolas Cage (nephew)

2 Talia Shire (sister)

3 Sofia Coppola (daughter)

4 Jason Schwartzman (nephew)

5 Bill Neil (brother-in-law)

The shark was circling later that year when Coppola produced *The Black Stallion*. The softer side of Francis was surfacing. He entered the eighties with the sappy *One from the Heart,* and the legendary director went sailing over the shark. This high-budget flop bankrupted Zoetrope, and Coppola was thankful for his vineyards.

The eighties brought us *Tucker,* which was pretty good, as well as a bunch of forgettable films. The nineties begat *The Godfather: Part III,* a decent flick despite unfortunate familial casting, but nowhere near the level of the first two. Coppola has rereleased a reworked version of his '79 masterpiece—*Apocalypse Now Redux.* This desperate hearkening back to his preshark days simply confirms what we already know. The new ideas are gone. The horror. The horror.

When did
Kevin Costner
1955–

jump the shark?

From dead stiff to superstar to Oscar-winning director to dead stiff . . . what a long, strange trip it's been.

Waterworld.

California native Kevin Costner has seen it all in a relatively short period of time. In all of his films he has mastered one key acting ingredient . . . playing Kevin Costner and getting the most out of the performance.

MODEL ROLES

Kevin Costner is an automatic for these casting calls if they involve:

1 JFK
2 A baseball veteran
3 Wearing a Civil War hat
4 An officer caught up in a conspiracy
5 A loner at the end of the world

We never had the chance to see his first big role because it ended up on the cutting room floor of *The Big Chill.* Lawrence Kasdan cast Costner as Alex, the college friend whose suicide provided the plot device that brought together all the characters. Allegedly it's him playing the corpse being dressed for the funeral at the beginning of the movie, and the more we think about it, he was a natural for the part.

His career consisted of bit parts and supporting roles in *Night Shift, Fandango,* and *Silverado,* until John Badham cast him in the lead of a horrible bike racing film titled *American Flyers* in the mid-eighties.

Brian DePalma then chose Costner to play Elliot Ness in his remake of *The Untouchables.* Kevin held his own against Robert De Niro's Al Capone and Sean Connery's Oscar-winning Jim Malone. He emerged as a major star and sex symbol, and started a great run that included *No Way Out, Bull Durham, Field of Dreams,* and his own Oscar-winning masterpiece, *Dances with Wolves.*

SPOILERS

In *No Way Out,* audiences were thrilled by the surprise ending. Here are some surprises for you, but you have to find the films:

1 Jeff Bridges did it
2 Rosebud was his sled
3 Norman did it
4 Bruce Willis has been dead the whole time
5 Kevin Spacey can walk straight

At the start of the nineties no actor was hotter than Kevin Costner, but the AC cranked up in a hurry. *Robin Hood: Prince of Thieves, JFK,* and *The Bodyguard* kept Costner on the map, but the shark smelled a sell-out. The shark circled with the Clint Eastwood–directed drama *A Perfect World,* which featured Costner as an escaped convict. Where was his baseball uniform?

In *Waterworld* Costner played a half-man, half-fish in a future, flooded world. The film was one of those flops that failed even before it reached the theaters. Stories of inflated budgets and overblown sets and special effects accurately predicted the doom of this ambitious project. It was supposed to be *The Road Warrior* in water, but it turned out to be the moment Kevin Costner jumped the shark.

Kevin unsuccessfully tried to go back to the sports well with *Tin Cup* and *For the Love of the Game.* He starred in and produced *The Postman,* which ended up being *Waterworld* in the desert of the future. *Message in a Bottle* was a light and fluffy love story, and *3000 Miles to Graceland* was a violent, one-joke bomb.

If a project featuring a baseball veteran who happened to be a JFK conspiracy buff left alone in the barren plains coping with a future world ever comes along, we know who to call.

Billy Crystal

1947–

jump the shark?

Billy Crystal is a modern extension of a Catskills comic and Oscar host, although we've heard the voices and jokes a few too many times.

Mr. Saturday Night.

After getting cut from *Saturday Night Live* on its opening night, we met Billy on *Soap* as Jodie Dallas, the first openly gay character in prime-time. Television wasn't *Will & Grace*-land in those days, but Billy pulled if off without a hitch. In 1985, he finally joined *SNL* for one season with Martin Short and Christopher Guest, and his star was on the rise.

Billy's film career got off to an inauspicious start with a costarring role in Joan Rivers's *Rabbit Test.* He hit his stride with *Running Scared, The Princess Bride,* and *Throw Momma from the Train.* Billy almost jumped with his own *Memories of Me,* but *When Harry Met Sally* and *City Slickers* established him as a feature-film star.

Billy, along with Whoopi and Robin, started hosting *Comic Relief* to benefit the homeless. In 1991, Billy hosted the Oscars for the first time. He looked marvelous, and remains one of its most popular hosts today. His opening monologue included a medley of tunes about Best Picture nominees and was a guaranteed crowd-pleaser despite being painfully corny. When he bowed out and Whoopi and Dave subbed in, it became clear that he'd been making a tough job look easy.

Following the success of *City Slickers,* Billy wrote and starred in *Mr. Saturday Night,* a nostalgic piece about the career of a Jewish comic in the 1950s. It wasn't fun or funny, and it tossed Billy right over the shark.

Since then, he's been merely likeable and dependable. His movies have been more misses than hits with *City Slickers II, Forget Paris, My*

NOT THAT THERE'S ANYTHING WRONG WITH THAT

Some of my best friends are gay:

1 Will on *Will & Grace*
2 Jack on *Will & Grace*
3 Sydney on *Love, Sydney*
4 Monroe on *Too Close for Comfort*
5 Ellen on *Ellen*

YANKEE FANS

He wore a Mets hat in *City Slickers,* but he's a Bronx Bomber fan, as are:

1 Rudy Giuliani
2 Sarah Jessica Parker
3 Chris Rock
4 George Costanza
5 Hillary Clinton (in an election year)

Giant, and *Analyze This.* In 2001, Steve Martin hosted the Oscars and became the first substitute to equal, and some say surpass, the master. Billy's tribute to his beloved Mickey Mantle in *61* was warmly received, but the Yanks ended up losing the World Series to the D-Backs, whom Crystal owns a piece of. I *hate* when that happens.

When did
Tom Cruise
1962–

jump the shark?

This good-looking guy is not only the number-one box office draw of the past twenty years, but he can actually act.

Eyes Wide Shut.

Thomas Cruise Mapother IV originally wanted to be a priest. He caught the acting bug as a teenager, made his debut in *Endless Love,* and has been packing them in ever since.

The Outsiders was supposed to be a breakout film for Tom, but it was another film released that year—*Risky Business*—where he made his mark. The handsome kid dancing around in his underwear was destined to be a superstar.

The eighties were hit and miss—actually blockbuster and flop—for Tom Cruise. He followed the dreadfully boring *Legend* with the blockbuster *Top Gun.* Martin Scorsese directed him in the disappointing but commercially successful sequel to *The Hustler, The Color of Money.* Tom married Mimi Rogers and then appeared in the horrendous bartender chronicle *Cocktail* with Bryan Brown. But it was Oscar nomination time for Tom when he turned in his finest performances as Charlie Babbitt in *Rain Man,* and then as Ron Kovic in Oliver Stone's *Born on the Fourth of July.*

The shark started to circle when *Days of*

QUOTABLE

Tom's films have been known to coin a phrase or two over time:

1 "I have a need for speed."

2 "You can't handle the truth."

3 "Sometimes, you just gotta say 'what the fuck.'"

4 "Ten minutes to Wapner."

5 "Show me the money."

Thunder and *Far and Away* came on the scene. Cruise left his wife for Nicole Kidman and renounced his Catholicism to become a Scientologist. Rather than jump the shark, Cruise rebounded with the quality flicks *A Few Good Men* and *The Firm*. He didn't disappoint in *Interview with the Vampire,* and headed up

another blockbuster with a remake of *Mission: Impossible.* Cameron Crowe cast Tom perfectly in *Jerry Maguire,* and he was on top of the world once again.

Tom had tempted the shark when he teamed with Nicole earlier, but he jumped the shark with their third collaboration, Stanley Kubrick's swan song *Eyes Wide Shut*. The film was not one of Kubrick's best, and the scenes with Tom and Nicole just felt wrong. This erotic thriller lacked two key ingredients—eroticism and thrills.

In his next role, Tom showed single guys how to seduce and leave a woman in *Magnolia.* He followed that performance by cashing in on a *Mission: Impossible* sequel and failing to carry the disappointing *Vanilla Sky.* He is now split from Nicole, seeing a lot less of Australia, and approaching forty. Will he age like Newman or Redford? We'll be watching . . .

When did
Robert De Niro
1943–

jump the shark?

He is the quintessential tough guy of the twentieth century, but these days, if pal Marty Scorsese isn't around, sound the shark alert.

Analyze This.

Robert De Niro is on the short list of the greatest actors of all time. He is one of the most magnetic performers in the business, and even in bad movies he's fun to watch.

The son of an artist, and a star pupil of the Actors Studio, De Niro paid

It was Joe Pesci's line, but De Niro was memorable as these comic characters:

1 Rupert Pupkin
2 Jack Walsh
3 Conrad Brean
4 Jack Byrnes
5 Jake LaMotta

his dues off-Broadway and in small film roles through the sixties and very early seventies. He gained national attention in *Bang the Drum Slowly* and *Mean Streets,* the latter of which would be his first of eight films with Martin Scorsese.

A plumb role as young Vito Corleone in *The Godfather: Part II* nabbed him his first Oscar and launched him on a prolific and impressive career.

His resume is distinguished by his work in *Taxi Driver, Raging Bull, The Deer Hunter, Brazil,* and *The Mission.* The versatile De Niro followed his heavy role of Capone in *The Untouchables* with a classic performance as Jack Walsh in the underrated *Midnight Run.*

We spotted a fin when he begged Jane Fonda to teach him to read in *Stanley and Iris,* but *Goodfellas* and *Cape Fear* kept the shark at bay. De Niro did solid work in the 1990s, with *Casino, Guilty by Suspicion, Wag the Dog,* and his directorial debut, *A Bronx Tale.*

At the end of the nineties, he finally jumped the shark in *Analyze This,* which marks the moment when De Niro started to become a caricature of himself. In *Meet the Parents* he was over the top and cartoonish, the opposite of his earlier comedic appearances. Travis Bickle as Fearless Leader in *The Adventures of Rocky and Bullwinkle*? He has since phoned in parts in *15 Minutes* and *The Score,* and sequels to *Analyze This* and *Meet the Parents* are on the horizon.

BOBBY AND MARTY

Not since Bergman and von Sydow have we seen such a rewarding match of director and actor. Here are the films De Niro and Scorsese have done together so far:

1 *Mean Streets*
2 *Taxi Driver*
3 *New York, New York*
4 *Raging Bull*
5 *The King of Comedy*
6 *Goodfellas*
7 *Cape Fear*
8 *Casino*

Notably, De Niro turned down the role of Jesus in *The Last Temptation of Christ.*

We'll always have Scorsese. But with his recent selection of roles, you can't help but wonder who De Niro is talking to these days.

Sally Field
1946–

jump the shark?

Whether she was an airborne nun or the Bandit's best gal, she could master any part . . . except the one with the gold statue.

> **"You like me, you really like me!"**

Sally Mahoney was literally born into the movie business. Her mother was an actress and her stepfather was a famous stuntman. She has been a star since her first gig in 1965 as the spunky teenager *Gidget.* Her cute, perky, girl-next-door look was a blessing in her early career, but difficult to overcome when she transitioned into serious acting.

Sally Field began in television, with *Gidget* and *The Flying Nun* both enjoying success. Almost a decade later, Sally played a woman with seventeen personalities in the made-for-TV movie *Sybil,* and deservedly won an Emmy. Coincidentally, she would win another Emmy twenty-five years later playing a bipolar character on *ER.* She makes a great nut.

The next year, Sally was Burt Reynolds's gal on and off the screen and had huge popular success with the *Smokey and the Bandit* series. But her transition into drama is where she hit her acting stride. She won a Best Actress Oscar as union organizer *Norma Rae* and clicked with Paul Newman as a reporter in *Absence of Malice.*

We spotted a fin with *Kiss Me Goodbye,* in which Sally played a widow still in love with the dead James Caan. In 1984 Sally unexpectedly jumped when she won the Oscar for *Places in the Heart.* During her acceptance speech, she declared, "You like me, you really like me!" and comedy writers had years' worth of material dropped right into their laps.

After the Oscars, Sally made average films like *Murphy's Romance* and *Punchline*, and martyr films such as *Steel Magnolias* and *Not Without My Daughter*. Comedy came calling and cheese like *Soapdish* and *Mrs. Doubtfire* were the result.

To her credit, Sally did some solid work in *Forrest Gump* and *ER*, but the words she uttered in '84 remain first in our thoughts whenever her name is mentioned. When that shark bites . . .

When did
Harrison Ford
1942–

jump the shark?

Sabrina.

Take John Wayne, give him a sense of humor and sex appeal, and you end up with the most bankable film star of all time.

Born in Chicago, Harrison Ford supported his early acting career as a professional carpenter. He later went on to help build two of the greatest modern film franchises (*Star Wars* and *Indiana Jones*) in existence.

His big break came in 1973 with a bit part in *American Graffiti*. Producer Francis Ford Coppola snagged him the following year for another small part in *The Conversation*. And then . . . there was *Star Wars*.

Ford's portrayal of Han Solo in the *Star Wars* trilogy was so strong that many blame the weakness of *The Phantom Menace* on the absence of a similar supporting character. Ford's subsequent run as Indiana Jones in *Raiders of the Lost Ark* and its sequels makes him a featured actor in half of the top ten movies of all time.

Not just an action hero, Ford has also shown more subtle acting talent in the excellent *Blade Runner, Witness,* and *The Fugitive,* the not-so-excellent *Frantic,* and the depressing *Regarding Henry.*

Comedy is hard, especially if you're Harrison Ford. He tried in *The Frisco Kid* and *Working Girl,* but his personality is not conducive to laughs. Following his successful stint as Dr. Richard Kimble and Jack Ryan, he once again tried for funny in a remake of Billy Wilder's *Sabrina.* Strike three . . . Harrison jumped the shark.

Since then, we've suffered for more than six days and seven nights with *The Devil's Own, Air Force One,* and the brutally tedious *Random Hearts.* Ford has hinted that he wants to do another Indy movie, and we can understand why. This great film star needs to be rescued . . . quickly.

FAMOUS HARRISONS

There aren't too many Harrison's around these days:

1 George Harrison
2 William Henry Harrison
3 Rex Harrison
4 Jenilee Harrison
5 Benjamin Harrison

THERE'S NO SUCH THING AS SMALL PARTS

A handful of Harrison's memorable roles:

1 Indiana Jones
2 Han Solo
3 Dr. Richard Kimble
4 Jack Ryan
5 John Book

When did
Jodie Foster
1962–

jump the shark?

Jodie Foster never takes a safe role, and we respect her for it. Unfortunately, she doesn't always choose the best ones, either.

We all watched Jodie grow up on screen, kicking off her career as the Coppertone girl at age three. She was an active child star, frequently appearing in television and films before the age of ten. Jodie had

She sat in the director's chair.

INNER CHILDREN

Jodie started early but has maintained her career over time. Other notable child film stars:

1 Tatum O'Neal
2 Haley Joel Osment
3 Brooke Shields
4 Robert Blake
5 Corey Feldman

the equivalent of a full showbiz career before hitting puberty.

In *Taxi Driver,* she held her own with Robert De Niro and earned her first Oscar nomination for her portrayal of a fourteen-year-old prostitute. Jodie came close to jumping with her next film, *Bugsy Malone,* and *Freaky Friday* and *Foxes* were anything but cinematic gems.

But the career of this Yale honors graduate is all about perseverance and taking chances. She has survived a lion attack, the unwanted attention of a would-be presidential assassin, and a feature film with Scott Baio.

Jodie's "adult" film roles have sealed her reputation as a major movie star. Her breakthrough was the Oscar-winning role of white-trash rape victim Sarah Tobias in *The Accused.* Three years later, she notched Oscar number two for her portrayal of Clarice Starling in *The Silence of the Lambs.* Jodie was Hollywood gold.

THE DIRECTOR'S CHAIR

Deep down, it seems like all actors want to direct. He are some Oscar-nominated directors:

1 Orson Welles
2 Kevin Costner
3 Mel Gibson
4 Ron Howard
5 Robert Redford

But like so many other actors, she really wanted to be on the other side of the camera. The timing for her first film couldn't have been worse, as she followed her Oscar triumph with the forgettable *Little Man Tate.* In the director's chair, Jodie Foster had finally jumped the shark.

She returned to acting in the post–Civil War drama *Sommersby,* costarring with Richard Gere. The lackluster *Nell* and *Maverick* were next, followed by her second directorial effort, the Thanksgiving turkey *Home for the Holidays.* We haven't seen as much of her since *Contact.* Maybe she's still trying to figure that one out.

We respect Jodie for turning down the *Lambs* sequel, but Dr. Lecter isn't the only one who yearns for the return of Clarice.

When did

Richard Gere

1949–

jump the shark?

Any friend of the Dalai Lama can't be all bad.

Once every decade or so, Richard Gere makes a good movie and is voted the Sexiest Man Alive. It's the time in between that frightens us.

Gere's initial arc of success started on Broadway in the 1970s with *Grease* and *Bent.* We got our first look at him on screen as the dangerous hustler in

> **At the Oscars— channeling to Tibet.**

Looking for Mr. Goodbar. He enjoyed critical praise the following year in *Days of Heaven* but audiences embraced him and the critics dumped him two years later with *American Gigolo.* His next film, *An Officer and a Gentleman* was his best, and positioned him for a great film career.

It seemed like Richard decided to take the eighties off as he plummeted off Hollywood's A-List. A remake of *Breathless, The Cotton Club, King David, Power,* and the appropriately titled *No Mercy* were not exactly Oscar caliber. It seemed that he could do no right.

A decade had passed, so it was time for Richard's renaissance. He did a good job playing a corrupt cop in *Internal Affairs,* and then he was Prince Charming opposite Julia Roberts's career-making whore in *Pretty Woman.* He married Cindy Crawford in 1991, and Richard Gere was back on top once again. His leap over the shark would happen not on the big screen, but on the small.

A Buddhist and supporter of Tibetan refugee holy-man the Dalai Lama, Gere has always been vocal about his politics and religion. However, during the Oscars ceremony in 1993, he made a poorly received, nasty remark about the Chinese as he asked the audience to channel

---

GREASE IS THE WORD

Gere caught an early break in *Grease* on Broadway in the early to mid-seventies. Here are some other *Grease* alumini from stage and screen:

1 John Travolta
2 Patrick Swayze
3 Tony Danza
4 Jeff Conoway
5 Michelle Pfeiffer
6 Olivia Newton-John
7 Stockard Channing
8 Adrian Zmed
9 Sid Caesar
10 Lorenzo Lamas

LEADING LADIES

At one point, Richard had Cindy Crawford at home and costarred with:

1 Julia Roberts
2 Debra Winger
3 Lauren Hutton
4 Uma Thurman
5 Jodie Foster

197

their thoughts to Tibet. He wasn't the first person to use the captive Oscar audience as a soapbox, but he followed Sally Field in jumping the shark while doing it.

If his eighties films were bad, the nineties were even worse. *Intersection, First Knight, Primal Fear,* and *Red Corner* are just few of his mediocre films. Cindy was out the door by 1995, and Richard needed to reunite with Julia in *Runaway Bride* to bring the box office back. The good news, though, is that it's a new decade, so look for Richard on the cover of *People* and in a quality film sometime soon.

When did
Mel Gibson
1956–

jump the shark?

It's been a heck of a ride from cult action star to Oscar-winning director for our favorite American-born Australian.

Mel Gibson was born in upstate New York, but his family moved to Australia after his dad won on *Jeopardy!*, and Mel ended up studying acting. He's got a great sense of humor and a Best Picture Oscar, but his career arc looks like a sine curve with a bad smack habit.

Conspiracy Theory.

Mel made his mark in 1981 with *The Road Warrior,* a sequel to a movie that we didn't get to see until after the sequel. Serious turns in *Tim, Gallipoli,* and *The Year of Living Dangerously* cemented Mel as something more than a brainless sex symbol . . . he was a damned good actor.

AUSSIE FLIX
Quality films from Australia:
1 *Breaker Morant*
2 *Mad Max*
3 *Babe*
4 *Gallipoli*
5 *Crocodile Dundee*

His follow up work in *The Bounty, The River,* and *Mrs. Soffel* made it look like he was going to commit to a serious dramatic career. *Mad Max: Beyond Thunderdome,* the third in the *Road Warrior* series costarring Tina Turner, was a mess and unintentionally steered Mel's career toward comedy. His next flick, *Lethal Weapon,* was intended to be a comedy, and

Mel's sense of humor and affinity for the Stooges came shining through.

The shark was tempted by *Tequila Sunrise, Bird on a Wire, Air America,* and *Forever Young,* but the *Lethal Weapon* sequels served as Mel's preserver. His first attempt at directing, *The Man Without a Face,* and a cheesy remake of *Maverick* seemingly spelled doom, but Mel's second directorial attempt would change all of that. *Braveheart* was his own *Dances with Wolves,* winning him the Oscar for Best Picture and Best Director.

We spotted a fin with his over-the-top performance in *Ransom,* but it was *Conspiracy Theory,* the laughable thriller costarring Julia Roberts, that vaulted Mel over the shark. The film didn't work on any level, and we expected more from William Wallace. Mel went back to the well for *Lethal Weapon 4* and tried playing the likeable bad guy in *Payback* without much success.

He earned $25 million for *The Patriot,* but its lukewarm reception recalled Costner's *Waterworld,* and we pray Mel steers clear of that path. He was a great chicken in *Chicken Run,* but Mad Max shaving his legs in *What Women Want* makes us wonder if we're forever going to be subjected to the softer side of Mel on screen.

When did
Whoopi Goldberg
1955–

jump the shark?

Every choice, whether it's her name or a feature film, is an adventure with Whoopi Goldberg. You never know what you're going to end up with.

Caryn Johnson grew up in New York City, and made her mark as a comedienne by portraying unique characters in her one-woman show. Mike Nichols caught her performance and brought the show to Broadway in the mid-eighties.

She hosted the Oscars.

Steven Spielberg sat in a dark, off-Broadway theatre and watched Whoopi do her thing. This gig landed her the plum lead role in *The Color Purple* in 1985—and in our collective consciousness.

It's safe to say that Whoopi has made some interesting choices during her career. After her stellar performance in *The Color Purple,* we were subjected to the alleged comedies *Jumpin' Jack Flash, Fatal Beauty,* and *Burglar.* Audiences wondered if the lady in dreadlocks was ever funny at any point in her life. A series of decent dramas like *Clara's Heart* (with a little Doogie Howser) and *The Long Walk Home* were well received, but commercial failures. Whoopi shared the stage with pals Robin Williams and Billy Crystal for *Comic Relief,* but her career had started to look like a fluke or, at best, a curiosity item.

In 1990, Whoopi took a supporting role in *Ghost* and scored huge with audiences and many critics. Her work as a goofy psychic made her the first black woman to win an Oscar since Hattie McDaniel for *Gone with the Wind* in 1939. Whoopi, now one of the highest-paid actresses in Hollywood, soon landed her biggest hit yet, *Sister Act,* where she portrayed a Vegas lounge singer hiding with a bunch of nuns. It worked.

We spotted a fin when Whoopi hosted her own talk show for less than a year, and made a sequel to the one-hit wonder *Sister Act.* Then, in the ultimate nod to her skill, the Academy invited Whoopi to host the 1996 Oscars. But Whoopi's loose and fun style was too constricted by the cue cards and unforgivably cheap visual gags—Whoopi in white face as Queen Elizabeth! This went over about as well as then-boyfriend Ted Danson's post-*Cheers* career, and Whoopi had jumped the shark.

Since then, we've had *Star Trek: The Next Generation,* more *Comic Relief,* and *Eddie,* to name a few. Whoopi has had a good run and is a talented, funny comedienne. She wisely left the Oscar hosting to others who do it better to find the edge that made her so special to see. Did she find it? Well, the host of the 2002 Oscar telecast was . . .

Hugh Grant

1960–

jump the shark?

Maybe it's a British thing, but if Liz Hurley were my girlfriend the last place you'd find me would be cruising Sunset Boulevard.

Meeting Divine on Sunset Boulevard.

Hailing from London, Hugh Grant had been a significant star in the U.K. for more than a decade by the time we first noticed him in *Four Weddings and a Funeral.* His immediate popularity in the U.S. was demonstrated by the seven films he did in the two years after his crossover hit.

Hugh's irresistible, foppish Englishman was a character not often seen on the American screen. He was the antithesis of macho, and women around the world fell hard for Hugh. He had Elizabeth Hurley on his arm, and *People* had named him one of the one hundred sexiest stars.

IN FLAGRANTE STUPIDO

We all have our secrets. Here is a small sampling of those who got caught with their pants down:

1 Bill Clinton
2 Eddie Murphy
3 Charlie Sheen
4 Jim Bakker
5 Pee-Wee Herman

All the attention went to his scruffy-haired head pretty quickly. We spotted a fin when we learned Hugh's next project was a buddy comedy with Tom Arnold called *Nine Months.* Baby films and Tom Arnold are a lethal combination. But it was what Hugh did offscreen in 1995 that sent him over the shark—getting arrested on Sunset Boulevard for "lewd conduct" with hooker Divine Brown. One might say that the shark jumped him.

Why Elizabeth Hurley's boyfriend needed to troll down Sunset Strip looking for love has perplexed us for years. It was a huge personal and professional embarrassment for Grant. He got some points back for apologizing publicly and profusely on *The Tonight Show,* but the damage had been done. He wouldn't have another strong role until *Notting Hill,* and his image will forever be tainted.

Hugh is now making the most of playing the charming villain, as we saw in *Small Time Crooks* and *Bridget Jones's Diary.* Clearly his

OUTRAGEOUS ACCENTS

Our favorite acting imports:

1 John Cleese
2 Peter Sellers
3 Anthony Hopkins
4 John Gielgud
5 Alec Guinness

range extends beyond the fumbling lovable goof on which he made his name. But every time we look at him now, we see a police-issue flashlight illuminating his million-dollar grin. Sometimes the shark comes in high heels and fishnet stockings. Bloody hell!

When did George Lucas

1944–

jump the shark?

American Graffiti. Star Wars. Raiders of the Lost Ark. Any questions?

> **Howard the Duck.**

George Lucas will be remembered as the force behind two of the largest film franchises ever—*Star Wars* and *Indiana Jones.* We watch most releases these days with THX sound developed by his company Lucasfilm, or with effects from his other creation, Industrial Light and Magic. George Lucas is "the man behind the curtain."

Like Steven Spielberg, Lucas began his career as a film school grad. He did a number of small films in the sixties, the most significant being *THX-1138,* first produced as a short, then as a 1970 feature with Robert Duvall. Three years later, he directed a low-budget nostalgia piece produced by his school buddy Francis Ford Coppola. *American Graffiti* was the sleeper hit of 1973, and it gave Lucas the juice he needed to make *Star Wars.*

Lucas decided to forgo his director's salary in exchange for forty percent of the box-office and merchandising rights for *Star Wars.* That move enabled him to spend the next five years building his Skywalker Ranch. *Episode IV* was his last directing job until *Episode I* surfaced more than twenty years later. Goodbye, director, hello, producer.

The Empire Strikes Back and *Return of the*

SAP FACTOR

The Ewoks led George Lucas straight to the shark. Other soft victims:

1 Francis Ford Coppola—
  One from the Heart
2 Steven Spielberg—*Hook*
3 Rob Reiner—*North*
4 John Carpenter—
  Starman
5 Mel Brooks—*Life Stinks*

Jedi rounded out the *Star Wars* legacy. Even though the films got progressively worse—typical of sequels—they were smash successes. Lucas teamed with Spielberg to create *Raiders of the Lost Ark,* a runaway smash and one of the best action movies of all time. They were the undeniable dream team in the movie industry.

The cheesiness of the cuddly Ewoks served as shark bait, and when George produced *Captain Eo,* Michael Jackson's Disney flick, with his buddy Francis Ford Coppola directing, we smelled danger. Later that year, Lucas jumped the shark with the release of *Howard the Duck,* an adaptation of a comic book that had two key flaws . . . it wasn't funny or entertaining. People stayed away in flocks, and George hasn't done anything great on screen ever since.

Willow gave him a chance to employ the small actors he puts in all his films, but it came off as a cumbersome reach. Lucas's career now consists of variations on his twin-pillared money machine: *Indiana Jones* and *Star Wars.* Jar-Jar Binks reminds us that the "cute" factor has not left George. May the force be with him.

MULTITASKING

Lucas has had his hand in many movies in the last thirty years. Here's a sampling:

1 *Finian's Rainbow*— Production Assistant
2 *Gimme Shelter*— Cinematographer
3 *Body Heat*—Executive Producer
4 *Leprechaun*—Producer
5 Pixar—Founder (sold to Steve Jobs)

When did
Demi Moore
1962–

jump the shark?

We can't pronounce her first name, but we do know that Demi was the most powerful actress in Hollywood during the mid-nineties.

Maybe you first spotted Demetria Gene Guynes on *General Hospital* as Jackie Templeton. There's a better chance that you first noticed this striking brunette with a sultry voice playing Michael Caine's

Demi dons the *A.*

daughter in *Blame It on Rio.* We're pretty sure you missed the New Mexico native as Holly in *Master Ninja I.*

Demi's big break came in 1985's *St. Elmo's Fire,* when she finally kicked her coke habit and started to become a star. This film, lumped together with *The Breakfast Club,* is responsible for the birth of the Brat Pack. Demi's character Jules personified her image . . . sexy, smart, and a little bit dangerous.

Demi stuck with fellow brat packers Rob Lowe and Emilio Estevez for her next films, *About Last Night* and *Wisdom.* Her notable bathtub scene with Lowe (his second most famous piece of video) gave us a nice "before" shot to compare with her post-silicone "after" work in *Striptease* a decade later. Once engaged to Emilio Estevez, Demi wed Bruce Willis and had three kids whose names are as difficult to pronounce as their mom's.

Ghost vaulted Demi Moore to superstar status as she became one of the highest-paid actresses in Hollywood. Any film with Patrick Swayze and Whoopi Goldberg is prime shark bait, but Demi managed to stay on top through the early nineties with *A Few Good Men, Indecent Proposal,* and *Disclosure.* The naked *Vanity Fair* covers didn't hurt either.

Demi then went the "I'm an actress and this is my craft" route, starring as Hester Prynne in *The Scarlet Letter*—a definitive jump right over the shark. Maybe it was motherhood, but we think it was that *A* on her chest that destroyed her sexy image. *Striptease* and *GI Jane* tried way too hard to be interesting. Much to the chagrin of Planet Hollywood, Bruce and Demi divorced, and she seems to have settled into the motherhood role. At least for now . . .

Eddie Murphy

1961–

A comic legend by the time he was twenty and a movie superstar a few years later, Eddie just couldn't resist the temptation to sing.

> **Eddie just wants to party all the time.**

Eddie Murphy joined the cast of *Saturday Night Live* as a teenager. He dominated one of the weakest casts in that show's shaky history. A master character-creator, Eddie gave us memorable characters including pimp-author Velvet Jones, Mister Robinson, John David Stutts, and Gumby. He nailed impressions of Stevie Wonder, James Brown, Jesse Jackson, and more. Nobody could touch him for funny.

Eddie segued smoothly into films. He achieved instant stardom with *48 Hours* and *Trading Places,* but hit the big time as Axel Foley in *Beverly Hills Cop. Delirious,* his 1983 HBO comedy special, is arguably the funniest ever done and reminded us how gifted a stand up comic he truly was.

We spotted a fin with *Best Defense* and when Eddie tried to act in *The Golden Child*. In 1985, Eddie wanted to pursue the dream of singing professionally, and released the Rick James produced *How Could It Be* with the dance hit "Party All the Time." When Eddie sang "Boogie in Your Butt" on a stand-up album, it was funny. But he was now serious about his singing career, and it took him right over the shark.

A reliance on sequels began with *Beverly Hills Cop II,* and self-penned/produced/directed ego-projects *Harlem Nights, Boomerang,* and *Vampire in Brooklyn* followed. Eddie would

WHERE ARE THEY NOW?

At least one of Eddie's *SNL* costars enjoyed superstardom. Can you find him/her?:

1 Joe Piscopo
2 Denny Dillon
3 Brian Doyle Murray
4 Robin Duke
5 Mary Gross
6 Christine Ebersole
7 Gilbert Gottfried
8 Brad Hall
9 Tim Kazurinsky
10 Julia Louis-Dreyfus
11 Charles Rocket
12 Tony Rosato

BUDDY PICS

Eddie has worked with an eclectic group of partners during his career:

1 Nick Nolte
2 Joe Piscopo
3 Arsenio Hall
4 Judge Reinhold
5 Dan Aykroyd

reclaim box office dominion in 1996 with a loose remake of *The Nutty Professor* and *Dr. Dolittle,* but his edge was gone.

In the spring of '97 the LAPD caught Eddie picking up a transsexual hooker. This happened during his transformation from rough, foul-mouthed urban comic to family-man comic à la Bill Cosby. Nothing is too weird for Hollywood.

We look at Eddie a little differently these days. His most popular role in years was an animated donkey in *Shrek.* But, when the ass breaks into song during the film, even the kids think twice about partying all the time.

When did **Paul Newman**

1925–

jump the shark?

From the hills of Bolivia to a hockey rink in Charlestown, we have nothing but respect for the man with the famous blue eyes.

> **It's in the way that you use it . . .**

There is nothing not to like about Paul Newman. He's a living legend, the last of a breed of superstar leading men. He is better looking in his seventies than most men are in their twenties. He is a dedicated husband and devoted humanitarian. He donates all the profits from his company, Newman's Own, to charity.

But this is about his movies.

Ignoring his first film (he apologized for *The Silver Chalice*), this Broadway actor got noticed as Rocky Graziano in *Somebody Up There Likes Me.* After a few more Broadway adaptations, Newman became a star as Fast Eddie Felson in *The Hustler.* He more than held his own with George C. Scott and Jackie Gleason, and began a memorable run in feature films.

Paul Newman made a slew of great movies. The sixties featured *Sweet Bird of*

STAYING HITCHED

There's an old saying, "I'm as serious as a Hollywood marriage," which reflects the cavalier attitude that movie stars seem to have about the institution of marriage. There have been some notable exceptions:

1 Paul Newman
2 Charlton Heston
3 Danny DeVito
4 Mel Gibson
5 Hume Cronyn

Youth, Hud, Harper, Cool Hand Luke, and *Butch Cassidy and the Sundance Kid.* The seventies began with *Sometimes a Great Notion, The Life and Times of Judge Roy Bean,* and yet another movie he should have won an Oscar for, *The Sting.* Paul was too busy racing cars to notice.

WOULD YOU LIKE BUTTER?

Now that's good popcorn:

1 Newman's Own
2 Orville Redenbacher
3 Pop Secret
4 Jiffy Pop
5 The "fresh," four-day-old bag that they pour at the movie theater

The shark began to circle with age in *The Towering Inferno* and *The Drowning Pool,* but he came back with our favorite role as captain Reg Dunlop in the hockey classic *Slap Shot* (that's what it says in the yearbook, Jim). He began the eighties with more serious roles in *Fort Apache, The Bronx; Absence of Malice;* and *The Verdict.* We finally spotted a fin when he wrote, directed, and starred in *Harry and Son* with Robby Benson.

Paul Newman jumped the shark in 1986 recreating Fast Eddie Felson for Martin Scorsese's *The Color of Money.* From the Eric Clapton soundtrack to the Tom Cruise performance, it was a sequel to *The Hustler* that never should have been made. Ironically, this would also be his first Oscar win after many nominations—a fitting cap to a phenomenal career. He still makes movies and is enjoyable to watch, but it just isn't the same (unless he's searching for the singing cats on Broadway).

We will probably never see a star like Paul Newman again. He jokes that his salad dressing makes more money than his movies. We have to love a guy who has such a natural sense of humor about himself and his career. Pass the popcorn.

Jack Nicholson

1937–

jump the shark?

When you're referred to by one name and never billed yourself as such, you know you're a Hollywood legend.

Batman.

That's a fact with Jack. The New Jersey native has become the face of Hollywood, offering great talent, a distinctive presence, and a radiant star quality. "My dog can do Jack Nicholson," a comic recently observed in a nod to the legend's idiosyncratic acting style.

Jack's film career started in the late fifties with *The Cry Baby Killer,* his first of several low-budget Roger Corman films. He'd been in seventeen movies by the time he did *Easy Rider.* A couple of years later, when he ordered a sandwich in *Five Easy Pieces,* we glimpsed the maniac troublemaker we would still love thirty years later.

Jack is an indelible part of American culture. He has given us some of the greatest characters in film history, including a hippie lawyer, stir-crazed hotel caretaker, mental patient, and general who can't handle the truth. Do we even need to list the films?

But Jack is not a one-note actor. He has excelled in complex and memorable turns in *Carnal Knowledge, Chinatown, Reds, Terms of Endearment,* and *Prizzi's Honor* (okay, we had to list those) among others. He is a rarity in Hollywood these days . . . a bonafide movie star who also happens to be an excellent actor.

A career as long as Nicholson's is fraught with shark bait. A number of paternity suits, some questionable film choices (*Tommy, Goin' South, Mars Attacks!*)—each could have spelled doom. Oddly, it seems that he got most of his bad movies out of the way in the beginning.

The shark began to circle with the depressing trifecta of *Heartburn, The Witches of Eastwick,* and *Ironweed.* Jack was great as an anchor in *Broadcast News,* but he jumped with his next film two years later as the Joker in *Bat-*

LADIES MEN

Jack still gets around with the young ladies. Seems like a good life. Other notable Casanovas:

1 Warren Beatty
2 Sam Malone
3 Don Juan (before hell)
4 Frank Sinatra
5 John F. Kennedy

man. The Joker was Jack and vice versa . . . plus the movie is particularly bad and Jack had become a caricature of himself.

His record since then has been spotty at best. A *Hoffa* or *Wolf* has become the rule rather than the *As Good As It Gets* exception. Everyone obligatorily bows to Jack at the Oscars or Laker games, but it seems shticky and not reverential. Jack is still fun to watch, but since *Batman,* some of his magic has gone.

When did

Al Pacino
1940–

jump the shark?

Al Pacino made going to the movies in the 1970s fun, interesting, and a little bit scary. He took method acting to a new place. Something in his eyes during the Italian restaurant scene in *The Godfather* reached us all. He was so damned real. We knew that there was something very right going on there.

"Hoo-hah."

Consider this brief résumé sampling: *Panic in Needle Park, The Godfather: Part I* and *Part II, Dog Day Afternoon, Serpico, . . . and Justice for All.* And that was just the seventies.

Al spoke some of the most memorable lines of the era, too: "I'm out of order? You're out of order!" "Attica!" "Never take sides against the family again. Ever." Classics.

We spotted a fin in 1980 when the softer

side of Al started appearing in *Cruising* and *Author! Author!* but he briefly avoided the shark with *Scarface.* The nineties gave us the tasty bait of *The Godfather: Part III* (sacrilege), *Dick Tracy,* and *Frankie and Johnny.* Finally, in 1992, *Scent of a Woman* vaulted Pacino right over the shark.

Michael Corleone could now only muster a "hoo-hah" as a blind, retired military man on a final suicide mission. He won a Paul-Newman-you-deserved-this-before Oscar, but he was now a cartoon of himself. He tried to get back to his roots with *Carlito's Way, Heat, City Hall,* and *Donnie Brasco,* but these characters fell short of Al's regular guy appeal.

He's done some memorable work in *Glengarry Glen Ross* and *The Insider,* but Al also went way over the top in *The Devil's Advocate* and *Any Given Sunday.* It's sad to see these days, but all of the Dons have now become caricatures.

When did
Michelle Pfeiffer
1957–

jump the shark?

They don't come any finer than this perennial entry on *People*'s Most Beautiful list, but we can't help but wonder who chooses her scripts.

Making whoopee.

Michelle Pfeiffer was born and raised in California and was a supermarket checkout girl before giving acting a shot. Her first role was as the aptly named Bombshell in *Delta House,* a follow-up TV series to *Animal House.* Her inauspicious film debut was opposite Tony Danza in the *American Graffiti* rip-off *Hollywood Knights.* She later followed this as

Stephanie Zinone in *Grease 2.* Who knew she was poised for superstardom?

Having nowhere to go but up, the former Miss Orange County scored her first major role as Tony Montana's wife in *Scarface.* Unfortunately, she followed with the forgettable *Ladyhawke, Into the Night,* and *Sweet Liberty.* Her performance in *The Witches of Eastwick* legitimized her standing with the big boys in Hollywood, but the next year would be her breakthrough with Oscar-caliber performances in *Married to the Mob* and *Dangerous Liaisons.*

After getting a piano excited in *The Fabulous Baker Boys* and making whoopee with both Bridges brothers, Michelle jumped the shark with a torrid streak of average movies with great actors including *Tequila Sunrise* (Gibson), *The Russia House* (Connery), *Frankie and Johnny* (Pacino), and *The Age of Innocence* (D. D. Lewis). No one will soon forget her "meow" as Catwoman in *Batman Returns* except maybe Fisher Stevens, who lost Michelle to the virtual TV network David E. Kelley.

Dangerous Minds made it seem like she might pull a Travolta, but worse films with good actors continued including *Wolf* (Nicholson), *Up Close & Personal* (Redford), and *One Fine Day* (Clooney). She hit rock bottom with *The Story of Us* (Willis), and just didn't fit in the thriller *What Lies Beneath* (Ford).

Don't get us wrong—Michelle Pfeiffer is a very talented actress who only grows more beautiful with age. We respect that she takes on atypical roles. But after twenty years in the business, you would think she'd find the right script to showcase her talent. Maybe her husband can jump on this?

Robert Redford

1937–

jump the shark?

Looks can get you only so far, but they got Robert Redford a long, long way.

This Santa Monica native began his career with a tremendous amount of TV work in the late fifties, including a memorable *Twilight Zone* and several *Alfred Hitchcock Presents* episodes. He segued smoothly into movies, notably *Inside Daisy Clover* with Natalie Wood, and *Barefoot in the Park* with Jane Fonda. He was an ideal leading man from the start.

Havana.

Robert Redford traded on his good looks and charisma to become the biggest box-office draw of the 1970s. In 1969, Redford teamed with Paul Newman in the classic *Butch Cassidy and the Sundance Kid,* his first of two partnerships that made him a household name.

The Way We Were, The Sting, and *The Great Gatsby* made Redford the number one box-office attraction. *The Great Waldo Pepper, Three Days of the Condor,* and *All the President's Men* featured great performances in quality films. The seventies belonged to the good-looking blond guy, but ended on an iffy note with *The Electric Horseman.*

> **ROY HOBBS**
>
> It's your baseball team. Who do you draft?
>
> 1 Crash Davis
> 2 Willie Mays Hayes
> 3 Gary Cooper
> 4 Moonlight Graham
> 5 Rudy Stein

Redford slowed down his acting career and discovered that he was also an excellent director and producer. He nabbed an Oscar with his directorial debut, *Ordinary People,* and later followed up with the *The Milagro Beanfield War, A River Runs Through It,* and *Quiz Show.*

But on screen, he would have his problems. The eighties started strong with *The Natural* and *Out of Africa.* We spotted a fin with the horrid comedy *Legal Eagles,* but he jumped the shark in 1990 by starring in the dreadful Casablanca rip-off *Havana.* Redford was showing his age.

Sneakers was harmless and fun. *Indecent*

> **ALMOST CORLEONE**
>
> Robert Redford was on the studio's short list to play Michael Corleone. Others considered:
>
> 1 James Caan
> 2 Robert De Niro
> 3 Martin Sheen
> 4 Ryan O'Neal
> 5 Harvey Keitel

Proposal was a bad joke. *Up Close & Personal* was weak. And we still haven't awakened from *The Horse Whisperer.* If Redford stays behind the camera, we can count on more good stuff. His Sundance Institute and its annual festival have given the American film industry a necessary shot in the arm. But if *Spy Game* is any indication, Roy Hobbs is not ready to hang up his cleats just yet.

When did

Julia Roberts
1967–

jump the shark?

It is difficult to argue that the highest paid and most bankable actress in Hollywood has jumped the shark—but we will.

Dying Young.

Julia Roberts hails from Georgia and wanted to be a vet until her brother Eric briefly made it in Hollywood. If he could do it, so could she (point well taken), and Julia got her break in the romantic comedy *Mystic Pizza*.

This led to Julia's first terminally ill role and Oscar nomination as Shelby in *Steel Magnolias*. She became a superstar with her second Oscar-nominated part and resurrected Richard Gere's career as a hooker with a heart in *Pretty Woman*. Julia was beautiful, she could act, and she was serious box office.

Flatliners and our favorite Moviefone spoken title, *Sleeping with the Enemy,* came next and were standard Hollywood junk. Her name made these films respectable financial successes. We spotted a fin when Julia appeared as Tinkerbell in the major Spielberg disappointment *Hook*.

But Julia went to the terminally ill well one too many times, and Joel Schumacher shoved her right over the shark with *Dying Young*. This boring, manipulative weep-fest was her first taste of failure and begat a string of disappointing films. In 1993, she married Lyle Lovett for a couple of years and forgot about her film career for a while. Her 1996 doubleheader of *Mary Reilly* and *Michael Collins* found Julia in Meryl Streep–esque roles, where she simply does not excel.

My Best Friend's Wedding brought the laughs back, and Julia began to exhibit Travolta-like tendencies in building a major comeback. She trod water with *Conspiracy Theory, Stepmom,* and the *Pretty Woman* cast reunion of *Runaway Bride,* but the self-referential *Notting Hill* showed Julia could laugh at herself, and that's what we wanted to see.

Her Oscar finally came as the tailor-made lead in *Erin Brockovich.* Julia and Steven Soderbergh elevated this made-for-TV movie into a better-than-average character drama. Julia has since said goodbye to Benjamin Bratt, but *The Mexican* and *America's Sweethearts* tell us the jury is still out as to whether or not this superstar has indeed jumped back.

BROTHERS AND SISTERS

Hard to believe that Eric was once the big draw in the Roberts clan. Other famous siblings:

1 John and Joan Cusack
2 Warren Beatty and Shirley MacLaine
3 Mary Kate and Ashley Olsen
4 Albert Brooks and Super Dave Osborne
5 Pick a Judd, any Judd

When did

Roseanne

1952–

jump the shark?

Roseanne is a gifted stand-up comic with a bit of a temper plus a nasty habit of changing her name and appearance every few years or so.

Born in Salt Lake City, Utah, Roseanne Barr had an eventful childhood, including a traumatic car crash and parents who allegedly abused her. After years of paying her stand-up dues, she landed the Holy Grail of comedy in 1985, a spot on Carson. She was great. She was funny. She touched a nerve with every woman in America, and Hollywood noticed.

"The Star Spangled Banner."

FUNNY LADIES

Perhaps it's chauvinistic, but good stand-up comediennes are rare. The exceptions:

1 Roseanne
2 Ellen DeGeneres
3 Rosie O'Donnell
4 Joan Rivers
5 Whoopi Goldberg

Three years later she transformed her act into a very successful sitcom. No one captured the lower-middle-class family with as much truth as Roseanne. However, as inevitably happens when somebody moves quickly from poverty to great wealth (how many lotto winners have kept it together?), she snapped. Money and success gave Roseanne the newfound ability to be outrageous on a much larger stage. And nobody wanted to see it.

Her first stab at a feature film, *She-Devil,* was hell. Things went a bit smoother when she voiced baby Julie in *Look Who's Talking Too* the next year, but the majority of her big-screen appearances feature Roseanne as herself. She's a ready-made character.

As we entered the nineties, Roseanne continued to dominate the television ratings. At home, she divorced Bill Pentland, her husband of fifteen-plus years, and married Tom Arnold. Roseanne and Tom were John and Yoko, completely inseparable while the world looked on in confusion. They lived to shock, and shock they did. The marriage lasted four years and made Tom a star, but Roseanne was soon to leave Tom for her driver, Ben Thomas.

Roseanne finally jumped the shark with her infamous rendition of "The Star Spangled Banner" at a San Diego Padres game. Her singing was bad, but her classless grab of her crotch was the straw that broke her fan base's back. She had crossed the line, and few people were interested anymore.

CELEBRITY UPHEAVALS

Roseanne jumped on the cosmetic surgery bandwagon in the nineties. Here are some notable regulars on silicon row.

1 Morgan Fairchild
2 Cher
3 Michael Jackson
4 Joan Rivers
5 Elizabeth Taylor

After Roseanne's stint on ABC came to a close, and a few plastic surgeries later, she resurfaced with a new look and a nationally syndicated talk show, *The Roseanne Show*. Roseanne hosting a talk show? It couldn't work and it didn't, lasting for less than two years. These days she's separated from third husband Ben and we can only hope she returns to being the great stand-up comedienne that she once was.

Meg Ryan
1961–

jump the shark?

Meg has taken the cute factor to an entirely new level and her bankable smile has made her one of the most sought after actresses in Hollywood.

> **She cut her hair short.**

The daughter of a casting agent, Meg Ryan was a journalism major who did some acting to earn extra money. To watch Meg was to fall in love

with her. She is bubbly and sexy—a killer combo for a comedic actress.

You probably missed her bit part as Candice Bergen's daughter in *Rich and Famous* and her two-year stint as Betsy on *As the World Turns*. She came on the Hollywood scene in 1986 as the grieving Mrs. Goose in *Top Gun* and hasn't looked back since.

Meg was solid in two of the first three films she made with future ex-husband Dennis Quaid, *Innerspace* and *DOA.* She approached superstar status when she costarred with Billy Crystal in *When Harry Met Sally.* She was the girl next door who could fake it with the best of them.

Meg played three roles in her next film, *Joe Versus the Volcano,* and it almost sunk not only her but costar Tom Hanks, as well. Meg balanced comedies like *Sleepless in Seattle* and *IQ* with *The Doors* and *Prelude to a Kiss.*

We spotted a fin when she went for the Oscar in the melodramatic women-love-it-guys-leave-the-room flick *When a Man Loves a Woman.* We don't want to see Meg the struggling alcoholic (or Andy Garcia as the caring stepdad).

She then cut her blond locks short for the comedy *French Kiss.* Like Samson's fateful snipping, her power was gone and she had jumped the shark. Her next three films were *Restoration, Courage Under Fire,* and *Addicted to Love.* She went back to the Nora Ephron/Tom Hanks well

---

SNIP, SNIP

A haircut is prime shark bait. Infamous snips:

1 Keri Russell
2 Madonna
3 Johnny Depp
4 Julia Louis-Dreyfus
5 Samson

with *You've Got Mail,* but it came up flat. Meg split with Dennis Quaid, and then had a reported fling with Russell Crowe during the filming of the lousy *Proof of Life.*

Meg can grow her hair back, but it might take more than that to make her America's sweetheart once again.

When did

Arnold Schwarzenegger
1947–

jump the shark?

Hollywood laughed in the seventies when Arnold said he'd be a movie star, but no one was more bankable in the eighties than this physically fit future Kennedy.

He became The Last Action Hero.

Arnold Schwarzenegger began his career as Mr. Universe, holding the Guinness record for "Most Perfect Male Physique." He vowed to conquer Hollywood and made his film debut as Arnold Strong in *Hercules in New York. Pumping Iron* brought his personality to the forefront, and earned him his signature role of *Conan the Barbarian.*

The Conan films led to a breakthrough role as *The Terminator.* Arnold was cool. Arnold was bad. Arnold was unbeatable. A series of solid action flicks followed including *Commando* and *Predator.* We thought we spotted a fin with the Jim Belushi buddy-flick *Red Heat* and his marriage to Maria Shriver. Arnold then flirted with comedy in the well-intentioned, not totally unwatchable *Twins* and *Kindergarten Cop.* But knowing where his bread was buttered, he quickly followed with *Total Recall* and *Terminator 2,* keeping the shark at bay.

Sadly, the 1993 Joel Silver catastrophe, *The Last Action Hero,* was strong enough to vault Arnold over the shark. Arnold played both Jack Slater and himself in a fable about movie action heroes. Ouch. Arnold tried to bounce

THEY'LL BE BACK

Don't mess with them:

1 Darth Vader—*Star Wars*
2 Keyser Soze—*The Usual Suspects*
3 Szell—*Marathon Man*
4 Hannibal Lecter—*The Silence of the Lambs*
5 Bruce, the shark—*Jaws*

back with *True Lies,* but something was missing and his charm seemed forced instead of natural.

Batman and Robin, Eraser, and The 6th Day were weak efforts at best, and we needn't even comment on *Jingle All the Way.* Nevertheless, we still respect Arnold as he tries to keep the nation Republican and healthy. Let's face it, he was never an actor. He has been our generation's John Wayne, always the same tough guy. We never expect him to bring us to tears or win any Oscars. And as long as he has the same expectations, we'll be back.

When did Brooke Shields

1965–

jump the shark?

With or without her Calvins, the only mistakes this Princeton grad has ever made are her script choices.

When Brooke played the nubile honey in the 1980 abomination, *The Blue Lagoon,* she was already a huge star. Brooke was fourteen and had been making movies for about six years; *Pretty Baby* was her first and most notable film. Her generous eyebrows and convincing vulnerability gave her enormous appeal. Surely, her acting skills would catch up, wouldn't they?

Brooke was a hot commodity in fashion and shined in the advertising world. She was Ivory Snow's most beautiful baby in America, and as a teenager the primary pitch person for Calvin Klein jeans. Nothing came between Brooke and her Calvins. Whoa.

The Blue Lagoon led to another awful

Brenda Starr.

early-eighties love story, *Endless Love*. Brooke escaped to Princeton and surfaced in an occasional Bob Hope special or at Michael Jackson's side. The Ivy League education apparently didn't help her film selection, and Brooke jumped the shark when she starred in the film adaptation of the comic strip *Brenda Starr*. This was to be a "comeback" for Shields, but the film was made in 1986 and released six years later . . . never a good sign.

Brooke's claim to fame in the nineties was being Andre Agassi's better half, but she was always able to make fun of herself, and her Special Guest Star appearance as a crazed soap fan on *Friends* gave her new life as a comedienne. She starred in *Suddenly Susan*, which aired for five years on NBC, and survived working with Judd Nelson and Kathy Griffin on a weekly basis.

When you scrape away the marginal movies, TV appearances (she was a regular on the *Circus of the Stars*), and her modeling career, you find someone simply famous for being a star. But beautiful Brooke is still very young, and *TIME*'s "Face of the Eighties" has plenty of time to jump back.

When did
Steven Spielberg
1946–

jump the shark?

The man can make movies.

A new Spielberg film is always a treat. He is one of the only modern directors whom everyone knows, even people who don't like movies. No director living or dead (with the possible exception of Frank Capra) possesses a better-honed ability to use the film medium to manipulate human emotion. He is an artist, a magician, and a kid in a candy store.

Schindler's List.

IN FRONT OF THE CAMERA

You can catch Hollywood's finest in:

1 *The Blues Brothers*—clerk
2 *Jaws*—guy on the radio
3 *Indiana Jones and the Temple of Doom*—tourist
4 *Gremlins*—guy in wheelchair
5 *The Lost World*—guy eating popcorn

Rejected twice by USC, Steven Spielberg studied at CSU Long Beach where he made *Amblin'*, a short that earned him a TV deal with Universal at the age of twenty. He worked on *Night Gallery, Columbo,* and other network shows and also created one of the best ever TV movies, *Duel.* His first feature, *The Sugarland Express,* got him the chance to create our personal favorite, *Jaws.* This shark fest was the first ever summer blockbuster, and he followed it with *Close Encounters of the Third Kind,* proving he wasn't a one-hit wonder.

It looked like Spielberg was going to end up as shark bait with his first stab at comedy, the disastrous *1941.* It was his first failure, and he responded with *Raiders of the Lost Ark* and *E.T.* The man can handle sharks. *Poltergeist* and an Indiana Jones sequel *Temple of Doom* followed next, and although these weren't classics, he seemed to be getting back on track.

Spielberg started a hit and miss pattern at this point. The dreadful *The Goonies* was followed by the classic *The Color Purple.* The tedious *Empire of the Sun* was backed up by the third Indy movie, *The Last Crusade.* As his consistency waned and his marriage to Amy Irving was coming to an end, we spotted a fin with *Always*.

THE PRODUCER

We all know Spielberg is a great director, but did you know he had a hand in producing:

1 *Used Cars*
2 *Back to the Future*
3 *Who Framed Roger Rabbit*
4 *Men in Black*
5 *Shrek*

Spielberg seemed to have jumped the shark with *Hook,* a big budget star-powered flop. But failure is what gets him going, and he responded with *Jurassic Park,* reminding us what a summer blockbuster should look like. Then, at year's end, *Schindler's List* presented the artist as mature man. Yes, it was manipulative. Yes, Nazis are easy villains (he's used them a half dozen times). Yes, it was his first—and admittedly well-deserved—Oscar winner.

But as good as *Schindler's List* was, it represents the moment when Steven Spielberg jumped the shark. His next film, *Jurassic Park: The Lost World,* was horrible, and *Amistad* was remarkably ineffective. *Saving Private Ryan* was good, but uneven, losing most of its punch after the opening battle scene. *A.I.* was interesting to look at considering it was a living/

dead collaboration between Spielberg and Stanley Kubrick, but it was not a great film.

We're admittedly splitting hairs. The man is the most important director in Hollywood and probably deserves "never jumped" status. But hey—that's what we're here for.

When did

Sylvester Stallone
1946–

jump the shark?

Yo, we love him as Rocky and Rambo, but if Sly wants to show his acting range, be afraid . . . be very afraid.

No actor in the $20 million club can boast a more crap-filled resume than Sylvester Stallone. Whether you look at his work critically or commercially he is, at best, batting .200. In fact, if you pull the Rockys and Rambos out of the mix, his career would be considered a flop. But people still come to see Sly.

Rhinestone.

The Italian Stallion got his start in the soft-porn *The Party at Kitty and Stud's*. He made his mark playing a hoodlum in a half-dozen movies in the early seventies. The most interesting of these are his bit part in *Bananas* as a subway mugger, and his costarring role in *The Lords of Flatbush*.

It was his gamble on *Rocky* that made him an overnight sensation. He wrote this legendary film by himself and for himself, and his tenacity and willingness to accept very little money up front got him the nod to play the lead. It is his best work and arguably one of the best films ever made, winning Best Picture and catapulting Stallone to superstardom.

Sadly, he never made a great movie again, starting with *F.I.S.T.* and *Paradise Alley. Rocky II* was solid, but the sequels became progressively

SLY THE WRITER

He's great on camera, but put a pen in Stallone's hand and you get:

1 *The Lords of Flatbush*
2 *Rhinestone*
3 *First Blood*
4 *Staying Alive*
5 *Rocky (I through V)*

worse, despite financial success. *Nighthawks* costarred Rutger Hauer and was somewhat entertaining, and *Victory* let us see Stallone, Pele, and Michael Caine in an acting tour de force!

Sly needed a new character for the eighties, and he got one with John Rambo in *First Blood*. This film, and its more profitable sequels, provided Stallone with a dependable money machine. The shark started to circle when he cowrote and di-

rected the *Saturday Night Fever* sequel, *Staying Alive*. Pain, Balboa, Pain.

He finally jumped in 1984 when he costarred with Dolly Parton in the comedy *Rhinestone*. Stallone and comedy just don't mix (see *Oscar* or *Stop or My Mom Will Shoot*), unless you're referring to his brief marriage to Brigitte Nielsen. If he's not making a Rocky or Rambo sequel, Stallone continues to take action roles like those in *Cobra, Cliffhanger, Demolition Man, The Specialist, Assassins,* and *Driven.*

One gets the sense that Stallone is aware of his acting limitations and we do respect him for that. However, it doesn't make the movies any easier to watch, particularly the ones that were intended to be funny.

When did
Sharon Stone
1958–

jump the shark?

Sliver.

She's blond, she's beautiful, and she's really, really smart . . . except when it comes to choosing film roles.

Sharon Stone hails from a small town in Pennsylvania and has an IQ of 154. Her first genius move was winning Miss Pennsylvania and becoming a successful Ford model.

Her first film appearance was as "pretty girl on train" in Woody Allen's *Stardust Memories* in 1980. She reprised the "pretty girl" role in TV classics such as *Calendar Girl Murders* and *Bay City Blues* and added some toughness in films such as *Police Academy 4* and *Action Jackson*.

Sharon became a star when she played the "pretty girl who kicks ass" alongside Arnold in *Total Recall,* and we couldn't take our eyes off her. Two years later she proved she wasn't a flash in the pan, costarring with Michael Douglas in *Basic Instinct*. It's not a good movie, but Sharon puts on one hell of a performance as a femme fatale. She was dangerous, sexy, different, and smart.

Unfortunately, her MENSA-caliber IQ didn't do her much good in choosing roles after *Basic Instinct*. We didn't even have time to see the shark coming in her next film, *Sliver.* Think of this movie and *Intersection* as the skis Sharon wore as she soared over the shark. All of the notoriety from *Basic Instinct* was gone and *The Quick and the Dead* pushed her further away from the Hollywood blockbuster.

Sharon has put in some solid work since the mid-nineties, most notably her drug-addicted hooker in *Casino* opposite Robert De Niro. It brought an Oscar nomination, but subsequent roles in *Last Dance* and *Sphere* were as forgettable as the films themselves. She was fun in her first big comedy lead, *The Muse,* but *Beautiful Joe* and *If These Walls Could Talk 2* remind us where Sharon is in show business today. Maybe Mrs. Bronstein has a comeback in the works. We can only hope.

When did
Barbra Streisand
1942–

jump the shark?

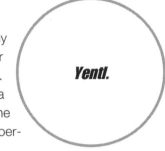

Yentl.

In 1970, Barbra Streisand received a special Tony for "Actress of the Decade." Broadway had never seen a star with her extraordinary talents before. She had a beautiful, exuberant voice and was a gifted actress, particularly in broad comedy. She was straight out of Brooklyn and one-hundred percent bankable.

After a series of TV specials, Elliott Gould's ex smoothly transitioned from the stage to the screen, reprising her award-winning performance in *Funny Girl*. She also pulled an Audrey Hepburn on Carol Channing and took the title role in 1968's *Hello, Dolly!*

In the seventies, Streisand could do no wrong. She brought back the long-dormant screwball comedy with *What's Up, Doc?* and *The Owl and the Pussycat*. We flocked to see her dramatic work in *The Way We Were* and *A Star Is Born*. And her voice (singing that is) . . . enough said.

Her film act started to wear thin with Ryan O'Neal in *The Main Event*, but Barbra wanted to get behind the camera. She took on a new challenge in 1983 by directing *and* starring in *Yentl*, and sent herself right over the shark. Barbra portrayed a young Jewish woman forced to pose as a boy so she could pursue her religious studies in this film version of the classic novel by Isaac Bashevis Singer. Papa, can you hear this?

Never a classic beauty, Barbra should have made a more convincing Jewish boy. She didn't. *Yentl* was a respectable financial success, critically appreciated, but not quite up to the usual level. Barbra hasn't been the same since.

She took a break from films, then appeared as a nut in *Nuts* and directed Nick Nolte in the critically acclaimed *Prince of Tides*. Barbra was more visible in the mid-nineties, hitting the road again and charging $1,000 per ticket for

---

BARBRA WANNABES

She sings, she dances, she tells jokes. So do they:

1 Bette Midler
2 Rosie O'Donnell
3 Liza Minelli
4 Carol Burnett
5 Neil Diamond

BROADWAY TO HOLLYWOOD

The transition is tough, but some have not only survived but thrived away from the theater:

1 Nathan Lane
2 Zero Mostel
3 Jack Lemmon
4 Kevin Spacey
5 Neil Simon

her sold-out musical concerts. She even showed up on *Saturday Night Live* for some "Coffee Talk." Her most recent directing effort, *The Mirror Has Two Faces,* reminds us that Barbra should stick to what she's best at and simply lower her ticket prices.

When did Patrick Swayze
1952–

jump the shark?

This dirty dancer should get a lifetime supply of shark repellent for saying "Nobody puts Baby in a corner" with a straight face.

Surfing with Keanu.

It's tempting to suggest that Patrick Swayze jumped the shark on day one. This Houston, Texan, is a fairly typical, athletic, good-looking Hollywood actor who often plays vapid, macho stereotypes. But the man can dance. We'll give him that.

Like many other young eighties leading men, Patrick got his film start with a solid performance in *The Outsiders*. Effective tough guy performances followed in *Uncommon Valor, Red Dawn,* and the half-decent hockey flick *Youngblood*. His breakout role was Johnny Castle, a tough guy who could dance, in *Dirty Dancing.* The performance is hopelessly dated and even comical now, but this was the part that made him a star . . . in spite of his soundtrack performance of "She's Like the Wind."

There was plenty of shark bait the next couple of years with *Road House* and *Next of Kin,* but lightning struck twice with the insanely popular chick flick *Ghost.* This was Patrick's biggest hit, but he had nowhere to go but down. He literally jumped the shark in *Point Break* as an undercover cop surfing with Keanu Reeves.

Although he continued to work through the 1990s, his films were pretty forgettable. He

FLY ME TO THE MOON

Swayze counts flying amongst his many hobbies. Here are some other actors who love to fly:

1 Harrison Ford
2 John Travolta
3 Jimmy Stewart
4 Tom Cruise
5 Robert Downey, Jr.

played a guy named Jack in three of his next five movies, and a daring drag role in *To Wong Foo, Thanks for Everything, Julie Newmar,* which only drifted him further into obscurity.

His best work since *Ghost* was in the *Saturday Night Live* skit where he auditioned for Chippendale's alongside Chris Farley. His self-deprecating performance was genuinely funny in the situation, no small feat for *SNL* in the nineties. It's too bad the shark had already moved on to its next victim.

INSIDE OUT, OUTSIDE IN

The Outsiders was the launch pad for many careers, including:

1 C. Thomas Howell
2 Matt Dillon
3 Rob Lowe
4 Emilio Estevez
5 Tom Cruise

When did

John Travolta

1954–

jump the shark?

He can fly circles around the shark, but we just love to watch him dance.

John Travolta is a New Jersey native who ruled the seventies, tanked in the eighties, came back in the nineties, and took a hall of fame jump into the millennium. Travolta hit instant stardom as Sweathog Vinnie Barbarino on *Welcome Back, Kotter.* He was the Fonzie of Buchanan High School, a breakaway star of a show that was really about somebody else.

Battlefield Earth.

LOSING MY RELIGION

Scientology has a large following in Hollywood. Members include:

1 Tom Cruise
2 Nancy Cartwright
3 Kirstie Alley
4 Jenna Elfman
5 Juliette Lewis

The TV movie *The Boy in the Plastic Bubble* and feature film *Carrie* were modest hits, but Travolta became a true superstar with *Saturday Night Fever* and *Grease.* He personified the seventies and all the disco trappings, and there was nowhere to go but down. He followed these classic musical flicks with a love story with older woman Lily Tomlin entitled *Moment by Moment.* The shark smelled blood.

The eighties began with the popular *Urban Cowboy* and a mercifully brief fad of fake bull riding in bars. Travolta followed this with a solid performance in *Blow Out*. The rest of the eighties is a laundry list of pain—*Staying Alive, Two of a Kind, Twist of Fate*, and *Perfect*. He couldn't jump the shark because the fish was laughing too hard. Travolta could do no right. It looked like he was done.

Look Who's Talking gave John new life, his first hit in over a decade helped by a Bruce Willis voiceover. But the success was short-lived, as *The Experts* (where he met his wife, Kelly Preston), *Shout,* and *Look Who's Talking Too* kept Travolta on the wrong side of the ramp.

Enter Quentin Tarantino and the plumb role of Vincent Vega in *Pulp Fiction*. John portrayed a junkie gangster and did more for the tourism trade in Amsterdam than one-hundred years of tulip festivals. He was back and bigger than ever. *Get Shorty, Face/Off*, and *Primary Colors* followed, and audiences were once again laughing with Travolta, not at him. He had set the tone for Bruce Willis and other comebacks by "pulling a Travolta."

A long-time Scientologist, Travolta finally had the juice to film his pet project, L. Ron Hubbard's *Battlefield Earth*. It was the *Plan 9* of Y2K, a hall of fame jump over the shark.

Hollywood and audiences can be forgiving, and Travolta is still working regularly and flying himself all over the country, but we're skeptical that the miracle man can pull off another major resurrection. If *Swordfish* and *Domestic Disturbance* are any indication, the reported sequel to *Battlefield Earth* can't get here soon enough.

When did
Robin Williams
1952–

jump the shark?

Toys.

The man is brilliant, but he cannot sit still.

The comic who would be *Popeye* took improv off the small stage and put it on the small box. The Juilliard-trained, Jonathan Winters–inspired Robin Williams was like a fireball on the American comedy scene from the late seventies through the nineties.

A brilliant stand-up comic, Robin came on the TV scene as Mork from Ork, as his own series got its start on *Happy Days* with his pal Fonzie (foreshadowing alert!). Television was too small a stage for Robin Williams, so he set his sights on the big screen. His debut, *Popeye,* sucked, but his performance in *The World According to Garp* was exceptional, and Robin would kick out an average of about two films per year from 1982 onward.

He made a few forgettable comedies during the eighties, but found the right part as military DJ Adrian Cronauer in *Good Morning, Vietnam.* This also segued Robin into deeper roles in *Dead Poet's Society, Awakenings,* and *The Fisher King.* We spotted a fin when he starred as Peter Pan in Spielberg's flop *Hook,* but recovered off-screen as the voice of the Genie in *Aladdin.*

Robin jumped the shark the next year in the horrendous film *Toys.* The cheese factor began to seep in with *Mrs. Doubtfire, Nine Months, Jack,* and *Father's Day.* We thought he

DOCTOR ROBIN

A selection of movies in which Robin wore scrubs:

1 *Dead Again*
2 *Awakenings*
3 *Good Will Hunting*
4 *Nine Months*
5 *Patch Adams*

might pull a Travolta when he won the Oscar for his role in *Good Will Hunting* and actually was mellow in a movie, but *Jakob the Liar* and *Bicentennial Man* assured us that such was not the case.

Still fun and engaging on any talk show or at his perennial hosting gig on *Comic Relief,* Robin never lets us forget what makes him so special.

When did

Bruce Willis
1955–

jump the shark?

He has made a career out of being the classic wiseass, and he's laughing all the way to the bank.

Born in Germany, Bruce Willis grew up in New Jersey and crossed the Hudson to become an actor

Hudson Hawk.

in the early seventies. A bartender with a great rap, a casting director met him and used him as . . . a bartender. It was Bruno's big break.

Most of us first met Bruce in 1985 as David Addison, the smart-ass private eye opposite Cybill Shepherd on *Moonlighting*. He was funny in a new, edgy way that we liked, talking to the camera in a way that made us feel that we were all in on the joke.

Willis hit the big screen softly in 1987 with *Blind Date*, but followed with a vengeance in *Die Hard* as smart-ass cop John McClane. This gigantic hit made him a film superstar, and we'd see more of John Mc-Clane down the road in two sequels. He married Demi Moore and voiced the baby in *Look Who's Talking*. He sang his Seagram wine cooler ads and recorded the top-five single "Respect Yourself" as "Bruno." Bruce was hot.

We spotted a fin with the *Look Who's Talking* sequel and the massively disappointing *Bonfire of the Vanities*. But the real jump came when he played a cat burglar in the horrendous *Hudson Hawk*. A torturously unfunny caper comedy with great prerelease buzz, *Hawk* flopped big-time and ushered in a horrible streak that included *The Last Boy Scout, Billy Bathgate, Striking Distance,* and *Color of Night*. Bruce began opening Planet Hollywoods all over the world, and his high-profile marriage began to fall apart, finally ending in divorce after thirteen years.

Yes, he was great in *Pulp Fiction,* and yes, *Twelve Monkeys* was pretty cool, but neither was good enough to make up for the crap mentioned in the last paragraph. Willis was overexposed in the nineties, period.

Oddly, the less-than-pleasant *Mercury Rising* got Willis pegged as being good with kids. This led him to his greatest success ever, *The Sixth Sense,* where he negotiated twenty percent of the gross on top of his salary. We never said Bruce wasn't good with numbers. If only he was as good at choosing roles. After *The Sixth Sense* came *The Story of Us* and *The Whole Nine Yards.*

Still wondering? Two words: *The Kid*. Actually three . . . Disney's *The Kid* (or "jumped the shark").

Sports

I'm a lifelong Pittsburgh Pirates fan. Thank you for your sympathy.

I will never forget (or forgive) Francisco Cabrera's base hit to score Sid Bream that sent the Atlanta Braves to the World Series and my precious Buccos right over the shark. Bonds, Bonilla, and Van Slyke would be gone, and my team would never be the same.

Sometimes it's an over-the-hill comeback. Or a change in uniform. Maybe it's a bad trade or free agent signing. Even a tailback from USC.

Players, teams, leagues, and owners have been jumping the shark since the first Olympic Games in Athens. And we, the moronic die-hard fans, just keep coming back for more torture. It's what keeps ESPN, twenty-four-hour sports talk radio, and first-time/long-time callers like Vinnie from Brooklyn going.

Sports is tricky when it comes to shark jumping since teams are constantly adding new talent and the balance of power constantly shifts. For example, the New York Yankees have been on top of the baseball world for the past few seasons, but it was only yesterday that they were on the opposite end of the spectrum with Don Mattingly in the lineup. Somehow the jump-the-shark moments manage to shine through it all.

Shark categories are consistent throughout most major sports. Here are a few samples:

Uniforms—The Chicago White Sox try on some shorts

Mascots—Bango of the Milwaukee Bucks loses his green "B" sweater

Drug Rehab—Darryl Strawberry, Dexter Manley, Lloyd Daniels, Lawrence Taylor . . .

Retirement/Comebacks—Sugar Ray, Magic, Michael, Mario . . .

Free Agency—Bobby Bonilla signs with the Mets

The Draft—The Portland Trailblazers take Sam Bowie ahead of a Tarheel named Jordan

Name Changes—Chris Jackson becomes Mahmoud Abdul-Rauf

Acting—Merlin Olsen is Father Murphy

League Rules—Designated hitters, three pointers, instant replay, the BCS . . .

Coaches—Rich Kotite takes control of the New York Jets

Play by Play—Jimmy "The Greek," Marv Albert, Frank Gifford . . .

USC Tailbacks—O.J. Simpson and . . . do I need to type this?

Hall of Fame—Sports Wing

The most blatant shark jumps in sports history (excluding O.J.) are:

10. Major League Baseball goes on strike and skips the World Series.

9. The Montreal Canadiens close the Forum.

8. Scott Norwood kicks it wide right.

7. Michael Jordan trades in number 23 for number 45.

6. Any sports-related item involving the city of Tampa (Lightning, D-Rays, Bucs, Gooden, Strawberry, Sheffield, Steinbrenner, Tropicana Field, etc.).

5. Herman Edwards picks up Larry Csonka's fumble at the Meadowlands.

4. Tonya Harding takes care of Nancy Kerrigan.

3. The New York Islanders don the fisherman jerseys.

2. Notre Dame signs up to be must-see TV.

1. The Boston Red Sox sell Babe Ruth to the New York Yankees.

Marv Albert

1941–

jump the shark?

Marv Albert was more than just a successful play-by-play man. The unprepossessing sportscaster with the obvious toupee was a celebrity of sorts, what with his appearances on *Letterman* and *SNL,* as well as his easily imitated catchphrase "Yes!" In 1997, however, he became more famous than he'd ever wanted to be.

Is Marv kinky? Yes!

Marv had been involved in trysts for some time. His sexual tastes apparently involved biting. One day the tryst bit back. His lover, Vanessa Perhach, accused him of throwing her down on a bed and forcing her to perform oral sex. He also bit her on the back a number of times.

Rumors were flying. Allegedly Albert liked threesomes and wearing feminine undergarments. (These kind of highlights were never played on *Letterman*). Supposedly he was mad at Perhach that day for not bringing a third party. Surprise witness Patricia Masden claimed Marv had bitten her and tried to force her to perform oral sex. That was more than enough for her: She ripped off his toupee and ran. Marv had just jumped the shark.

On the other side, Albert's defense team claimed that Perhach had a history of making inflated allegations against boyfriends who ended relationships with her. Albert's attorney, Roy Black (who'd gotten William Kennedy Smith off in his rape trial), claimed Perhach was angry with Albert since he was about to marry someone else. Much of Marv's argument couldn't come out in court due to rape shield laws preventing the victim's sexual past from being discussed.

BEHIND THE MIC

Hall of Fame broadcasting legends:

1 Bill Stern
2 Curt Gowdy
3 Mel Allen
4 Jim McKay
5 Harry Caray
6 Ernie Harwell
7 Vin Scully
8 Howard Cosell
9 Keith Jackson
10 Pat Summerall

ALLEGED WIGS

Rumor has it that it's not their hair up there:

1 Burt Reynolds
2 William Shatner
3 Sam Donaldson
4 Charles Grodin
5 Rip Taylor
6 Tony Randall
7 Jack Klugman
8 Larry Hagman
9 Steve Martin
10 Don Knotts

Marv knew it was time to throw in the towel. He decided to plead guilty to the biting in order to have the rest of the case dismissed. He was charged with a misdemeanor, and with no previous record, he avoided jail time.

Still, the scandal was out. NBC fired him. (The joke was they gave him a pink slip . . . and he put it on.) Albert laid low for about a year after jumping the shark, but eventually got back into sports broadcasting. It's really the perfect job for him, since TV is full of backbiting.

When did

The Boston Celtics
1946–

jump the shark?

From the parquet floor to Red's cigars, the men in green defined basketball excellence . . . until the 1990s.

Len Bias dies.

The Celtics are one of the original NBA franchises and steeped in a history of tradition. The winking leprechaun and the players were legendary— and the teams were even better.

They became "the Celtics" when Red Auerbach took over as head coach in the early fifties. He drafted Tom Heinsohn and K.C. Jones, and traded for Bill Russell in the middle. Between 1957 and 1969, the Celtics failed to win the title only twice (in '58 and '67). That's a dynasty.

Havlicek stole the ball and the wins kept coming with a memorable championship over the Suns in '76 and a great rivalry with Dr. J's Sixers. GM Auerbach worked his magic by drafting Larry Bird as a junior. The eighties belonged to the Lakers and the Celtics, featuring the Magic/Bird rivalry. Having McHale, DJ, and the Chief didn't hurt either, and the Celts found themselves in the Finals, winning in '81, '84, and '86. We spotted a fin when number 23 entered the NBA and dropped fifty on the Celtics in a first-round playoff game, a sign of things to come.

In 1986, the Celtics had the number-three draft pick and selected Len Bias, a future all-star. Bias was later found dead from cocaine, and the

Celtics had jumped the shark. The once proud franchise would never recover from this unexpected blow.

As Bird, McHale, and Parish retired in the 1990s, no one could fill their shoes. M.L. Carr became coach and GM, and the Celtics' slide continued. In 1993, their one all-star, Reggie Lewis, died from a heart attack while shooting baskets, amongst unproven rumors of cocaine use.

Rick Pitino, savior of many a franchise, was brought in and given full control to restore Celtic pride. The Boston Garden was knocked down and the parquet moved to the Fleet Center. Pitino lasted three years before returning to the safety of Kentucky bluegrass. Put out that cigar . . . the Celtics are just another team in the NBA.

When did

The Boston Red Sox

1901–

jump the shark?

1919. 1946. 1948. 1949. 1967. 1972. 1975. 1978. 1986. So close, yet so far.

The curse of the Bambino.

The Boston Red Sox are steeped in tradition and one of the most respected franchises in the American League. Yet it's been eighty-three years since their last championship. That's right, 1918. Ouch.

The Red Sox won five of the first eighteen World Series ever played, including three in four years ('15,'16,'18), mostly thanks to the acquisition of a pitcher named Ruth. In 1914, the Red Sox purchased the contract of George Herman Ruth from the Baltimore Orioles. One of the best lefties of his day, the Babe also played outfield to get his bat in the lineup.

Following Ruth's stellar season in 1919, owner Harry Frazee sold the

Babe to the New York Yankees for $100,000 and earned his entrance into the Jump the Shark hall of fame. Neither team would ever be the same. Prior to this trade, the Yankees had zero World Series titles. Since this trade, the Red Sox have caught that disease while the Yankees have gone on to win more titles than any other franchise.

The Red Sox have had their chances, but something always seems to get in their way. They had the best team in the league in the late forties, but that didn't seem to help matters. In 1946, Enos Slaughter's baserunning won the Cards a World Series as Johnny Pesky held the ball. Yaz's triple crown couldn't stop Bob Gibson from defeating the Sox three times in the 1967 fall classic.

The seventies were no better. In 1972, the Red Sox were a half game up on the Tigers with three to play . . . Detroit won. And that was just the start. In 1975, the Red Sox won Game Six, the greatest World Series game ever played, as Carlton Fisk waved his homer fair. But heartbreakingly, they still managed to lose Game Seven. The '78 Yankees made up a fourteen-game deficit and Bucky Dent homered off Mike Torrez to win a one-game playoff.

1986 was the worst yet. Ahead in the series with the Mets three games to two and leading 5–3 in the tenth inning of Game Six, the Red Sox were one out away. Base hit, base hit, base hit, and it was 5–4. Enter Bob Stanley who brought the Sox to one strike away . . . and then threw a wild pitch to tie the game. Mookie Wilson hit a grounder right through Bill Buckner's legs, and the Sox were on the way to yet another gut-wrenching defeat.

The nineties saw Roger Clemens in a Yankees uniform, Mo Vaughn's bat disappear in the playoffs, and Pedro Martinez win Cy Youngs, but no rings. The Yankees are the envy of Major League Baseball, and the Red Sox continue to drift in the wake the shark left behind more than eight decades ago.

The Buffalo Bills
1960–

jump the shark?

Everyone remembers the Super Bowl champs, but no one remembers the losers. Unless it's the Buffalo Bills.

Ralph Wilson brought the Bills into the AFL in 1960, and in five short seasons Lou Saban made the Bills league champs. In 1966, Buffalo lost to the Kansas City Chiefs and fell just short of becoming Green Bay's opponent in Super Bowl I. It was a sign of things to come.

> **Scott Norwood hooks it wide right in Tampa.**

HELMET HEADS
Our favorite NFL helmets:

1 New England Patriots (with the snapping Minuteman)
2 Pittsburgh Steelers (with the logo only on one side)
3 Cleveland Browns (I could've done that)
4 San Diego Chargers (white helmet, yellow bolt)
5 Tampa Bay Buccaneers (1976, not that there's anything wrong with that)

O.J. Simpson made the Bills a respectable team during the 1970s, but never a champion. Chuck Knox took over the coaching reins in the late seventies and brought the Bills into the playoffs, but he couldn't advance them to the big game.

In a move that has caused many a franchise to jump the shark, the Bills radically changed their uniforms in 1984, adding a bright red helmet. Two years later, Marv Levy brought his no-huddle offense to rookie Jim Kelly, Thurman Thomas, Andre Reed, and crew, and the Bills became a dominant force in the AFC. Starting in 1990, Levy led the Bills to four straight Super Bowl appearances, but no victories.

The Bills simply dominated the 1990 regular season with a 13–3 record, and earned their first Super Bowl appearance with a 51–3 thrashing of the Los Angeles Raiders. They traveled to Tampa for Super Bowl XXV where they were favored to beat Bill Parcells's New York Giants. The Giants successfully shut down the Bills' potent offense, yet Jim Kelly drove the Bills to the Giants' thirty-yard line with four seconds remaining. All-Pro kicker Scott Norwood tried a

SUPER LOSERS
It's not whether you win or lose, but these teams are great at dropping the big one:

1 Minnesota Vikings
2 Denver Broncos
3 Los Angeles/St. Louis Rams
4 Cincinnati Bengals
5 Miami Dolphins

forty-seven yard field goal and hooked it wide right. Giants 20, Bills 19, Shark 1.

The Bills returned to the Super Bowl the next three years, but were beaten once by the Washington Redskins and trounced twice by the Dallas Cowboys. They continued to post winning records during the regular season with help from their "Twelfth Man," the Rich Stadium crowd. But when the playoffs rolled around, the Bills could never win the big game.

When did

The Chicago Cubs
1876–

jump the shark?

The Chicago Cubs have one of the richest histories in all of sports. They've always had great players—from Tinker to Evers to Chance to Hack Wilson, Ernie (Mr. Cub) Banks, Ferguson Jenkins, and current superstar Sammy (Sr. Cub) Sosa. They've always had a great ballpark—the Friendly Confines of Wrigley Field. But they've been looking back at the shark since 1945.

William "Billygoat" Sianis put a hex on the Cubs in 1945.

It wasn't always like that for the Lovable Losers. From their inception in 1876 as the White Stockings, the Colts, and the Orphans (the team didn't have the official nickname of Cubs until March of 1902 when the name was used by the *Chicago Daily News*), until the curse was enacted in 1945, the Cubs won eleven National League pennants and two World Series titles. Since then, no World Series, no pennants. While the Cubs have had a modicum of success recently, including trips to the playoffs in 1984, 1989, and 1998, on that fateful afternoon in September 1945, the Cubs ran into a shark (or goat, as the case may be) that they couldn't avoid.

DOUBLE TROUBLE

Two Chicago teams share the nickname of the same animal (Cubs and Bears). Other dual nickname cities over the years:

1 St. Louis Cardinals (football and baseball)
2 New York Giants (baseball and football)
3 Colorado Rockies (hockey and baseball)
4 Baltimore Orioles and Ravens
5 Detroit Lions and Tigers

William "Billygoat" Sianis, the owner of a local tavern, bought two tickets to a World Series game between the Cubs and the Detroit Tigers at Wrigley Field. One ticket was for himself, the other was for his goat Murphy. The ushers refused to allow them into the stadium, citing his odor (the goat's, not Sianis's). Sianis stormed out and placed a hex on the Cubs, and with that, the Cubs completed their leap and were rarely to be heard from again. Over the years, the curse was "taken back" several times, the first such occurrence in 1969, a year before Sianis's death. The Cubs actually led the league most of that season, but an unprecedented collapse to the Amazin' Mets prevented the Cubs from jumping back.

And while the Cubs official leap came in 1945, there are those who insist the Cubs jump every year with a promising start to the season followed by the inevitable June swoon. The shark is an epidemic with the Cubs, attaching itself to everything they touch. Wrigley Field jumped when they installed lights in 1981. The Cubs made the leap when they traded Lou Brock for Ernie Broglio (although they may have jumped back when they got Sammy Sosa for George Bell). Harry Caray vaults posthumously every night when celebrities butcher his tradition of singing "Take Me Out to the Ballgame" during the seventh-inning stretch. Even Ronnie "Woo Woo" Fields, the notorious Cubs superfan, jumped with his arrest for public urination.

Sure, the Cubs provide daily summer entertainment for nearly forty thousand fans in the largest beer garden in the world. Sure, the Cubs have produced dozens of All-Stars and Hall of Famers. Sure, the Cubs will win a World Series again. Sure.

NO GRAMMY FOR YOU

Some of the less memorable performances of Take Me Out to the Ballgame

1 Mike Ditka
2 Susan Hawk, *Survivor*
3 Barney
4 Steve McMichael (believed to be the only announcer ever thrown out of a game)
5 The Backstreet Boys

HOME SWEET HOME . . .

Changing ballparks has always been a cause for teams to jump the shark and in some cases, to jump back:

JUMP

1 The Cubs put lights up in Wrigley Field
2 The White Sox open new Comiskey Park
3 The Expos move to Olympic Stadium
4 The Marlins open Pro Player Stadium
5 The Astos move to Enron Field

JUMPED BACK

1 The Indians open Jacobs Field
2 The Mariners open Safeco Field
3 The Orioles open Camden Yards
4 The Blue Jays open SkyDome
5 The Giants open Pac Bell Park

The Chicago White Sox

1900–

jump the shark?

Best-selling books and Oscar-caliber films chronicle when the Sox changed colors back in 1919.

Joe says it ain't so.

Whether owned by Charles Comiskey or Bill Veeck, the Chicago White Sox have always been an intriguing baseball franchise. The "pale hose" won their first championship in 1906, upsetting their crosstown rivals—the 116-win Cubs. The Sox took their second title in 1917, and have been trying to repeat the victory ever since.

SOX STUNTS

The Cubs may be more popular, but Comiskey has had its share of infamous moments:

1 Disco Demolition Night

2 Beer Case Stacking Night

3 Jogging Night

4 Harry Caray throws back another Falstaff

5 The Sox in shorts

The 1919 Chicago White Sox were the equivalent of today's New York Yankees. It seemed like nothing could derail this powerhouse team from winning its second World Series in three years . . . except a gambler named Joseph Sullivan. Owner Charles Comiskey was notorious for paying his players next to nothing, making them prime targets for a fix. Arnold Rothstein was the Manhattan gambler who provided most of the money and only bet on what he could fix.

First baseman Chick Gandil led the players who threw the Series to the Cincinnati Reds, but never got the big payday when the gamblers reneged. Joe Jackson was the best of the eight men that Commissioner Kenesaw Landis booted out of baseball, subsequently helping the White Sox jump the shark.

The White Sox won the pennant in 1959, but fell to the Dodgers in the World Series. It's the closest they've come to a championship since the Black Sox scandal. When Bill Veeck took over the team in the seventies they didn't win any more often, but they had a good time losing. Veeck brought minor league stunts to major league baseball, including Disco Demolition Night and pajama-style uniforms featuring pullovers and shorts.

IT'S HOW YOU LOOK

The White Sox have had some heinous outfits. Others:

1 1979 Pittsburgh Pirates

2 1972 San Diego Padres

3 1976 Cleveland Indians

4 1982 Chicago Cubs

5 Houston Astros (any year)

The 1980s brought Harry Caray, Carlton Fisk, Tony LaRussa, and a playoff appearance, but ended up with the same old results. The nineties saw old Comiskey Park go down, and a sterile new Comiskey Park open its doors. Frank Thomas, Robin Ventura, and Jack McDowell won a division title in stylish black uniforms, but the pennant remained far away. The Sox continue to pay the price for giving the Series away.

When did

The Cincinnati Bengals

1968–

jump the shark?

The history of the Bengals' uniform changes is just as compelling as their thirty-plus seasons playing professional football.

Ickey shuffles.

In the late sixties Paul Brown wanted to get back into professional football, but at the time the Browns were the only game in Ohio. He decided to create a team, and the Bengals were born. They played in the AFL with Brown as their first head coach.

In 1971 the Bengals drafted quarterback Kenny Anderson, who remained at the helm over the next sixteen years. The team had some early success, but didn't really progress until they dumped the classic "Bengals" uniform for their current striped look. That season, they almost hit the jackpot as coach Forrest Gregg took them to Super Bowl XVI—only to fall short to the 49ers 26–21.

CHANGE THOSE SHIRTS

The Bengals switched jerseys, and ended up in the Super Bowl. Other championship switches:

1 Denver Broncos
2 Pittsburgh Penguins
3 Duke Blue Devils
4 Minnesota Twins
5 Houston Rockets

It took seven years, but Sam Wyche brought them back to the big game with Boomer Esiason and all-world tackle Anthony Munoz marching the Bengals down the field. But Joe Montana and the 49ers were waiting and defeated the cats in the Super Bowl once again.

The Bengals never cycled through QBs, but running backs were a different story. Boobie Clark, Pete Johnson, and James Brooks were standouts, but no one could rival the notoriety of Ickey Woods. In their Super Bowl year, Ickey rushed for a league-record fifteen scores, but that paled in comparison to the other way he moved his feet. After each score, he danced "The Ickey Shuffle," a number that would have made Elaine Benes look good. Sadly, a knee injury soon took care of Ickey.

As for the Bengals, they haven't been able to shuffle ever since, becoming one of the most inept franchises in the NFL.

When did

The Cleveland Browns

1946–1995, 1999–

jump the shark?

The came, they saw, they dominated, they struggled, they got moved, they returned, and they were always the Browns.

Drew Carey's favorite football team has the richest history of any NFL franchise. In 1946, coach Paul Brown signed Otto Graham and the Browns started winning. After their first losing season ten years later, the Browns drafted the best running back ever to play the game, Jim Brown. Art Modell purchased the team in 1961 and let Paul Brown go two years later . . . a sign of things to come.

Art Modell leaves town.

They won their final championship in 1964 but remained respectable on the field over the next twenty-five years. Brian Sipe, Greg Pruitt, Bernie Kosar, and Ozzie Newsome all kept the Dawg Pound barking for a champion, and came the closest when John Elway and the Broncos finished them off with "The Drive." As painful as that loss was, it

WHO ARE THOSE GUYS?

You can tell from the helmet that the Browns are the Browns. Other simple approaches:

1 Penn State helmets
2 New York Yankees home uniforms
3 Boston Celtics home uniforms
4 Montreal Canadiens home jerseys
5 Alabama Crimson Tide helmets

couldn't compare to what was coming in 1995.

Following an uncharacteristic 5–11 season, Art Modell announced he was relocating the team to Baltimore. There Modell found luxury boxes and a Super Bowl championship, and he sent the Browns straight over the shark. The city was rightfully up in arms, and it struck a deal with the NFL to not only maintain its name, colors, and heritage, but also to resurrect the Cleveland Browns in four years.

The Cleveland Browns came back to the NFL, losing their opener to their archrival Pittsburgh Steelers 43–0. The rivalry is still there and although they are winning once again, the Browns will never be the same. The history and colors now reside in Browns Stadium, where there will never be a seat available for the man who sent the franchise over the shark.

When did
The Dallas Cowboys
1960–

jump the shark?

Love 'em or loathe 'em, the boys of big D will always be America's Team.

Jerry Jones purchases the club.

The Dallas Cowboys entered the NFL in 1960 with Tex Schramm as GM, Gil Brandt as director of player personnel, and Tom Landry as the head coach. Not a bad hiring class. It took five years for the Cowboys to become winners, but they didn't lose for another twenty after that, despite playing home games with a hole in their roof.

Dallas often got to the big game in the late sixties and early seventies but they couldn't put away Green Bay or Baltimore. They trounced the Dolphins in Super Bowl VI and the Broncos in Super Bowl XII. Revenge was sweet in Super Bowl XXX as they avenged Super Bowl X and XIII losses to their longtime nemesis, the Pittsburgh Steelers. They also beat the Bills a couple of times, but who didn't? Still, winning wasn't the only thing that mattered in Irving, Texas—the cheerleaders did as well.

The Dallas Cowboys Cheerleaders had enough of a following to have their own TV movie. Fans, broadcasters, and opponents were often distracted by the star-spangled gals kicking on the sidelines. They were a key component in making America's Team, although Roger Staubach, Bob Lilly, Tony Dorsett, Robert Newhouse, and Randy White helped matters as well.

When Dallas had its first losing season in twenty years in 1986, we spotted a fin. The once mighty Cowboys won only three games in 1988, and Jerry Jones stepped in to buy the franchise. Although Jerry did bring a Super Bowl to Big D, America's team jumped the shark the day he became the owner. He fired an institution, Tom Landry, and had his college teammate Jimmy Johnson take over the team. Dallas became the best team money could buy, and a lot of winning came with it. But the salary

cap and the aging players have made Big D just another NFL team struggling to get by.

Drug Rehab

jump the shark?

In the good old days of pro sports, no one cared. You could drink yourself silly, shack up with hookers, whatever, so long as you performed on the field. The press knew some players had wild private lives but chose to look the other way.

Thanks to a couple of fellas named Woodward and Bernstein, however, that sort of blind-eye journalism

> **Steve Howe's re-re-re-re-re-re-rehab.**

PATRON SAINTS OF REHAB

Our favorite cases:

1 Robert Downey, Jr.
2 Steve Howe
3 Darryl Strawberry
4 Jerry Garcia
5 Lawrence Taylor

is out. Athletes' lives are as much fodder for reporters as their stats. Throw in the war on drugs and you've got trouble. It goes like this: Pro ball players are young, rich, and popular, and have lots of money. This sort of cohort is bound to be tempted by drugs, and often succumbs to it. When the usage comes to light, teams have to snap to and do something about it, publicly.

The best answer is drug rehab. Not that it succeeds all the time, but at least the player gets to keep playing. Big-time sports have had some well-known cases of drug rehab gone awry. But no one made the concept look more ridiculous than a reliever named Steve Howe.

Howe pitched for the Dodgers and the Yankees, with short stints on the Twins and Rangers in between. He won Rookie of the Year in 1980, and his potential seemed limitless. Unfortunately, he developed a cocaine habit he simply could not shake.

Howe went through a series of drug busts, suspensions, and rehabs. It used to be three strikes you're out, but Major League Baseball no longer saw it that way. Howe didn't have one chance, or two chances—he blew it *seven times* and still the Yankees took him back. That's right, seven drug suspensions, seven new chances. Apparently, he only understood the first word in "drug rehab."

His story demonstrates that drug rehab is

R-O-L-A-I-D-S

This is how we spell relief:

1 Bruce Sutter
2 Mariano Rivera
3 Goose Gossage
4 Dan Quisenberry
5 Rollie Fingers

a p.r. move that allows teams to keep talented players. Meanwhile, Howe redefined the phrase "career high." Ultimately, Howe was barred from coaching his daughter's softball team. At last, a league that had the nerve to stand up to him.

When did
George Foreman
1949–

jump the shark?

George Foreman was not only tough, but downright nasty early in his boxing career. His second career and transformation into the King of the Grill is simply unbelievable.

George **the sitcom.**

Big George was born in Marshall, Texas, in 1949 and won Olympic gold as a heavyweight at age nineteen. Five short years later, he bested Smokin' Joe Frazier to become the heavyweight champion of the world. He seemed unbeatable to everyone except Muhammad Ali, who mocked George's lack of personality before defeating him in 1974's Rumble in the Jungle.

After losing a fight three years later, George experienced a religious awakening, gave up boxing, and became a preacher. He would spend a decade spreading the word of God, but 1987 found George back in the ring at the age of thirty-eight. George was always big, but now he was *wide*—and his preaching showcased a personality never seen before in Foreman the heavyweight. Sponsors lined up as the wins and wisecracks kept coming.

In 1991, at age forty, George went the distance with heavyweight champion Evander

SEVENTIES HEAVYWEIGHTS
Simply the best era for heavyweight boxing:
1. Muhammad Ali
2. Joe Frazier
3. Ken Norton
4. Ernie Shavers
5. Jerry Quarry

COMEBACKS
It was thirty years between titles for George. Now that's a long time to wait. Some others:
1. New York Rangers
2. Montreal Canadiens
3. Boston Celtics
4. St. Louis Cardinals
5. Green Bay Packers

Holyfield, gaining plenty of respect and notoriety in the process. When George started guaranteeing Mieneke mufflers and becoming a pop culture fixture, the sharks were circling.

He took it a step too far in 1993 in the Tony Danza–produced TV comedy *George.* The fans didn't want to see George in a sitcom, and he and his credibility jumped right over the shark. Still, at the age of forty-five, he did manage to knock out the twenty-six-year-old Michael Moore to become heavyweight champ, but boxing had become the Don King equivalent of the World Wrestling Federation. George refused to fight the number-one contender and eventually lost his title. These days, Big George has ten kids (including five boys all named George) and spends his time selling Lean Mean Grilling machines. Shark-kebab, anyone?

When did

Bo Jackson
1962–

jump the shark?

Bo knows
a hip injury.

Before the flamboyant two-sport Deion Sanders, there was the humble two-sport Bo Jackson, whom Nike helped conquer the sporting world.

Bo knows college. Hailing from Alabama, Vincent Edwards Jackson became a high-school sports star in track, baseball, and football. He was drafted by the Yankees, but turned them down to attend Auburn, where he continued to excel in all three sports. His college career culminated with the Heisman Trophy in 1985.

JUST DO IT

Bo is one of many memorable Nike pitchpeople:

1 Michael Jordan
2 Tiger Woods
3 Marion Jones
4 Mia Hamm
5 Greg Maddux and Tom Glavine

Bo knows baseball. Bo was drafted by Tampa Bay as the first selection in the NFL draft, but he rejected their offer to follow his dream of becoming a major league baseball player. Football—despite the Heisman—was his hobby. He signed with the Kansas City Royals in 1986 and had a cup of coffee in the minors before getting called up in September.

Bo knows football. The next year, he was drafted again (since he never signed with Tampa Bay) in the seventh round by the Los Angeles Raiders, and Al Davis had no problem with Bo's baseball career. Bo was not only playing two professional sports, he was the MVP of the 1989 baseball all-star game and an NFL All Pro in 1990.

Bo knows Nike. Oregon shoemakers quickly realized that Bo Jackson had universal appeal, and they developed a campaign around all the different things Bo could do. It was an unprecedented success and further boosted Bo's notoriety around the world. Around the same time, Bo got into the habit of snapping bats across his leg to vent anger, keeping the shark on alert.

Bo knows pain. In a 1991 NFL playoff game against Cincinnati, Bo destroyed his left hip and the invincible two-sport star had jumped the shark. He would never play football again, and the Royals released him. The White Sox picked him up after his hip replacement surgery, but this athletic marvel had been reduced to a DH and limped noticeably when running the bases. He ended his baseball career playing for the California Angels in 1994.

Bo knew it was time to quit.

> **OTHER BOS**
>
> Bo is one of many with the famous moniker:
>
> **1** Bo Derek
>
> **2** Beau Bridges
>
> **3** Bo Duke (*The Dukes of Hazzard*)
>
> **4** Beau De Labarre (*Welcome Back, Kotter*)
>
> **5** Bo Diddley

When did

Michael Jordan
1963–

jump the shark?

Michael Jordan playing in the NBA is like your thirteen-year-old brother playing with your fellow six-year-old friends. The difference is that the NBA consists of the best basketball players on the planet. Yet not one of them could stop number 23.

Michael was born in Brooklyn, New York, and grew up in Wilmington, North Carolina. As a high school sophomore, Michael was passed over by the varsity team, which jump-

Number 23 becomes number 45.

started his competitive drive and work ethic. He became a Tarheel and hit the winning shot for the NCAA Championship his freshman year. The next year, he was selected as the third pick in the NBA Draft (behind Akeem Olajuwon and Sam Bowie) by the lowly Chicago Bulls.

The professional trophies started to pour in with Rookie of the Year honors, but Michael gained true superstar status by winning two slam dunk contests and giving birth to Air Jordan. MJ perennially led the league in scoring, and in the 1985 playoffs he dropped fifty on the Boston Celtics during a Bulls first-round series loss. Michael surpassed the game of Bird and Magic with his spectacular dunks and infectious smile, bringing the NBA to new marketing heights.

The nineties saw MJ carry the Bulls past the Pistons and on to three consecutive NBA titles. Nike, Gatorade, and other endorsements made him a marketing gold mine. It seemed that nothing could stop Michael Jordan. Then, tragedy struck in 1993 when two teenagers murdered Michael's father. Michael retired from basketball (although some conspiracy theorists suggest he was suspended from the NBA due to gambling) and surprised us all by attempting to become a professional baseball player. The shark was circling.

The Bulls' owner allowed Michael to play for his baseball team, the Chicago White Sox, for which MJ donned number 45. Although Jordan was very serious about baseball, he looked like a mere mortal on the diamond. The next season, Michael returned to the NBA with an "I'm back" fax, but he kept his number 45 on the basketball court and subsequently jumped the shark. The Bulls were knocked out of the playoffs by the Orlando Magic, and for the first time in the nineties Michael left the NBA Playoffs empty-handed.

Michael returned as number 23 the next season and brought home three more NBA Championships before retiring again in 1998. He then became a part owner of the Washington Wizards, but suffered in the skybox as he watched his team lose. In 2001 he returned again, but without the triangle offense or coach Phil Jackson, and surrounded by Wizards, things just aren't the same. Still among the league leaders in scoring, Michael is on a mediocre team and soaring at a lower altitude. Now when fans say they want to be like Mike, they mean one thing . . . rich.

When did

Bobby Knight
1940–

jump the shark?

The technical foul wasn't created specifically for the General, it only seems that way.

Robert Montgomery Knight grew up in Ohio as a tough, stubborn, and brutally honest man. By the time the Ohio State grad was twenty-five years old, he was the head basketball coach for Army, the youngest in Division I history. His temper was there from day one, but so were the results—winning.

After his success at Army, Bobby Knight had his choice of prime jobs, and chose Indiana University to be close to home and in the heart of hoop country. He brought the discipline of West Point with him and reached the Final Four in only his second year of coaching IU. In 1975,

The chair toss.

they won thirty-one straight before succumbing to Kentucky in the regional final. The next year the team went 32–0 and garnered a national title, and the General's only response was that it should have been two. This was not a "player's coach."

Bobby Knight won two more NCAA titles in the eighties and a pre–Dream Team Olympic gold medal in 1984. It was the method to his March madness that was always in question. He wouldn't hesitate to literally grab a player and berate him "for his own good," going so far as to kick his own son Patrick to make a point. He was revered and feared by the IU faithful. What often got lost in the shuffle of the endless winning seasons at IU was the fact that most of Knight's players actually graduated and went on to lead successful lives outside of basketball. Bobby Knight's version of tough love has generated mixed results, but it has also shown his passion to win.

His tirades were legendary, and no one was spared. We spotted a fin at the 1984 Pan Am games when he was tried (and convicted in absentia) over a dispute with a cop about time in a practice gym. In a game against Purdue the next year, he got everyone's attention—and another T—by hurling a chair across the court. He received a standing ovation from the Assembly Hall faithful, but Bobby Knight had jumped the shark and would never again command the respect he had become accustomed to from players, coaches, and fans.

IU did keep winning, but its championship days were over. First- or second-round NCAA tournament losses became the rule, not the exception. Investigations into Coach Knight's abuse of players, both verbal and physical, kept cropping up. The University finally placed him on probation when a videotape featuring his hands around the neck of a player surfaced. In 2000, when student Kent Harvey said "Hey, Knight, what's up?" the Coach grabbed his arm and gave him a lecture on respect. Knight was dismissed, and the student body, former players, and coaches all protested the firing, underscoring the respect Bobby Knight had earned over time.

Sugar Ray Leonard

1956–

jump the shark?

There's an old saying in comedy—"Always leave 'em laughing." If there were a similar saying in boxing it would be "always leave before you get brain damage." Sugar Ray Leonard didn't do any permanent damage when he stuck around too long—except to the memory of his career.

The fourth comeback.

Sugar Ray was one of the greatest boxers ever to grace the squared circle. Born Ray Charles Leonard (named after the singer, though his later nickname was in honor of fighter Sugar Ray Robinson), he had won the Olympic boxing gold medal as a light-welterweight by the age of twenty. He had planned to retire, but then decided to go pro instead.

In 1979, Sugar Ray became the welterweight champ by defeating Wilfred Benitez. He then lost the title and won it back from Roberto Duran. In probably his greatest fight, he defeated Tommy Hearns by a TKO in the fourteenth round in 1981. They reversed roles that night, with the slugger Hearns outboxing Leonard and Leonard outslugging Hearns.

No Más

He came back one too many times, but Sugar Ray Leonard took on some great opponents during his career:

1 Roberto Duran
2 Marvin Hagler
3 Thomas Hearns
4 Wilfred Benitez
5 Hector Camacho

Leonard got a detached retina during training in 1982. Before it got worse, he announced his retirement. In 1984, missing the spotlight, he came back, and the shark began to circle.

He hoped to fight middleweight champ Marvelous Marvin Hagler. After an unimpressive win against Kevin Howard, an unranked boxer, Sugar Ray decided to retire for good. Turns out "for good" in Leonard-speak meant a few years; the shark was closing in.

Leonard faced Hagler in 1987 and won. In fact, he kept fighting and (mostly) winning until he lost to Terry Norris in 1991. Predictably, Leonard retired yet again. This time he didn't return to the ring until 1997, when he finally jumped the shark.

Hector "Macho" Camacho slaughtered Leonard, an old man of forty. The fight was stopped in the fifth round. Leonard had sullied his beautiful career by leaving his fans with the memory of him at his worst. We'd almost rather see him pontificating with Larry Merchant on HBO. Almost.

Major League Baseball

1903–

jump the shark?

If you've seen *The Natural* or the Ken Burns documentary, you know what baseball means to America . . . and how dramatically "the game" has changed over the years.

> **The 1994 strike.**

From the first World Series in 1903, America identified with baseball as its game and national pastime. Baseball's first commissioner, Judge Kenesaw Mountain Landis, oversaw the Black Sox scandal and was awed by Murderer's Row. Happy Chandler and Ford Frick presided over the battles of the Yankees, Giants, and Dodgers during the forties, fifties, and early sixties, when every kid growing up wanted to be a baseball player. The game expanded with new franchises, the Dodgers, Giants, and Senators headed west, and the business of baseball was booming.

MLB MISHAPS

Baseball has its notable watershed moments:

1 The Strike
2 Free agency
3 The designated hitter
4 Interleague play
5 Establishing, and abolishing, the Commissioner's office

Everything started to change, for better or worse, when Bowie Kuhn became the commissioner of baseball. He successfully prevented a strike early on, but when Curt Flood challenged the reserve clause in 1970, the game was to change forever. Five years later, Andy Messersmith and Dave McNally were the first free agents—they could sign with any team for the right price. It was hard to root for your favorite team now that the players would be changing frequently. But baseball continued to thrive.

New generic Astroturf stadiums were popping up all over, and each league was divided into two divisions. We spotted a fin in 1973 when the American League was seeking more offense and instituted the designated hitter. Ron Blomberg stepped in for the Yankees, and the game and its strategy were sharply altered.

There had been baseball strikes, but none was as devastating as the 1994 work stoppage. The game was stopped for 234 days, no World Series was played, owners and players were

FLIPPING

Our favorite brands of baseball cards:

1 Topps
2 Upper Deck
3 Fleer
4 Donruss
5 Bowman

vilified, and the game had jumped the shark. The owners got rid of an "objective" commissioner and promoted one of their own for the position. Basketball and football had passed the game by, and even hockey threatened to become a more popular pastime. Interleague play was an attempt to spice things up. It worked in cities with two teams, but failed elsewhere throughout the league. The McGwire/Sosa home run challenge brought many fans back to the game, but it just wasn't the same. World Series games now take place in November and rarely end before midnight.

The youth of America is filled with hoop dreams these days, and baseball has no one to blame but its greedy self.

When did **Men's Tennis**
1875–

jump the shark?

The fate of men's tennis is remarkably similar to boxing . . . the seventies had the all-time greats, the eighties started the slide, the nineties featured a great rivalry, and no one is paying attention today.

> **John McEnroe hangs up his racquet.**

Years before Bud Collins ever invited us for breakfast, the first Wimbledon championships were played on the famed green lawns of England. The tourney and the game haven't changed much since 1875, but the players certainly have.

The golden age of men's tennis came in the 1970s—when Arthur Ashe, Rod Laver, John Newcombe, Jimmy Connors, and Bjorn Borg dominated the sport. John McEnroe and Ivan Lendl made their respective marks in the early eighties, and tennis was as popular as any other sport. Prince racquets were popping up all over the country.

TENNIS ANYONE?

Can you really get pumped to tailgate at any of the championship locations?:

1 Roland Garros—The French Open
2 Wimbledon—The Lawn Tennis Championships
3 Flushing Meadow—The U.S. Open
4 Melbourne Park—The Australian Open
5 Forest Hills—The U.S. Open (previously)

Andre Agassi and Pete Sampras carried the sport into the nineties with some help from Stefan Edberg and Boris Becker. But fans were really tuning in to see if an aging McEnroe and Connors had one more special match left in them. The Mats Wilander vs. Jim Courier final just doesn't pack the same kind of heat.

When John McEnroe finally hung it up in 1992, the emotion of men's tennis seemed to leave with him, and the sport jumped the shark. Unless Agassi and Sampras are playing these days, no one is tuning in to this sport of champions. The talent is still there, but the personality is gone and it feels like the top players have been created, not born. Who is the next wunderkind? More importantly, who cares? Tennis desperately needs a Tiger Woods with a backhand.

When did The Montreal Canadiens jump the shark?

1910–

No NHL franchise has sipped from the Stanley Cup as many times as le Club de Hockey Canadien. The "organ-i-zation" is widely considered to be the class of professional hockey. Winning twenty-four championships probably has something to do with that.

The Habs bid *au revoir* to the Forum.

The Canadiens were one of the four founding teams of the National Hockey League in 1917, and won the league's first championship (with the classic CH logo emblazoned across their jerseys). Westmount Arena, the Canadiens' home ice, was destroyed by a fire and eventually replaced in 1924 by the Forum on St. Catherine's. The owner of the Rangers was mistakenly told the *H* in the logo stood for Habitant and referred to the team as the Habs. It stuck.

Many a superstar graced the famed ice of the Forum as the Habs piled up Cups over the next few decades. Captains Toe Blake, Maurice "The Rocket" Richard, Jean Beliveau, Henri Richard, and Yvan Cournoyer not only carried the team's legacy, but had great-sounding hockey names as well. Gump Worsley, Jacques Plante, Rogie Vachon, and Ken Dryden kept the pucks out from between the pipes.

In 1978, Molson took over the ownership of the Canadiens, and a fin was spotted circling the ice. The New York Islanders and later the Edmonton Oilers put a stop to the Habs' string of titles. The Habs managed a twenty-fourth Cup in 1993 when they defeated the Wayne Gretzky–led Los Angeles Kings in five games, and then began construction on a new stadium. The Canadiens were leaving the Forum—hurtling themselves directly over the shark.

The storied franchise hasn't come near the Stanley Cup finals since its move to the Molson Centre. The Habs did the unthinkable in trading away the game's best goaltender, Patrick Roy, to Colorado—where he would pick up some additional championship hardware. The captains' names were now Muller and Koivu, and even Guy Lafleur came out of retirement to play with the Rangers! Perhaps San Jose jerseys would be more appropriate for the Canadiens these days.

The National Basketball Association

1946–

jump the shark?

> **Number 23 hangs it up for the second time.**

The only sure things in this life are death, taxes, and watching the last three minutes of any NBA game and not missing a thing.

Although the NBA logo hasn't changed at all, the game of basketball has evolved from peach baskets and 2–0 defensive struggles into the slam- and three-fest we see today. Professional basketball was a second-tier sport in its early going. George Mikan's retirement and the 24-second shot clock in the mid-fifties brought much needed offense into the game as the Celtics began their run of eleven championships in thirteen years.

The sixties welcomed the Big O, Jerry West, and Wilt Chamberlain to the NBA. Havlicek stole the ball and Bill Russell won more Celtic titles. The seventies began with Willis Reed's heroics, Lew Alcindor's name change to Kareem, and the integration of the ABA into the NBA—along with its star Julius Erving. The NBA became marketing-savvy as well, and was poised for a huge leap as hoops became the sport of the streets.

Magic Johnson and Larry Bird took the league to the next level in the early eighties. Pat Riley's Showtime battled the Celtics, Sixers, and Pistons for most of the decade. But the 1984 draft was the launch pad to NBA superstardom, as marketing guru David Stern was now the league commissioner. Akeem Olajuwon, Charles Barkley, John Stockton, and some guy named Jordan joined Magic and Bird, and the league had the marquee talent it had always sought. This was the nucleus of the future Dream Team that was matched against the Lithuanian starting five . . . true Olympic spirit.

A LEAGUE OF THEIR OWN

Other basketball leagues are out there . . . until the NBA sucks them in:

1 CBA
2 ABA
3 USBL
4 WNBA
5 Harlem Globetrotters take on the Washington Generals

THE WACK PACK

These NBA players would have been great guests on Howard Stern:

1 Manute Bol
2 Muggsy Bogues
3 Mark Eaton
4 Shawn Bradley
5 Dikembe Mutombo (he is!)

Michael Jordan won the slam dunk contest, got a Nike deal, and became an international superstar. The NBA wisely hitched a ride with number 23 and put all their balls in his basket. Everyone around the world wanted to be like Mike. When MJ retired to play baseball in 1993 the league lost a step, but stabilized itself with the Rockets on top. Michael returned to guide the Bulls to three more titles, but NBA action was not as fantastic.

When Jordan retired for the second time in 1998, the NBA had jumped the shark. The NBA logo was everywhere, but in practice lacked its superstar power. The league spent its time looking for the next Michael Jordan and forgot about the rest of the teams. Shaq and Allen Iverson just don't have Jordan's appeal, and many fans seem to have gone elsewhere. But with Michael back for a third run, this time as a Washington Wizard, the NBA hopes there's some magic left.

When did

The National Hockey League
1946–

jump the shark?

Florida has two teams.

The happy little trees on *The Joy of Painting* draw more fans than a National Hockey League telecast. Unless you're watching in Canada, of course.

The NHL got its official start in 1917 with the Montreal Canadiens winning their first of twenty-four championships. Less than a decade later, American teams began to be integrated—making the NHL the first international professional sports league.

The Detroit Red Wings, Chicago Blackhawks, New York Rangers, Boston Bruins, Toronto Maple Leafs, and Montreal Canadiens were the NHL's "original six" in the early forties. It took twenty-five years for the Zamboni to usher

THE BIG SCREEN

The movies draw more fans than the league does. Our favorites:

1 *Slap Shot*
2 *The Mighty Ducks*
3 *Youngblood*
4 *Mystery Alaska*
5 *Strange Brew*

in six more teams, the St. Louis Blues, Philadelphia Flyers, Los Angeles Kings, Pittsburgh Penguins, Minnesota North Stars, and Oakland Seals. Expansion meant a dilution of talent and more offense, and Bobby Hull, Phil Esposito, and Gordie Howe became the league's first 100-point scorers. In the seventies hockey's claim to fame was its fighting, and Dave Schultz, Terry O'Reilly, and Tiger Williams rarely let us down.

At the start of the eighties, the WHA was folded into the NHL to create its "everyone makes the playoffs" format. The game was cleaned up a bit as the Lake Placid "Miracle on Ice" brought hockey to another level. The Great One came on the scene and his Edmonton Oilers dethroned the Islander dynasty. European players joined the Canadians and Americans, and the league became high-scoring end-to-end action. Mario Lemieux and Wayne Gretzky, two of the all-time greats, were playing in their prime, but few south of Niagara Falls tuned in.

NBA wunderkind Gary Bettman was brought in as league commissioner to make the NHL the next sports marketing success story. Expansion was everywhere, but the fans weren't. Canadian teams couldn't keep up with the costs, and Quebec and Winnipeg became Colorado and Phoenix. Wayne Gretzky was an L.A. King. Canada was abandoned, Florida had two teams, and the NHL had jumped the shark. The league continues to search for national recognition, but we'd take the Hansons over the left wing lock any day.

TROPHY CASES

The ultimate championship trophy is Lord Stanley's cup. Honorable mentions:

1 Vince Lombardi Trophy (silver football)

2 Lawrence O'Brien trophy (gold basketball)

3 World Series trophy (gold stadium with flags flying)

4 Wimbledon plate (there's one in your grandma's living room)

5 America's Cup (doesn't matter what country's boats are better)

When did

The New York Giants

1925–

jump the shark?

Early on, all was humming along for the New York football Giants. Since their formation by Tim Mara (for a $500 expansion fee) in 1925, they were one of the most successful teams in the NFL. From 1925–1963 the Giants won sixty-three per-

> **The Miracle in the Meadowlands.**

cent of their games, four NFL Championships, and appeared in eleven other Championship games.

During the 1950s Tom Landry handled the defense and Vince Lombardi the offense for head coach Jimmy Lee Howell. It was widely understood that Howell was just a front man and Lombardi and Landry were the force behind the Giants' success. At the end of the decade both Lombardi and Landry were offered jobs to build (or rebuild in Lombardi's case) franchises from the ground up. The loyal Tim Mara would not ask Jimmy Lee Howell to step down in order to promote either of his coaching prodigies to the head coach position and keep them in the organization.

Mara's loyalty would cost him. Just one year after Lombardi and Landry left, Howell retired and we spotted a fin. While new coach Ally Sherman was able to win with a talented team for three years, he proved incapable of rebuilding the team as it aged. By 1964 the Giants were losers, winning just thirty percent of their games over the next twenty years. Lombardi and Landry, on the other hand, combined for ten NFL/NFC Championships between 1961 and 1978.

After more than two decades of mediocrity, the Giants jumped with the "Miracle in the Meadowlands." By this time, Mara had passed

DOUBLE TEAMS

Teams that coexisted with the same name:

1 New York Giants (NFL & MLB)
2 Brooklyn Dodgers (MLB & AAFC)
3 New York Yankees (MLB & NFL)
4 St. Louis Cardinals (MLB & NFL)
5 Pittsburgh Pirates (NFL & MLB)

SAME NAME, DIFFERENT CITY

Active franchises that share their nickname with another city:

1 New York & San Francisco Giants (NFL & MLB)
2 Chicago/Arizona & St. Louis Cardinals (NFL & MLB)
3 Texas & New York Rangers (MLB & NHL)
4 Carolina & Florida Panthers (NFL & NHL)
5 Sacramento & Los Angeles Kings (NBA & NHL)

away and his heirs were feuding, running the team without actually speaking to each other. The two Mara factions each controlled fifty percent of the team, making for an impossible situation and lots of embarrassment for the NFL. On November 19, 1978, rather than taking a knee and running out the clock against the Eagles, QB Joe Pisarcik attempted a handoff to Larry Csonka. *Attempted* is the key word here, as the handoff bounced off Csonka and popped up into the air, where Eagle rookie DB Herman Edwards caught it. The future Jets head coach returned the fumble for a TD and won the game for the Eagles. Things couldn't get any worse.

The Mara family eventually responded by hiring former Colts GM George Young. He drafted Phil Simms and Lawrence Taylor, and in 1982 promoted defensive coach Bill Parcells to head coach. Parcells managed to lead the Giants to two Super Bowl victories, but then left the team in the incapable hands of Roy Handley. There were bad times and good times ahead, but every Giants fan still feels the bite from that fateful fumble in '78.

When did
The New York Islanders
1972–

jump the shark?

In less than thirty years, the Islanders have experienced more highs and lows than any other NHL franchise.

The Isles came on the scene in the early seventies when New York Nets owner Roy Boe brought a hockey team to Long Island. The Islanders and Nets would share the Nassau Veterans Memorial Coliseum, still known as one of the worst sports arenas ever built.

The fisherman jerseys.

After a predictably lousy first season, GM Bill Torrey hired head coach Al Arbour, drafted Denis Potvin, and began to build a hockey dynasty—all in a very short period of time. They made their mark by knocking the crosstown-rival

---

TREASURE ISLAND

They weren't stars, but these were Islanders:

1 Bob Bourne
2 Stefan Persson
3 Ed Westfall
4 Anders Kallur
5 Garry Howatt

Rangers out of the playoffs only two years later. Bryan Trottier, Mike Bossy, and Billy Smith joined the club, which improved each year. In 1979, Butch Goring was the missing piece of the puzzle, and original Islander Bob Nystrom took a feed from John Tonelli to defeat the Flyers in overtime and gave Long Island its first Stanley Cup.

The Islanders would win four Cups in a row and were poised to take a fifth, but Wayne Gretzky and the Edmonton Oilers put an end to that with a dynasty of their own. The Isles haven't seen the finals since then, and have made it to the conference finals only once in the past twenty years. They remained a formidable franchise in the early eighties, but Pat Lafontaine and Pat Flatley weren't Bossy and Gillies, and Kelly Hrudey was no Chico Resch.

The Islanders seemed to come out of their doldrums with their 1993 playoff upset of the two-time defending Cup champion Pittsburgh Penguins. The next season Bill Torrey left for Florida, Al Arbour moved to the front office, and big boss John Pickett continued his run as an absentee owner. The '94 season brought an end to the "1940" chants as the Rangers finally won a cup. The Isles answered the next year with a new jersey featuring the Gorton's fisherman wielding a hockey stick and an angry look. All tradition had been abandoned with this hall of fame jump over the shark.

Mike Milbury became the new GM, and the Isles were having a permanent fire sale, dealing their all-stars around the league. Pickett not only was never there, but he didn't want to sell the team. When John Spanos came along to rescue the Isles, he was arrested for fraud and the team went back to Pickett. Howard Milstein and Steven Gluckstern bought the team as a real estate purchase and deemed the Coliseum unsafe, attempting to move the Isles without success. The memories of championship hockey hang from the rafters of the Coliseum . . . assuming it hasn't collapsed yet.

When did

The New York Jets

1960–

jump the shark?

Gang Green fans have experienced so much frustration with their beloved "J-E-T-S, Jets! Jets! Jets!" it's difficult to pinpoint the precise moment when the team jumped.

The fake spike.

The Jets began in the AFL in 1960 as the New York Titans, with Sammy Baugh as the head coach. Three years later, Leon Hess and four others purchased the team and renamed it the Jets, hiring Weeb Ewbank as the new coach. The Jets, led by Matt Snell and Joe Namath, were winners who, by 1967, sold out every Sunday.

The next season, the Jets battled the Raiders in a crucial game that the Jets led by three with one minute left. In a move that almost sent a network over the shark, NBC cut to a telecast of *Heidi* as the Raiders scored twice in the last minute to win the game. But even the "Heidi Bowl" couldn't keep Gang Green from its destiny. After revenging the Raiders loss in the AFL Championship, Joe Namath guaranteed the underdog Jets a Super Bowl victory over the Baltimore Colts . . . and he delivered.

Jets fans have been suffering ever since. The seventies featured a perennially injured Joe Namath, Lou Holtz taking and leaving the head coaching job in less than a year, and a horrendous uniform change. The Jets reached the AFC Championship in the early eighties, only to be shut out by the rival Miami Dolphins. They moved from Shea Stadium to the Meadowlands and their new home field, Giants Stadium. Joe

---

BROADWAY JOE

Who says football players can't act? Our favorite primetime thespians:

1 Fran Tarkenton (*That's Incredible*)
2 Alex Karras (*Blazing Saddles*)
3 Lawrence Taylor (*Any Given Sunday*)
4 Rolf Bernischke (*Wheel of Fortune*)
5 O.J. Simpson (various killer roles)

DON'T GO CHANGING

Thankfully, the Jets have returned to their original uniforms. Other NFL gaffes:

1 Cincinnati Bengals (too many stripes)
2 Denver Broncos (where's the orange?)
3 Tampa Bay Buccaneers (not that there's anything wrong with the Buccaneer)
4 Atlanta Falcons (bring back the red helmet)
5 Baltimore Ravens (should still be the Cleveland Browns)

Walton had followed Walt Michaels without much success, but the coaching carousel was just getting started.

The shark was closing in when head coach Bruce Coslet took over, but it was under the one-year reign of Pete Carroll that the Jets finally jumped the shark. The Jets were battling the Dolphins for first place and had a 24–6 lead when Dan Marino rallied his team in the second half to get within three points. In the closing seconds, Marino faked a spike and threw a TD over the stunned Jets D. The team finished last in the division, and has not been the same since.

Leon Hess's handpicked successor Rich Kotite coached for the next two seasons and won a total of four games. Enter coach/GM/deity Bill Parcells, who resurrected the Jets for a season and took them to the AFC Championship in 1998. Eddie the fireman wasn't the only one believing the Jets had jumped back. But by the next season, Parcells was gone and his hand-picked successor, Bill Belichick, turned down the head coaching job, heading to the division rival and future Super Bowl champion New England Patriots. The Jets have burned through two coaches since then as they try to make their way back to the site of Broadway Joe's finest moment.

When did
The New York Mets
1962–

jump the shark?

Love them or hate them, the New York Mets have displayed plenty of personality over the past forty years.

Mike Scioscia takes Doc Gooden deep.

The New York Metropolitans, whose colors remind us of the departed Dodgers and Giants, played their first game in 1962 under manager Casey Stengel and were simply dreadful. Two years later they were playing in their new home at Shea Stadium, accompanied by the sound of planes flying overhead from LaGuardia Airport. In 1966, the Mets acquired Tom Seaver and began their ascent to becoming World Series champions as the Miracle Mets of 1969.

During the early seventies Willie Mays came home as a Met and the team returned to the Series in '73, only to fall to the powerful Oakland A's. The late seventies were horrific times, featuring the trade of Tom Seaver, the dominance of the New York Yankees, and George Foster promising us forty games on SportsChannel. Things improved when Dwight Gooden, Keith Hernandez, Darryl Strawberry, and Gary Carter came into the fold and brought a swagger with them.

In arguably the most exciting baseball postseason run of all time, the Mets took the Astros in a dramatic six game series, and then beat the Red Sox in seven games (thank you Bob Stanley and Bill Buckner) for their second World Series victory. Davey Johnson's Mets were unbeatable and happy to tell everyone about it. Two years later, they won one hundred games and were poised to win another title.

Enter Mike Scioscia. The Mets were poised to take a 3–1 series lead with Gooden on the mound up by three runs, but Scioscia took him deep, tied the game, and the Mets had jumped the shark. The trades next year were horrendous, dealing Lenny Dykstra and Roger McDowell for Juan Samuel, and later trading Samuel for Mike Marshall and Alejandro Peña. The next season Bud Harrelson replaced Davey Johnson, Darryl Strawberry left for L.A., and free agent/tarp expert Vince Coleman was brought in.

Unable to ever get by the Atlanta Braves, the Mets finally returned to the World Series in 2000 to face the dreaded nemesis New York Yankees. The Mets were on their way to winning Game One in Yankee Stadium when Armando Benitez gave up four runs and a Yankees victory. Where are Jesse Orosco, Doug Sisk, and Roger McDowell when you need them?

The New York Rangers

1927–

jump the shark?

"1940!" It took fifty-four years to silence the chant, but only one more to see the team jump.

> **They let the captain ride away.**

The NHL gave Madison Square Garden a franchise in 1927, and Garden president Tex Rickert built a winner. Tex's Rangers finished lower than second only twice in the team's first sixteen years in the league, culminating with their third Stanley Cup in 1940.

Rangers fans suffered for the next thirty years, pinning their hopes on star players like Gump Worsley, Andy Bathgate, and Harry Howell. When the NHL expanded in 1967, coach and GM Emile "the Cat" Francis led the Rangers to nine consecutive playoff appearances. Jean Ratelle, Vic Hadfield, and "Mr. Ranger" Rod Gilbert powered the team, with Ed Giacomin between the pipes, but the Blueshirts continued to come up short when it was playoff time.

> ## KEENAN'S TRAVELS
>
> A few of the memorable stops during Iron Mike's career
>
> 1 Philadelphia Flyers
> 2 Chicago Blackhawks
> 3 Boston Bruins
> 4 St. Louis Blues
> 5 Florida Panthers

The Rangers made "the trade" in 1975, sending Brad Park, Jean Ratelle, and Joe Zanussi to the hated Bruins in exchange for Phil Esposito and Carol Vadnais. Joined by Anders Hedberg, Ulf Nilsson, and goaltender John Davidson, the Rangers would have plenty of winning during the regular season, but the rival Islanders were busy building a Stanley Cup dynasty of their own. Hall of Famers Craig Patrick and Espo couldn't get a cup as GMs in the eighties, but when Neil Smith took over, the Rangers' fortune was about to change.

Smith brought in head coach Mike Keenan and captain Mark Messier to show the team how to win. It took four years, but after thrilling series with the Devils and Canucks, the Rangers captured the elusive Stanley Cup. One month later, Keenan quit over a pay dispute and the shark was cir-

> ## MATTEAU! MATTEAU!
>
> Memorable overtime goals that won the Stanley Cup:
>
> 1 Bobby Orr—1970 Boston Bruins
> 2 Bobby Nystrom—1980 New York Islanders
> 3 Brett Hull—1999 Dallas Stars
> 4 Pete Babando—1950 Detroit Red Wings
> 5 Bryan Hextall—1940 New York Rangers

cling. The great Wayne Gretzky rejoined his teammate Messier in New York for a season, but the two failed to get another Cup together.

Messier was not only the captain, but the heart and soul of the team. In 1997, with both sides to blame, he left to play in Vancouver, and the Rangers subsequently jumped the shark. Under three different head coaches and a new GM the Rangers have not only failed to make the play-offs, but are one of the worst teams in the NHL. Messier has since returned, but the chant of "1994!" has already started to make its way through arenas across the country.

When did

The Notre Dame Fighting Irish

1918–

jump the shark?

The boys from South Bend became must-see TV.

Cheer, cheer for old Notre Dame, and then be sure to catch a Very Special *Blossom* on NBC.

When it comes to college sports, few universities can rival this small school in South Bend, Indiana. The Fighting Irish are steeped in tradition and synonymous with the words "college football."

FIGHT SONGS

The Notre Dame victory march is one of the best. Other showstoppers:

1 "The Victors"—Michigan
2 "On Wisconsin"—Wisconsin
3 "Boomer Sooner"—Oklahoma
4 "Yea Alabama"—Alabama
5 "Ramblin' Wreck"—Georgia Tech

The "Notre Dame Victory March" was first played in 1908, and has since become one of the nation's most popular college fight songs. Head coach Knute Rockne built the Irish tradition with his famed speeches, the four horsemen rode and were immortalized by Grantland Rice.

Frank Leahy picked up where Knute left off, and Paul Hornung carried on the tradition by winning the Heisman in 1956. Head coach Ara Parseghian took the Irish to the next level in the sixties and early seventies. Despite having

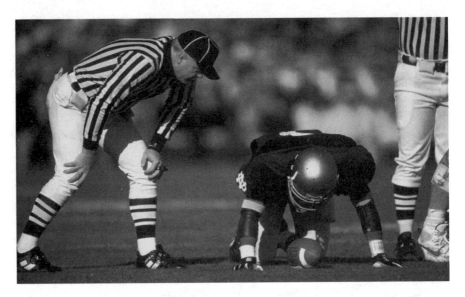

adopted the leprechaun as its mascot, Ara and his successor Dan Devine just kept winning.

We saw the shark circling when Gerry Faust took over in the early eighties, but he was replaced by Lou Holtz, who built Notre Dame into the most commercially popular school in all of college athletics. Not only did Holtz win, but he let everyone know how good the Fighting Irish were.

The early nineties saw Notre Dame enter into an exclusive contract with NBC to broadcast all Irish home games. Touchdown Jesus hasn't been the same since, and the commercial breaks have caused Notre Dame to jump the shark.

Lou Holtz left the Irish, and is now coaching the Gamecocks in South Carolina. Successor Bob Davie struggled each year and was let go. His replacement, George O'Leary, lasted less than two weeks when inaccuracies on his coaching resume were spotted. The once-feared Irish languish near .500 and fail to carry the aura of earlier seasons. The highlight of Irish football for the past decade was the film *Rudy*. This once-proud football school is now a middle-of-the-road squad. If you don't believe it, tune in to NBC all season to witness it for yourself.

When did

Olympic Basketball

1932–

jump the shark?

Canadian Dr. James Naismith may have invented basketball in 1891, but from the very beginning the U.S. has ruled. Nowhere was this dominance made more evident than at the Olympic Games.

> **The Soviet "victory" in '72.**

Basketball first became an Olympic sport in 1932. The U.S. won every gold medal up to 1968, never losing a single game. The teams were made up of top college players and no other country seemed able to match their talent. In 1972, there was no reason to believe the streak would end. The team had little trouble reaching the finals, where they met the underdog Soviet Union team. If the U.S. prevailed, it would mean seventy-two consecutive wins and another gold.

The game was surprisingly hard-fought, with the Soviets matching the Americans basket for basket. With three seconds left, Doug Collins sunk two free throws to put the U.S. ahead 50–49 (even though a buzzer went off during his second shot). The Soviets would have to inbound the ball, cross the entire floor, and score in three seconds. It didn't look good.

In the last three controversial seconds, however, they'd get more than one chance.

The Soviets inbounded once and failed to score, but for some reason a ref had whistled the play dead with one second left. The clock was reset but the ball was inbounded, this time before the timekeeper was ready. The Soviets failed to score a second time and the Americans started celebrating. But after discussions at the highest level, the clock was reset yet again.

The third time was the charm for the

MEMORIES OF MUNICH

Lowlights from the 1972 Olympics:

1 Murder of eleven Israeli athletes
2 U.S. basketball loss
3 Rick DeMont stripped of gold medal for asthma medication
4 Runners Vince Matthews and Wayne Collett banned after screwing around on victory podium
5 U.S. fails to get gold for the first time ever in the pole vault

---

LOVE ME TWO TIMES

These cities have hosted the Olympics more than once:

1 Athens
2 Paris
3 St. Moritz
4 Lake Placid
5 Innsbruck

Soviets. One long pass and an easy basket later, they had won the gold medal. The stunned Americans unanimously voted not to accept their silvers, and those medals remain unclaimed to this day.

Olympic basketball jumped the shark at this point. Pros are now allowed to play and the U.S. wins by enough points that last-second officiating can't change the result. But no matter how great our Dream Team is, it can never wipe out the nightmare of 1972.

When did Olympic Gymnastics
1896–

jump the shark?

Gymnastics has not always been kind to the U.S.A. The Soviet Union and their Eastern Bloc specialized in turning out pint-sized young women who could toss their bodies around with unmatched skill and precision.

Mary Lou Retton.

In the seventies two women revolutionized the sport. Olga Korbut on the Soviet team became the darling of the 1972 Olympics with her famous backflip. In 1976, Romanian Nadia Comaneci scored the first perfect 10 (and six more). Women's gymnastics, far more popular than men's, became the province of teenagers, and any girl over five feet looked like a giraffe.

Lots of American girls were inspired by these performances. One of them was Mary Lou Retton, who, if she stood on her tiptoes, might make 4'9". She was lucky enough to get some old-school training from infamous coach Bela Karolyi. When Bela defected from Romania, the shark had begun to circle.

The U.S. team got a break in 1984. America had boycotted the Moscow Olympics in 1980 to protest the Soviet invasion of

PERFECT TEN
Gymnastic events that the Olympics force you to watch:
1 Parallel bars
2 Floor exercise
3 Vault
4 Horizontal bar
5 Rings
6 Pommel horse
7 Trampoline
8 Balance beam
9 Uneven bars
10 Rhythmic gymnastics

Afghanistan. In retaliation, most communist nations boycotted the Los Angeles Olympics. The U.S. dominated like never before.

America hadn't medalled in gymnastics often, but here was a golden opportunity. The only country they had to worry about was Romania, which featured the best gymnast around, Ecaterina Szabo. The U.S. team, with Mary Lou, was more than up to the task. Szabo got her medals, but when it was over, Mary Lou had two bronzes, two silvers, and became the first U.S. woman to win the all-around competition. A perfect vault gave her the gold by .05 points over Ecaterina.

Mary Lou's success vaulted Olympic gymnastics right over the shark. You could hardly turn the corner without seeing Mary Lou and her blinding, almost frightening, smile. She did ads, shows, magazine covers, Wheaties' boxes—whatever came her way.

The U.S. gymnastics team went from underdog to overbearing. The commercialization of Olympic gymnastics had begun. The "innocence" of Olga and Nadia became the overindulgence of Mary Lou, Shannon, Dominique, and any other female gymnast.

When did
Olympic Hockey
1920–

jump the shark?

Sometimes, a perfect moment can cause something to jump the shark because you know it's never going to be that good again. Enter the 1980 U.S. Olympic hockey team.

We believed in miracles.

The Olympics were often a proxy for bigger things. Jesse Owens's gold medals in the 1936 Berlin Olympics seemed to refute Hitler's racist ideology. After

WINTER SPORTS

The Olympics showcase these otherwise unseen sporting events:

1 Curling
2 Luge
3 Halfpipe
4 Slalom
5 Two-Man Bob

WWII, the cold war was fought on these international playing fields. When the games were over, we'd count up the medals and see which culture was superior.

The 1980 Winter Olympics in Lake Placid brought little doubt about which system was better at hockey—the Soviets were unbeatable. Their team hadn't lost an Olympic game in twelve years. The present squad had already beaten the NHL all-stars. Meanwhile, the inexperienced U.S. team was not even expected to medal.

But from the start the Americans played above expectations. They tied a tough Swedish team and crushed the Czechs 7–3. Maybe these guys had a chance—at a bronze or silver. First, though, they had a date to lose to the Soviets.

The first period saw the most scoring. The Soviets had pulled ahead 2–1 when the U.S. tied the score with exactly one second left on the clock. The Soviets threatened to pull away in the second period, outshooting the Americans 12–2, but only managed to put one puck in the net.

Rather than folding under pressure, the U.S. gave it their best shot in the third period. Eight minutes and thirty-nine seconds later they tied the game. Precisely at the ten-minute mark, team captain Mike Eruzione put in a twenty-foot wrist shot, and suddenly the Americans were ahead.

One goal isn't much of a lead against a determined Soviet attack, even for ten minutes. But as the clock counted down, goalie Jim Craig kept making amazing saves. It didn't seem possible, but when the game ended, the U.S. had won, 4–3. As announcer Al Michaels put it, "Do you believe in miracles?"

U-S-A! U-S-A!

Our favorite members of the 1980 gold medal squad:

1 Jim Craig
2 Ken Morrow
3 Dave Christian
4 Buzz Schneider
5 Mark Johnson

Oddly enough, that was when Olympic hockey jumped the shark. Sometimes you fight so hard for something that once you reach your goal, everything changes. No Olympic hockey game would—or could—ever matter quite so much again. Even the 4–2 U.S. victory over Finland that actually won the gold medal was an anticlimax. Most of us have forgotten that game, but we will never forget the U-S-A victory over the boys from the CCCP.

Olympic Figure Skating

1924–

jump the shark?

The grace of Peggy Fleming. The beauty of Katarina Witt. The left hook of Tonya Harding. In 1994, Olympic figure skating rivaled old-time hockey and hasn't been the same since.

Tonya versus Nancy.

Tonya Harding was a blond, blue-eyed sprite, 5'1" and 105 pounds. But don't let that fool you—she was one tough broad. She grew up poor, had a rough childhood, and tied the knot at nineteen with Jeff Gillooly. This may be the story

of millions of women (except the Gillooly part), but few can skate like the devil. That was Tonya's way out. Her specialty was the triple axel—no American woman before her had done it in competition.

Tonya topped the 1991 U.S Ladies' Freeskating rankings. By 1993, however, the top woman was the tall, dark-haired Nancy Kerrigan. Nancy was a complete contrast in style to Tonya. During the U.S. Olympic trials on January 6, 1994, as Kerrigan was leaving the ice in Detroit's Cobo Arena, a man struck her in the knee with a blunt object. The attacker, Shane Stant, had been hired by Tonya's husband as her bodyguard. Tonya denied she knew of the attack beforehand, though her husband and her bodyguard claimed otherwise. The national soap opera had begun.

It was framed as America's Sweetheart versus the Princess of the Trailer Park, though some preferred the feisty bad girl against Little Miss Perfect. Upping the ante, the U.S. Olympic Committee decided both Harding and Kerrigan could compete that year. Suddenly, the Winter Olympics figure skating competition was as big as the Super Bowl. Nancy and Tonya merely

---

GOLDEN SKATERS

U.S. Olympic gold medal winners for skating include:

1 Peggy Fleming (1968)
2 Dorothy Hamill (1976)
3 Eric Heiden (1980)
4 Kristi Yamaguchi (1992)
5 Sarah Hughes (2002)

DICK BUTTON SAYS . . .

Olympic figure skating has some great terms:

1 Axel
2 Blur spin
3 Camel spin
4 Choctaw
5 Flip
6 Lutz
7 Loop
8 Mohawk
9 Salchow
10 Stroking

practicing together got the kind of media you'd expect at an Ali weigh-in.

Harding's performance was a nightmare. She came onto the ice late, missed her first jump, and started crying. Turns out a shoelace was broken. She got another chance, yet still only managed to finish eighth. Meanwhile, Kerrigan was close to perfection. Unfortunately, so was the Ukraine's Oksana Baiul. She beat out Kerrigan for the gold by a tenth of a point.

Soon after, Tonya pleaded guilty to hindering an investigation. She got three years probation, $160,000 in fines, and five hundred hours of community service. The U.S. Figure Skating Association concluded she knew about the attack beforehand, stripped her of a 1994 national championship, and banned her from competition for life. Nancy became a national hero, did soup commercials, and hosted *Saturday Night Live*. Tonya had made figure skating more popular than ever by mixing it with pro wrestling. The next thing you know, those Olympic judges will be handing out two gold medals . . . but that could never happen.

When did

The Pittsburgh Steelers

1933–

jump the shark?

A blue-collar team for a blue-collar town, the late seventies Steelers were the best football team of all-time.

One for the thumb.

Art Rooney founded the Steelers in 1933 and watched them struggle for the next forty years. The most notable thing about the Steelers was the "steel" logo that was displayed on only one side of the helmet.

Chuck Noll signed on as head coach in 1969 and drafted Joe Greene as his first choice. Noll was a master at the draft, choosing Terry Bradshaw,

Mel Blount, Jack Ham, Franco Harris, and other future hall of famers in his first two years. The Steelers improved dramatically and played at the new Three Rivers Stadium. The first playoff game ended with the Immaculate Reception, and the Steelers were rolling.

It took two more years for the Steelers to win their first Super Bowl, and they would continue to win three more over the next five years. The Steel Curtain defense was complemented by Swann and Stallworth on offense, and the Steelers were the model for football success. The terrible towels and ardent fans cheered the Steelers on to victories over the archrival Houston Oilers and the Oakland Raiders, as well as two Super Bowl triumphs over the Dallas Cowboys.

Following their Super Bowl XIV win over the Los Angeles Rams, Joe Greene and crew declared their quest for a fifth Super Bowl ring, or "one for the thumb." The catch phrase was embraced in Pittsburgh, and fans today still twirl their terrible towels and pine for that elusive ring.

Terry Bradshaw to Lynn Swann became Cliff Stoudt to Louis Lipps. The 4–3 Steel Curtain was alone in a land of 3–4 defenses. The Steelers have had some winning campaigns, and even returned to the Super Bowl in 1995 only to fall to the Cowboys for their first Super Bowl loss. Seven years later, the Steelers fell to the underdog Patriots, leaving the Heinz Field faithful harkening back to the days of Lambert, Webster, and Gerela.

Dennis Rodman

1949–

jump the shark?

He shocked people with his unique style, but the NBA has never seen a rebounder quite like the Worm.

Dennis grew up in Dallas, Texas, and didn't play hoops throughout high school. The year after he graduated, he grew eight inches and tried out for a junior college. By the time he was through, Dennis was drafted by the Detroit Pistons and would help carry them to two championships.

Dennis, along with Bill Laimbeer, transformed the Pistons into the bad boys of basketball. They did whatever it took to win, and stood in the way of Michael Jordan's title aspirations for years. The Worm focused primarily on rebounding and defense, and he won numerous league honors and titles for both of those aspects of his game.

In 1993, Dennis was dealt to the San Antonio Spurs—who didn't know how to handle him. He rebelled by dying his hair different colors each game and only occasionally showing up to practice, kicking his bad-boy image up a notch.

> **Double Team.**

NICE D

Dennis Rodman was a rare all-star who was appreciated for his defense (and hair products).

Others include:

1 Joe Dumars
2 Dikembe Mutombo
3 Michael Cooper
4 Sidney Moncrief
5 Mark Eaton

Michael Jordan knew what the Bulls needed, and Phil Jackson felt he could handle Dennis's antics. The Worm joined the Bulls in 1995, created plenty of controversy, and won three titles in Chicago. It was around this time that Dennis began to become a celebrity, and the shark smelled blood.

Dennis was spotted with Madonna, and later married Carmen Electra for a few minutes. He was photographed in a bridal gown and other androgynous clothing, and always had something to say for any microphone nearby. He jumped the shark when he starred with Jean-Claude Van Damme in the movie *Double*

NUMBER PLEASE

The Worm wore 10, 91, and 70 during his pro career. More math:

1 Shawn Bradley—76
2 Wilt Chamberlain—13
3 George Mikan—99
4 Larry Bird—33
5 Michael Jordan— 23, 45, 23

Team. The man with the green hair pushed his luck, and was viewed as a freak versus a quirky showman.

Dennis released an autobiography, *Bad As I Wanna Be,* which sold well due to his kiss-and-tell revelations about Madonna. He left the Bulls and joined the Lakers for a few games, but couldn't hold it together and left the NBA. When we spotted him in a WCW wrestling event, we knew the shark had swum away.

When did
Pete Rose
1941–

jump the shark?

Pete Rose is one of baseball's all-time greats. He holds the record for most hits, most singles, most games, and most at-bats. He was Rookie of the Year in 1963 and MVP in 1973. He won batting championships, gold glove awards, and was a perennial All-Star. Charlie Hustle always gave it his all.

Wanna bet?

So why isn't he in the Hall of Fame? Rose had a serious gambling problem. This doesn't necessarily get you into trouble with the Major Leagues, unless you are accused of the cardinal sin—betting on baseball.

THE BIG RED MACHINE

Who could compete with the starting eight from Cincinnati in the 1970s?

1 Johnny Bench
2 Tony Perez
3 Joe Morgan
4 Dave Concepcion
5 Pete Rose
6 George Foster
7 Cesar Geronimo
8 Ken Griffey

While still a player, Pete hung out at a gym in Cincinnati. He met certain people there, the "fellaheen," as they were called. Unsavory characters, they were involved in tax evasion, drug dealing, and worst for Rose, illegal gambling. Rather than running, Rose allowed them to hook him up with bookies.

When the fellaheen were investigated in an FBI probe, Rose's name and huge gambling debts came up. His "friends" were more than happy to inform on him. Not only was Rose a compulsive gambler, but he bet on his own

team, they said. The word got out to baseball commissioner A. Bartlett Giamatti, who placed Rose, now a retired player, on the ineligible list. Once one of baseball's brightest stars, Rose was banished and excluded from election to the Hall of Fame.

Plenty of ballplayers have jumped the shark, but Rose was probably the first willing to bet on whether he'd make it across. To this day the argument continues as to whether he should be a Hall of Famer. If it were based on stats alone, there'd be no question. Moreover, Rose still denies he bet on baseball, and most of the testimony against him comes from felons.

Some claim he's paid his debt. Others argue that plenty of Cooperstown inductees have made similarly questionable decisions. Still, others say Rose dishonored baseball and that betting on the game—which he probably did—is inexcusable. Only one thing is certain: He deserves an honorary plaque in the Jump the Shark Hall of Fame.

Sports Illustrated
1954–

jump the shark?

If you are a true sports fan, you read *SI*.

Henry Luce, the founder of *TIME* and *LIFE*, created *Sports Illustrated* as a rival to the popular *Sport* magazine. The first issue hit the stands August 16, 1954, complete with replica Topps baseball cards, and a legend was born.

ESPN.

The writing in *Sports Illustrated* has always been exceptional, and its photography is certainly memorable. In the fifties and sixties, sports reporting was a brief recap in your local paper. *SI* changed all that with its national perspective on sports.

The sixties brought *SI*'s memorable block-lettered logo and an ever-expanding readership. In 1964, the infamous swimsuit issue was born and continues to generate more controversy, drooling, and ad pages with each passing year. The 19th Hole, Faces in the Crowd, and the Sportsman of the Year became staples for any literate sports fan.

THE COVER

SI loves these cover boys:

1 Michael Jordan
2 Muhammad Ali
3 Jack Nicklaus
4 Joe Montana
5 Insert Olympic hero here

As television brought the games to more people and sports gained in popularity, *SI*'s influence continued to expand. "*SI* jinx" rumors began, claiming that a cover photo led to an inevitable defeat the very next week. Changes continued as Billie Jean King and Chris Evert were Sportspeople of the Year during the seventies, and the cover of the 1980 U.S. Olympic hockey team included no words.

In the mid eighties, *SI* put a box around its famous logo and awarded its Sportsmen of the Year to "eight athletes who care." The shark began to circle. But four letters are what caused this institution to jump the shark . . . ESPN. Other sports entities had come and gone, having little success at knocking *SI* off its elite pedestal. But the sports network from Bristol became the true fan's resource for scores, analysis, and humor.

I READ IT FOR THE ARTICLES

Our favorite *SI* swimsuit models:

1 Christie Brinkley
2 Paulina
3 Elle McPherson
4 Cheryl Tiegs
5 Vendela

In 1997, *SI* realized its need to diversify and teamed with CNN to create a rival sports network. They compete with ESPN on the newsstands (*SI* wins), cable (*SI* loses), and the Web (*SI* gets hammered). The swimsuit issue, like the magazine's golf coverage, grows more and more revealing each year. *SI* is still an excellent read, but no longer the only game in town.

When did

The Superstars

1974–1983

jump the shark?

There was no better way to spend an off-season Sunday afternoon than watching the world's best athletes compete in Hawaii and Florida.

> **The obscure soccer or cycling star wins every time.**

The Superstars featured athletes from all different sports competing against each other in a variety of physical challenges. No athlete could compete in his or her own sport, and each show culminated with an obstacle course that no one seemed to be able to get through.

The show did a great job of filling the January to March void of major sporting contests. ABC cranked up its sports hype machine using Keith Jackson as the primary commentator, often paired with Reggie Jackson, O.J. Simpson, and other superstars of the current times. The show spawned *Battle of the Network Stars,* which had television celebrities competing in various sports challenges. But I digress.

BACK TO YOU, KEITH

Great *Superstar* sideline reporters:

1 Donna DeVerona
2 Bruce Jenner
3 Frank Gifford
4 Billie Jean King
5 Al Michaels

The Superstars was successful in its early run with Renaldo Nehemiah and Lynn Swann showing their stuff. Attempting to capitalize on its success, *The Superteams* was born, pitting that year's sporting finalists against each other in even more obscure sporting contests. Swimming linemen, cycling outfielders, and bench-pressing golfers were commonplace on the show.

The Superstars jumped the shark when every winner ended up being some obscure cyclist or bowler. The stars of the "major" sports never seemed to show up to this competition, and after a while we simply lost interest. The athletes certainly enjoyed themselves and the climbing wall and hurdles on the obstacle course will not soon be forgotten.

SPINOFFS

The success of *The Superstars* gave us these classics:

1 *Battle of the Network Stars*
2 *Almost Anything Goes*
3 *The Challenge of the Sexes*
4 *Us vs. The World*
5 *American Gladiators*

When did

Mike Tyson

1966–

jump the shark?

Iron Mike was a heavyweight champ who dominated the boxing world before being destroyed by it.

Mike and Robin talk to Barbara Walters.

Mike Tyson was born and raised in Brooklyn. A troubled youth, Mike was rescued by trainer Cus D'Amato, who molded him into the best young heavyweight the world would ever see. D'Amato died tragically when Mike was only eighteen. Promoters Jim Jacobs and Bill Cayton took over the reins, with trainer Kevin Rooney at the boxer's side.

By November of the next year, Mike Tyson was the heavyweight champion of the world. He literally destroyed anyone he fought and brought boxing back into the spotlight in a way it hadn't been since Ali's run in the early seventies. Mike was universally feared and had zero problems in the ring, but his life outside was a different story. In late 1987, he married actress Robin Givens (and her mother Ruth), and the sharks began to circle.

One of Mike's managers, Jim Jacobs, died suddenly from leukemia, and Bill Cayton was left in charge. Robin and Ruth poked their heads into Mike's financial affairs, and Don King began

BABA WAWA

Mike was only one of Barbara Walters's infamous interviews:

1 Michael Jackson and Lisa-Marie Presley
2 Fidel Castro
3 Katharine Hepburn
4 Anwar Sadat and Menachem Begin
5 Monica Lewinsky

to weasel his way in. Amidst all this personal controversy, Iron Mike pissed off Pay-Per-View customers everywhere when he dropped previously undefeated Michael Spinks in ninety-one seconds and unified the heavyweight title.

THE GREATEST
Our favorite heavyweights:
1 Muhammad Ali
2 Joe Frazier
3 Rocky Marciano
4 George Foreman
5 Clubber Lang

Tyson's performance began to suffer inside and outside of the ring. He had a street fight with Mitch "Blood" Green, drove a car into a tree, and constantly denied reports of abusing his wife. In an attempt to set the record straight, Mike and Robin appeared on *20/20* with Barbara Walters. As his wife let the world know what was going on at home, the soft-spoken Tyson sat there watching his career sail right over the shark. Shortly after the interview he was divorced, got rid of Kevin Rooney, and signed a promotional contract with Don King.

Back in the ring, an overmatched Frank Bruno held Iron Mike at bay, only getting knocked out in five. But no one expected what happened in Japan when James "Buster" Douglas knocked a listless Tyson out. Suddenly, Mike was mortal. An epic battle was later set between him and new champ Evander Holyfield, but not before Mike was sent to prison on rape charges.

Upon his release, the now-Islamic Mike eventually got his Holyfield fight, but suffered the second loss of his career to an older and more effective boxer. The eventual rematch led to Tyson's biting Holyfield's ear and being banned from boxing for one year. Mike had always been feared in the ring and respected as a great heavyweight. The Holyfield rematch transformed him into a circus act and an unfortunate casualty of the state of boxing today.

The UCLA Bruins

1920–

jump the shark?

UCLA dominated NCAA Division I basketball like no other team. From 1964 to 1975 they won ten out of twelve championships. It's no coincidence that the coach during all those years was John Wooden.

> **The Wizard of Westwood retires.**

Wooden himself had been a basketball great. He was College Player of the Year in 1932 at Purdue. In the late forties, he took over the mediocre UCLA basketball program. He spent the fifties rebuilding that program and putting his basketball philosophy into practice.

By 1960, everything was in place for a dynasty. In the '60–'61 season the Bruins finished second in their conference. They finished first in both '62 and '63. In 1964, UCLA broke through—Wooden's team was a perfect 30–0 and won the national championship. In fact, before Wooden was done, they'd have four perfect 30–0 seasons and in one streak win eighty-eight games in a row. From '64 on they would win every championship—except in '66 and '74—until Wooden's retirement in 1975.

DYNASTIES

Simply the best:

1. Pro baseball—New York Yankees
2. Pro hockey—Montreal Canadiens
3. Pro basketball—Boston Celtics
4. Collegiate wrestling—Iowa Hawkeyes
5. Women's college basketball—Tennessee Lady Vols

Wooden emphasized fundamentals. Passing and dribbling were just as important as shooting. He also believed strongly in teamwork. While he had great stars, such as Lew Alcindor (now Kareem Abdul-Jabbar) and Bill Walton, he never depended on any single player to carry the team. Anyone showboating got benched. The strength of his team (and his name) allowed Wooden to recruit the best high school players, but his true success was in molding each team into something bigger than the sum of its parts.

X'S AND O'S

Great college hoops coaches not named Wooden:

1. Adolph Rupp
2. Dean Smith
3. John Thompson
4. Jerry Tarkanian
5. Hank Iba
6. Bobby Knight
7. Mike Krzyzewski
8. Jim Boeheim
9. Lute Olsen
10. Roy Williams

Wooden turned sixty-five in 1975. He retired with nothing left to prove. Since 1977, the John R. Wooden award is given to the best college basketball player.

His shoes were simply too big to fill. While UCLA has had good seasons since, only once has the team been able to hang another banner from the rafters of Pauley Pavilion. Still, as they say, it's better to have jumped the shark and lost, than never to have jumped at all.

When did
The USC Trojans Tailbacks
1925–

jump the shark?

If you played tailback at USC behind its All-American offensive line, you were destined to become a starter in the NFL—but a troubled one.

The University of Southern California football tradition began in 1925, and it took only three seasons for the Trojans to produce their first thousand-yard rusher in Morley Drury. USC has won almost seventy percent of its games and has had the most first-round draft picks by the NFL. Despite the notoriety of the Marching Band and "Tusk," much of this success can be attributed to the ability of their backfield.

It took forty years until Heisman trophy winner Mike Garrett emerged as the next thousand-yard rusher, the start of an unprecedented string of successful tailbacks to play for the Trojans. He became an all-pro for the Kansas City Chiefs and also played for the San Diego Chargers. Three years later, O.J. Simpson won his Heisman and went on to become the first pro to rush for over two thousand yards in a season. He later had some problems off the field that you may have heard about.

> **Marcus Allen wins the Heisman.**

RIVALS

USC has built some classic rivalries over time with:

1 UCLA
2 Notre Dame
3 Cal
4 Stanford
5 Michigan

Clarence Davis started the seventies where O.J. left off and had a moderately successful career as an Oakland Raider. Anthony Davis was another thousand-yard rusher for two years, but flopped as a first round pick of the Tampa Bay Buccaneers. Ricky Bell was overshadowed by Archie Griffin and Tony Dorsett and never really established himself in Tampa, either. Charles White eclipsed two thousand yards, won the Heisman, and was then a bust as a back for the Cleveland Browns.

Marcus Allen came on the scene next and rushed for an all-time best 2,427 yards in his Heisman-winning season. Marcus would succeed in the pros as a back for the Raiders, meeting up with O.J. again at a later date. But when Marcus left, USC tailbacks stopped running behind the All-American line up front and jumped the shark. During the past two decades, the retired USC tailbacks have made more headlines than any of the current crop.

When did

Wide World of Sports
1961–

jump the shark?

ESPN.

"Spanning the globe to bring you the constant variety of sport. The thrill of victory, and the agony of defeat. The human drama of athletic competition. This is ABC's *Wide World of Sports!*" This opening still sends a chill down the spine while conjuring the vision of a guy flying off the side of a ski jump.

Starting with the show's debut in 1961, those words prefaced countless episodes of

INSTANT REPLAY

Notable advancements in sports television broadcasts:

1 Instant replay
2 Isolated action coverage
3 Instant pitching-speed stats
4 Animated first-down line
5 Score and running time in the corner

Wide World of Sports. Announcer Jim McKay allegedly penned this magical opening on the back of an envelope, just the way Lincoln legendarily wrote the Gettysburg Address. McKay's words are almost as famous.

Throughout the sixties and seventies, sports fans couldn't get enough of the show. It truly showed a wide world: soccer, dogsledding, billiards, fencing, mountain climbing, chess, yachting, karate—no sport was foreign to them. They really did span the globe, and that included covering humble American events like rattlesnake hunting, frog jumping, and the Soap Box Derby. Of course, there was also plenty of meat-and-potatoes stuff, like track and field, basketball, tennis, and so on.

No TV sports show could compete for the first couple of decades that *Wide World* was on the air. But then coverage got fancier at the networks and, more significantly, cable started spreading. Suddenly, TV was offering sports around the clock. As the years went on, *Wide World* seemed to matter less and less.

Jim McKay was unquestionably beloved, but he was also past retirement age. Born in 1921, he suddenly seemed a bit tired compared to the hip, young, trash-talking dudes at ESPN. And hey, we still loved *Wide World of Sports*, but how much cliff diving can you take?

It's hard to place the exact moment when the show jumped the shark. It happened bit by bit, a function of ESPN's growth. Sort of the same way it happens to an athlete: Each season he loses a step, and eventually he knows it's time to go. How many athletes born in '61 are still at the top of their games?

Politics

"Paradoxically, politicians, unlike television shows, can sometimes become more intriguing, if less electable, once they jump the shark. . . ."

—Maureen Dowd, *The New York Times*

The 2000 presidential election gives a clear indication that politics is no stranger to jumping the shark.

Drug and sex scandals. Archaic voting methods. Bad photo ops. Drunken siblings and offspring.

The amazing thing about politicians jumping the shark is how they handle the aftermath. Some survive, and even thrive in a quirky kind of way, while most sink deep into the undertow and become fodder for late-night talk show hosts.

The shark doesn't feast only on politicians. Countries, political parties, and doctrines are all fair game.

Some of our other Shark categories apply to politics, but there are a few that could only be here. Samples include:

The Other Woman—Jim Bakker meets Jessica Hahn

Power Hunger—Alexander Haig is in control

Sex—That blue dress from the Gap

I Do—Jackie Kennedy becomes Jackie O

Photo Ops—Dewey defeats Truman

Mass Media—Oliver North, the talk show host

Drugs—Marion Barry gets some crack

Family—Billy Carter, Roger Clinton . . .

Transparencies—Hillary Clinton, Yankees fan

Larry King appearances—If your name's not Duke Ziebert, you've probably jumped the shark

Fashion—Nixon's sweat, Carter's cardigan

Hall of Fame—Political Wing

The most blatant shark jumps in political history (excluding Gary Condit) are:

10. Communism crumbles along with the Berlin Wall

9. General George Custer at Little Big Horn

8. The jewel of the crown leaves the British Empire

7. Alexander Haig decides he is in charge

6. Florida and the recount

5. Ted Kennedy at Chappaquiddick

4. Napoleon at Waterloo

3. Michael Dukakis in the tank

2. Dan Quayle spells "potatoe"

1. Gary Hart on the *Monkey Business*

When did
Jim Bakker
1939–

jump the shark?

In the late sixties, a young preacher and his wife had a great act. Tammy Faye Bakker brought out naughty sock puppets and Jim Bakker would set them straight with proper Biblical teachings. They got their big break when Pat Robertson asked them to perform their act on his Christian Broadcasting Network. The audience loved them—they were the Steve and Eydie of televangelism. A few years later, they had created their own network, PTL (Praise The Lord). It grew by leaps and bounds, beaming out by satellite, and in a few more years they created Heritage, USA, a popular religious theme park.

Hello, Jessica.

By the 1980s, the Bakkers were among the biggest Christian stars on TV. Jim, bearing an uncanny resemblance to a middle-aged Rick Moranis, and Tammy, a sprite who cried often, ruining her heavily made-up face, made a cute couple. Viewers felt good about sending them money. But there was trouble in paradise: behind the scenes, Jim mismanaged funds and Tammy was addicted to painkillers.

> **PUPPET SHOW**
> Some classic puppets:
> 1 Pinocchio
> 2 Punch and Judy
> 3 Charlie McCarthy
> 4 Howdy Doody
> 5 Lamb Chop
> 6 Gumby
> 7 Topo Gigio
> 8 Kermit the Frog
> 9 Lester
> 10 Madame

Still, what really blew up the act was a little dalliance Jim had with church secretary Jessica Hahn in 1980. It was a single encounter in a Florida motel, followed by years of regret. Understandably interested in keeping it quiet, Bakker ended up paying Hahn over a quarter-million dollars in hush money. When this all came out in 1987, millions were outraged that a so-called moral leader could be involved in such sin. Others were outraged that he had paid so much for a single session. The Bakker tears never stopped flowing.

> **CAN I GET AN AMEN?**
> They're extensions of the Lord and TV stars:
> 1 The God Squad
> 2 Billy Graham
> 3 Pat Robertson
> 4 Mother Angelica
> 5 Jimmy Swaggart

Jim had to step down, and was replaced by Jerry Falwell. From there, he went from jumping sharks to getting fed to them. The court looked into his finances, and in 1989 Jim was convicted on twenty-four counts of broadcast fraud, mail fraud, and conspiracy. His judge was Robert "Maximum Bob" Potter, who gave him forty-five years. The sentence was later reduced to eight years on appeal.

Tammy Faye, suffering from hallucinations, landed in the Betty Ford Clinic. In 1992, she filed for divorce. Meanwhile, Jessica Hahn got somewhere in the neighborhood of a million to pose for Playboy and became a featured guest on *Howard Stern*.

All that damage and sadness for a few moments of pleasure. If only Jim had practiced what he preached to those sock puppets so long ago.

When did
Marion Barry
1936– Mayor of Washington, D.C. 1978–1990, 1994–1998

jump the shark?

Marion Barry was born poor and black in the South (no, this isn't Steve Martin in *The Jerk*). He became a civil rights crusader and eventually moved to Washington, D.C. After serving on the city council— and being shot attempting to defend the District Building—he was elected mayor in 1978.

The mayor smokes crack.

There were high hopes for Barry. The city thought they had elected a new type of leader, and they had—a party animal. There were allegations that as early as 1981 he had been seen snorting cocaine during a Christmas party at the This Is It nude bar. Barry admitted to nothing more than being a "night owl."

Things got worse as Barry was also accused of money mismanagement and sleeping around. Well, he may have been a rascal, but he was Washington's rascal. They elected him to three consecutive terms. The shark was champing at the bit.

WE BUILT THIS CITY

America has its fair share of crooked city governments, most notably:

1 Chicago
2 Washington, D.C.
3 New Orleans
4 Las Vegas
5 Salt Lake City

On January 18, 1990, the FBI had former girlfriend Hazel Diane "Rasheeda" Moore lure Barry to a room at the Vista Hotel. Once there, in full view of hidden cameras, the mayor commenced to smoke crack. And he smoked it like it wasn't his first time. He got in a couple of long drags before agents rushed the room and arrested hizzoner. Barry, seeing his career go up in smoke, could only mutter, over and over, "Bitch set me up. . . . I shouldn't have come up here. . . . Goddamn bitch!"

If you think a videotape like this would be enough to convict a man, you clearly don't know D.C. Of the fourteen charges brought against him (in the court of Judge Thomas Penfield Jackson, who's now best known for the Microsoft antitrust case), the jury was able to convict him on only one count. The charge arising out of the 1990 sting ended up in a hung jury, as several jurors felt the government was out to get their mayor.

Barry was convicted of misdemeanor possession and served six months. After such national humiliation, some men would retire from public life, but not Barry. It's hard to leave the life once you're used to it. He got out and by 1994 was elected mayor yet again. Put that in your pipe and smoke it.

BUSTED

D.C. has had its fair share of drug-related scandals:

1 Bill Clinton's last-minute pardon of drug dealer Carlos Vignali

2 George W. Bush's underage daughters try to purchase alcohol

3 Hamilton Jordan, President Carter's chief of staff, investigated for possible cocaine use (no indictment)

4 Supreme Court nominee Judge Douglas Ginsburg admits he smoked marijuana (must withdraw from consideration)

5 Al Gore admits he smoked marijuana (no one cared)

Joe Biden

1942– U.S. Senator from Delaware 1973–

jump the shark?

Some Presidential candidates get felled for sex scandals, some for fiscal mismanagement, but it takes a very special person to fail due to plagiarism.

The Senator tells a story not his own.

Joseph R. Biden Jr. is one of the Senate's power brokers. He's currently serving his fifth term and should have no trouble gaining a sixth. He runs the Foreign Relations Committee. You'd think a guy like that would run for president. Well, he sorta did, and it's precisely when he jumped the shark.

Biden hoped to be the Democrat's presidential nominee in 1988. His stump speech included stirring evocations of the hardscrabble life of his ancestors. He asked, rhetorically, why he was the first of his clan to attend college. There was nothing wrong with his ancestors—why, they'd dig "in the coal mines . . . and would come up after twelve hours and play football for four hours." They were smart, hard workers, and who knows how high they could have risen if they'd just had a little help from the government.

It was an effective speech, playing up Biden's past and appealing to resentment at the same time. The only problem was that British politician Neil Kinnock had already given the speech, almost word for word. Biden adapted Briticisms and changed names. He also upped his ancestors' workday from eight to twelve hours. Still, there it was: Biden's touching past wasn't even his own, and he had sailed over the shark.

Operatives of Biden's opponent Michael Dukakis

SPEECH THERAPY

Who could forget these classic American speeches?

1 George Washington's Farewell Address
2 Patrick Henry's "Give me liberty or give me death" speech
3 Lincoln's Gettysburg Address
4 William Jennings Bryan's "Cross of Gold" speech
5 FDR's "Day of Infamy" speech
6 JFK's Inaugural Address
7 Martin Luther King, Jr.'s "I Have A Dream" speech
8 Richard Nixon's Resignation
9 Ronald Reagan's *Challenger* disaster speech
10 George Bush's 1988 Republican National Convention acceptance speech

found out about the theft and quickly distributed tapes with the two speeches side by side. It also turned out that Biden had borrowed sections of Robert Kennedy's speeches and had even been caught plagiarizing in law school. Biden was forced to drop out of the race in September 1987, before the first primary.

It's been a while. Word has it Biden is thinking of running again for President in 2004. If he gets the nod, one can almost hear his acceptance speech: "Four score and seven years ago . . ."

When did

Napoleon Bonaparte

1769–1821 Emperor of France

jump the shark?

Waterloo.

This famous Frenchman was more than just a vertically challenged general with a tasty dessert as his namesake.

Napoleon's rise was breathtaking. Born in Corsica on August 15, 1769, he had a natural aptitude as a soldier and rose to the rank of brigadier general by 1793. Soon after his success at quelling mob violence in 1795 Paris, he was given command of the ragtag Army of Italy.

Napoleon went into high gear, winning battles against Italians, Sardinians, and Austrians. He did run into trouble in Egypt fighting the British, which showed he could be beaten. He returned to France, launched a coup d'etat, and was soon running the country. His ambition was not to be quelled, however, and he demanded to be crowned Emperor of the French. In 1804, he granted himself this wish. (Beethoven, who was about to dedicate his "Eroica" symphony to Napoleon, was so repulsed that he ripped the title page from his score.)

Napoleon set his sights elsewhere, gaining victories over the Italians, Prussians, Russians, and Spaniards. Only Great Britain seemed able to repel him. In 1810, however, we spotted a fin when he invaded Russia for refusing to buckle under to his rule. It was a disastrous campaign that cost him hundreds of thousands of soldiers.

Like Mike Tyson after Buster Douglas, Napoleon suddenly didn't look so tough. Europe as one turned against France. Napoleon's army retreated as Paris fell. Morale crumbled, defections mounted, Napoleon abdicated. He was exiled to Elba (hence the classic Napoleonic palindrome "Able was I, ere I saw Elba").

But you can't keep a good dictator down. He escaped the island and in almost no time was head of France again, replacing the unpopular Louis XVIII. The stage was set. He'd either hold his country, or jump the shark.

The allies arose once more. After some preliminary battles, Napoleon met Wellington's British army ten miles south of Brussels at Waterloo. Brilliant strategist though he was, Napoleon blundered by sending a detachment under the command of the Marquis de Grouchy (rumored to love trash) to prevent the Prussian reinforcements from joining the battle. Grouchy utterly failed in his mission and, while his thirty-three thousand men were out of the action, the Prussians joined the British troops. Napoleon was routed. He would die six years later, and would never fight again.

To this day, the phrase "to meet one's Waterloo" means to suffer a crushing defeat. It also was the impetus of a hit single for Abba. If that's not jumping the shark, we don't know what is.

When did

Robert Bork

1927– Judge, Federal Circuit Court of
Appeals 1982–1988

jump the shark?

During the Reagan presidency, we all knew Robert
Bork was on the short list for the Supreme Court.
A federal judge, he was also an intellectual leader
of the conservative movement, having done
groundbreaking work on antitrust issues. It was only
a matter of time.

> **The judge makes it a
> Blockbuster night!**

The nomination came in 1987. Bork was highly qualified, but also
quite controversial. Realizing a strong conservative like Bork could change
the balance of the court, Democrats spared no expense in going after him.
Senator Edward Kennedy summed up
their ferocity when he said:

OVERRULED

Judges who have been rejected for
the Supreme Court:

1 John Rutledge (1795)
2 Alexander Wolcott (1811)
3 Ebenezer Hoar (1869)
4 George H. Williams (1873)
5 Caleb Cushing (1873)
6 John J. Parker (1930)
7 Clement F. Haynsworth, Jr.
   (1969)
8 G. Harrold Carswell (1969)
9 Robert Bork (1987)
10 Douglas Ginsburg (1987)

"Robert Bork's America is a land
in which women would be forced into
back-alley abortions, blacks would sit
at segregated lunch counters, rogue
police could break down citizens' doors
in midnight raids, schoolchildren could
not be taught about evolution, writers
and artists would be censored at the
whim of government, and the doors of
the federal courts would be shut on the
fingers of millions of citizens for whom
the judiciary is often the only protector
of the individual rights that are at the heart of our democracy." We had spotted a fin.

Bork's enemies investigated everything he'd ever done, looking for a
weakness. They read every opinion, every paper, every speech, and found
plenty. But that wasn't enough. Someone decided to check out what
movies he rented. This should have been a sign to Bork that he was in real
trouble. Old speeches are one thing, but what business is it if you want to
watch *C.H.U.D.*? With that sort of opposition, you might as well give it up.

Okay, he didn't rent *C.H.U.D.* But he did rent *A Day at the Races, Ruthless People,* and *The Man Who Knew Too Much.* In other words, nothing em-

barrassing. The public was revolted enough by this overreaching that Congress passed the Video Privacy Protection Act of 1988. Too late for Bork, though it probably helped Clarence Thomas a few years down the road.

Bork was rejected for his extreme views. His name has become a verb—to be "Borked" means to be turned down for a position due to ruthless opposition. The man himself has become a bitter curmudgeon, denouncing U.S. culture in a series of articles and books. Reading them, some people may think it's a good thing he's not on the court today. Then again, if he hadn't been Borked, maybe he wouldn't be so bitter.

When did

The British Empire
1642–1947

jump the shark?

India becomes independent.

In 1937, the sun literally never set on the British Empire. That's a lot of real estate.

At its peak, the British had possessions in all twenty-four time zones. Approximately one-fifth of all inhabitable land was under British dominion. From New Zealand to Nigeria, Canada to Hong Kong, anywhere you traveled you could see the Union Jack.

The jewel in the crown was India. British involvement in India goes back to the early 1600s, when the merchants of the British East India Company were granted monopoly rights to trade with the East Indies. The infamous Black Hole of Calcutta incident took place in 1756. It was claimed (incorrectly) that 146 British citizens were imprisoned in a small, airless dun-

WHAT'S WITH THE
ACCENT?

The British Empire has extended everywhere, including:

1 Falkland Islands
2 Malta
3 Kuwait
4 Sri Lanka
5 Maldive Islands
6 Fiji
7 South Africa
8 Myanmar
9 Malaysia
10 Bahama Islands

geon and that 123 of them died overnight. This provided England with an excuse to rule over such a primitive people. In 1757 the British effectively began to take control of India with the Battle of Plassey.

We spotted a fin nineteen years later when there was an uprising in the American Colonies, and the British surrendered the territory. But India's inexpensive raw materials helped the United Kingdom grow into a great economic power. In 1857, a century after first taking charge, the British were challenged by the natives in a war for independence. The "Indian Mutiny" was harshly suppressed, and the British Crown held on all the more dearly to their jewel.

Rudyard Kipling, the great fan and poet of the British Empire, was born in Bombay in 1865. His became the famous justification for empire: It was the "white man's burden" to conquer the earth and teach darker-skinned people to be civilized.

As the twentieth century arrived and colonialism in general came into question, the jewel in the crown grew ever more tarnished. British influence began to waver, Jawaharlal Nehru called for complete independence, and Mahatma Gandhi practiced civil disobedience. The British attempted to repress these movements with ugly violence, but the tide of history was against them. Slowly, often begrudgingly, they gave in—the Empire had jumped the shark. Indians were granted limited self-government in 1935, and in 1947 won complete independence.

All through the nineteenth century the British had slowly been losing their lands. But this loss—more of an idea than of a place—was most obvious in India. It was an occupation born in violence and maintained by violence. Once time caught up with it, it could not stand.

LOOK IT UP

British words borrowed from India:

1 bungalow
2 dinghy
3 bandana
4 loot
5 thug
6 jungle
7 cummerbund
8 dungaree
9 juggernaut
10 pundit

George Bush

1924– U.S. President 1989–1993

jump the shark?

No question about it, George Bush had put in his time. U.S. ambassador, CIA Director, vice president—it was his turn to be president. He had trouble with his image, though. Some thought he was a wimp, and he didn't appeal to women. So he promised a "kinder, gentler" nation, said "read my lips, no new taxes," and threatened that if his opponent were elected the country would be overrun with felons out on furlough. Just like that, he was President.

> **A bad meal in a foreign country.**

But he still had a problem with the image thing. His term followed on the heels of a president who was such a confident leader that Bush had trouble defining himself in comparison. If you don't define yourself, someone else—or something else—will. And that defining moment came upon him violently in Japan.

FORTUNATE SON

My boy is gonna be like me:

1 George W. Bush
2 Ken Griffey, Jr.
3 Robbie Kneivel
4 Freddie Prinze, Jr.
5 John F. Kennedy, Jr.

During Bush's term, America stood tall. The Berlin Wall fell, Iraq was defeated, and the U.S. became the world's single superpower. Still, there were economic fears, many focused on Japan, whose bubble had yet to burst. Bush went there on a trade mission in 1991.

Attending a state dinner in Tokyo, Bush felt ill. Perhaps it was the Halcion he took to counteract jet lag. Perhaps it was a virus. Perhaps it was bad sushi. Whatever it was, it wasn't staying down. Before he knew it, he had thrown up in the prime minister's lap. Bush had spent years as a diplomat, but it's hard to maintain one's dignity after unleashing a bout of projectile vomiting.

YOU SEE SUSHI

Common ingredients found in sushi:

1 Vinegar
2 Soy sauce
3 Wasabi
4 Gari (ginger root)
5 Nori (seaweed)

It was the spew heard round the world. The comedians had a field day. *SNL* did a whole sketch with Dana Carvey as Bush throwing up over and over. On Japanese TV, they had a similar skit with a retching monkey representing Bush.

Bush did not win reelection. Most say it was the economy that turned the electorate against him, but who knows? One thing we do know is that Bush was replaced by Clinton, a man with a grin that suggested he could keep anything down.

When did
Jimmy Carter
1924– U.S. President 1977–1981

jump the shark?

Jimmy Carter was elected to save America from shame. We were a country trying to put Watergate and Vietnam behind us. Here was a peanut farmer and a governor from Georgia, an outsider untainted by the dirty politics of Washington. As he promised, "I will never lie to you."

Billy Beer.

But there was plenty to be ashamed of during his single term of office. There was his "malaise" speech where he seemed to blame Americans for lacking confidence in themselves when it seemed more likely we lacked confidence in him. There was the Iranian Hostage crisis that would not go away as long as he was president. There was uncontrollable, sky-high inflation.

But there was nothing quite so cringe-inducing, and therefore so shark-jumping, as what Carter's election unintentionally unleashed on America—his brother Billy. If Jimmy was the good boy, Billy was the black sheep. While Jimmy campaigned, good ol' boy Billy partied. While Jimmy ran a farm, Billy ran a gas station that sold more liquor than gas. Jimmy gave millions hope that America would move ahead. Billy made rednecks look bad.

It wouldn't have been so bad if Billy had just kept quiet, but he tried to cash in. Okay, he

BROTHERS IN ARMS
Notable sibling combos:
1 The Allman Brothers
2 The Blues Brothers
3 The Brothers Grimm
4 The Marx Brothers
5 The Menendez Brothers
6 The Ritz Brothers
7 The Smith Brothers
8 The Smothers Brothers
9 Warner Brothers
10 The Wright Brothers

didn't open up a lemonade stand on the White House front porch, but there were times when Jimmy probably wished he would just so he could keep an eye on him.

Billy was willing to sell his name, and it most famously landed on Billy Beer. Billy Beer was "Brewed expressly for and with the personal approval of one of America's all-time great beer drinkers—Billy Carter." His quote on the can: "I had this beer brewed just for me. I think it's the best I ever tasted. And I've tasted a lot. I think you'll like it, too." No word if it was ever served at White House functions.

Even worse, Billy was willing to sell whatever influence he had. After being paid over $200,000, he became a registered agent for Mohammar Qaddafi's Libya. In their defense he noted "there's a hell of a lot more Arabians [sic] than there is [sic] Jews." They sure got their money's worth.

Jimmy Carter had a lot to overcome during his presidency, but nothing tarnished his legacy more than his brother. By the way, Billy Beer flopped and to this day is not even a collector's item.

THIS BUD'S FOR YOU

Memorable beer slogans:

1 Miller Time
2 Whassup!
3 When you're out of Schlitz, you're out of beer
4 Tap the Rockies
5 When you say Budweiser, you've said it all
6 If you've got the time, we've got the beer
7 Weekends were made for Michelob
8 Tastes great, less filling
9 Head for the mountains
10 Tonight, let it be Löwenbräu

When did

Bill Clinton

1946– U.S. President 1993–2001

jump the shark?

The U.S. economy was never better under Bill Clinton's term, but unfortunately that's not what he'll be remembered for.

Even before Clinton was elected the forty-second president of the United States there were signs of trouble. As governor of Arkansas, he was known to have a weakness for the ladies. So much so, in

The blue Gap dress.

EXECUTIVE CLOTHING

Memorable presidential garb:

1 Abe Lincoln's stovepipe hat
2 Teddy Roosevelt's pince-nez glasses
3 Sherman Adams's vicuna coat
4 Pat Nixon's "respectable, Republican cloth coat"
5 Adlai Stevenson's hole in his shoe

fact, that his handlers had a name for accusations of past love affairs—"bimbo eruptions." Enter Gennifer, stage left.

Gennifer Flowers, during the presidential campaign, claimed she and Bill were lovers. Unfortunately (for Bill), she'd taped their secret phone conversations. Clinton appeared on *60 Minutes* and masterfully denied the affair while tacitly admitting he'd still slept around. With his wife's steadfast support, the public bought it. Thank you, Hillary.

After having him on the ropes, there was no way the "vast right-wing conspiracy" was going to let a little thing like his winning the election slow them down. They continued to investigate his background with a fine-toothed comb, hoping to find something—anything—to discredit him. Then came Paula.

Paula Jones sued Bill Clinton for sexual harassment in 1994, claiming that as governor he had invited her to his hotel room, propositioned her, and dropped trou. In what now seems like a massive miscalculation, Clinton agreed to be deposed. This opened up the entire landscape of his love life to the opposing attorneys. Which brings us to Monica.

Monica Lewinsky was the beret-wearing intern who met with the prez for semi-regular gropefests in and around the Oval Office. Clinton was unpleasantly surprised when the lawyers started asking questions about her. Under oath, he denied any sexual relations. And that statement might have stood, if not for Linda.

Linda Tripp was Monica's gal-pal phone friend (at the time). Monica told Linda all about her affair with Clinton, a.k.a. "The Big Creep." Turns out during one session the overexcited

NEVER A DULL MOMENT

During the Clinton era, if it wasn't sex, it was something else:

1 Whitewater
2 Vince Foster
3 Pardongate
4 Chinagate
5 IRS-gate
6 Travelgate
7 Filegate
8 Draft dodging
9 "I didn't inhale"
10 Boxers or briefs

Clinton left some presidential residue on her dress. Tripp (who was secretly taping the phone calls—does everyone do this?) advised her to save the evidence.

The dress, replete with Clinton DNA, was turned over to independent counsel Ken Starr. This piece of Gap-bought evidence helped prove the president hadn't been entirely forthcoming. The upshot? Clinton was impeached. The blue dress became symbolic of a larger stain on his presidency and vaulted him over the shark. Ultimately, Clinton was not convicted and served out his term. It's not for nothing that they called the Slick Willie.

When did

Hillary Clinton

1947– U.S. Senator from New York 2001–

jump the shark?

Hillary Clinton was almost as controversial as her husband during their eight-year stay in the White House. Her fumbling on the health care issue would probably have gotten a nonspouse fired, and it certainly got the shark circling. Her involvement in travelgate and cattlegate made her a subject of investigation. And even after tasting the bitter world of politics, she still wanted to know what it felt like to actually be elected herself.

The Yankees hat.

So she decided to be a Senator. "What state?" she must have asked. There was no going back to Arkansas, and her native Illinois was out. Noting an opening in heavily Democratic New York, she set up residence. All local Democrats who might have considered running thoughtfully stepped aside.

DAMN YANKEES

New York Yankees who won the MVP:

1 Babe Ruth
2 Lou Gehrig
3 Joe DiMaggio
4 Phil Rizzuto
5 Yogi Berra
6 Mickey Mantle
7 Roger Maris
8 Elston Howard
9 Thurman Munson
10 Don Mattingly

Her Republican competition went from Yankees die-hard Rudy Giuliani (who was diagnosed with cancer) to Rick Lazio (who?). Lazio actually thought rushing the former first lady during their debate would make him look tough.

As long as she avoided any major gaffes, it would be smooth sailing. But it's not easy to avoid gaffes in New York. The people there can be very demanding, and you've got to be ready to kiss a lot of babies and eat a lot of ethnic food. A novice like Hillary couldn't help but make some mistakes along the way.

For instance, Hillary embraced Suha

Arafat after Suha made a speech claiming Israelis were gassing Palestinian children. Hillary flip-flopped on clemency for violent Puerto Rican nationalists. But nothing struck home like the story of a simple little cap.

Before Hillary had officially declared her candidacy, the World Series Champion New York Yankees had been invited to the White House. Who should show up to meet them but Hillary, looking uncomfortable in a Yankees cap? When the Chicago native claimed to be a life-long fan it seemed like the most shameful sort of pandering. Who knows? Maybe she was telling the truth, but she never seemed more like a carpetbagger.

She went on to win the election, of course. Yet that jump the shark moment is burned in her constituents' memories. She may represent New York citizens, but not their teams. Like any Senator, Hillary attempts to appear in forums where she comes off best. This would mean, then, that for the rest of her term, she'll avoid New York sports stadiums and arenas like the plague. It can be tough on the ego to be booed on sight.

FIRST LADIES

Hillary was a first lady who made her presence felt. Others include:

1 Martha Washington
2 Abigail Adams
3 Dorothea "Dolly" Madison
4 Mary Todd Lincoln
5 Eleanor Roosevelt
6 Bess Truman
7 Lady Bird Johnson
8 Pat Nixon
9 Betty Ford
10 Nancy Reagan

When did
Communism
1848–1989

jump the shark?

Marx and Engels strove for the liberation of the proletariat, but the best thing communism ever produced was the hockey team that bore CCCP on its jerseys.

Marx proved scientifically that the class struggle led to socialism, where the state would control the means of production and eventually wither away into an egalitarian, classless utopia known as communism.

The Berlin Wall comes crumbling down.

THINK ABOUT IT

Marx was one of many in-
fluential German thinkers:

1 Kant

2 Hegel

3 Nietzsche

4 Heidegger

5 Beckenbauer

Isn't this book about *Happy Days*?

But Marx's theory didn't add up. First, all-powerful states don't tend to wither away. Second, successful capitalist countries could withstand Marx's imagined threats. It was only the less-developed countries whose governments could be toppled and then run despotically in the name of the people.

The most striking example of this phenomenon occurred in 1917. Communists took over Russia in a revolution that shook the world. (Mao taking over China in 1949 didn't have quite the same impact. The world had been shaken plenty by that point.) As the Great Depression arrived on the scene, many saw communism as the unavoidable future.

The Soviets were materially behind the West, but with each Five-Year Plan, they claimed to be catching up. As the decades marched on and the West got richer, however, all the propaganda in the world couldn't cover up the failures of communism. It was the worst of both worlds: no freedom and no money.

SEEING RED

The remaining Communist
countries in the world:

1 China

2 Cuba

3 North Korea

4 Vietnam

The Berlin Wall was erected in 1961, becoming *the* symbol of communism. For years, millions of East Germans had been escaping into West Germany through Berlin. Fully closing off Communist East Berlin from free and prosperous West Berlin, the Wall showed the supposed will of the Soviets. "We'd rather shoot our people than let them leave."

In 1963, President Kennedy proclaimed "Ich bin ein Berliner." In 1987, Ronald Reagan demanded "Mr. Gorbachev, tear down this wall!" and that's just what happened. In 1989, the Wall was opened, and in 1990 it was torn down. The few states that were still communist were using capitalist techniques to help their failing economies. Communism had jumped, and the Soviet hockey team hasn't been the same since.

When did

George Custer

1839–1876 U.S. General

jump the shark?

George Armstrong Custer's rise through the ranks had been meteoric. After finishing last in his class at West Point, he soon distinguished himself as a Civil War general. He was a fearless fighter, leading to shockingly high casualty rates in his units. Before the war ended in 1865, he was the youngest general in U.S. history.

Little Bighorn.

Custer remained in the army after the war and took charge of the 7th Cavalry. In 1874, he led an expedition to open up the Black Hills of western South Dakota, even though the land had earlier been guaranteed to the Indians. In 1875, the Sioux and Cheyenne left their reservations to protest this encroachment. They gathered in Montana with the great warrior Sitting Bull and led successful attacks against the U.S. Cavalry. In 1876, the U.S. military decided to force this Indian army back to the reservation.

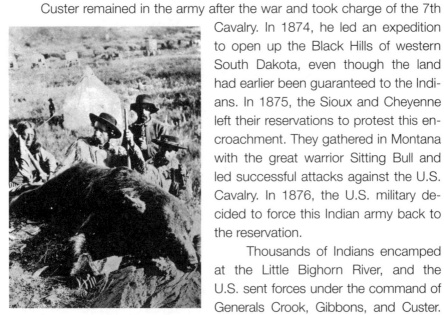

Thousands of Indians encamped at the Little Bighorn River, and the U.S. sent forces under the command of Generals Crook, Gibbons, and Custer. Custer advanced more quickly than ordered, moving far ahead of Gibbons's infantry. Meanwhile, General Crook had been turned back at Rosebud River by Crazy Horse.

On June 25, Custer jumped the shark when he split his forces into three parts and rashly attacked the Indian village. Custer personally led over two hundred men into battle, not realizing he was hopelessly outnumbered. Thousands of

MILITARY FIASCOS

The don't all have Abba songs named after them, but here are some notable military defeats:

1 Hannibal defeats the Romans
2 The fall of the Spanish Armada
3 Waterloo
4 Gallipoli
5 Any battle involving France

Sioux, Cheyenne, and Arapaho surrounded Custer's unit at Little Bighorn. Custer ordered his men to shoot their horses and hide behind the carcasses, but it was no use. Within an hour, Custer and all his men were wiped out in perhaps the greatest U.S. military fiasco ever.

Ironically, the foolish charge turned the tall, blond, blue-eyed Custer into a great folk hero of the nineteenth century. Numerous ballads and books were written about "Custer's last stand." These days, however, he's portrayed as the vain and impetuous white oppressor of the sympathetic Native Americans. In a way, he has jumped the shark in death just as he did in life.

When did
The Democratic Party
1792–

jump the shark?

There were times in the twentieth century when it seemed the Democratic Party had wiped out its rival. FDR was elected so often that Bob Hope joked that it was illegal to vote Republican. The Democrats might have held on to the White House if Eisenhower hadn't switched over to the GOP.

> **The Mondale-Ferraro ticket.**

After Watergate, polls showed the public running from the Republicans once again. They ran right to Jimmy Carter, took one look, and ran right back. So if the Democrats couldn't hold on to leads when the going was good, it could sure get ugly when they knew they were losing.

THE LAND OF A LOTTA LAKES

Some notable politicians from the great state of Minnesota:

1 Robert La Follette
2 Harold Stassen
3 Hubert Humphrey
4 Eugene McCarthy
5 Jesse Ventura

Such was the situation when Ronald Reagan ran for reelection. He'd pretty easily taken down Carter in 1980, yet who should the Democrats pick to represent them in 1984 but Walter Mondale? Mondale, who couldn't even cut it as Carter's veep in the previous election. Mondale, the man who campaigned on a promise to raise taxes. (That's not a typo.)

Mondale knew he was losing. He understood he needed some sort of thunderbolt to awaken the populace. His solution—pick a woman as his running mate.

Democrats like to make statements. For instance, when Bill Clinton was choosing the Attorney General, his first two choices—Zoe Baird and Kimba Wood—fell through. He then went with Janet Reno, making it clear that no one with a penis need apply. But there was a difference: Clinton was in office, Mondale was trying to get elected.

Geraldine Ferraro had served in Congress for three terms, and it's doubtful she would have been considered were it not for her sex. When Mondale announced "I looked for the best Vice President and I found her in Gerry Ferraro," it was about as convincing as George Bush saying Clarence Thomas was the best person for the job.

If that weren't bad enough, there were questions about her husband, John Zaccaro. Rumors included that he was connected to organized crime and that he wasn't paying his taxes. When he refused full financial disclosure, many saw it as an admission of guilt.

Ultimately, the public saw Mondale's choice for what it was—not some glorious advance for women, but a strategic move that reeked of desperation. Reagan took forty-nine of fifty states and almost took Mondale's home state of Minnesota. Mondale did prove one thing, though. He showed that a woman could fail in politics as miserably as any man—even Walter Mondale.

Thomas Dewey

1902–1971 Republican Presidential
Nominee 1944, 1948

jump the shark?

Thomas Dewey had been a crime-fighting District Attorney and a three-time governor of New York when he ran as the Republican candidate for President in 1948. He had previously run against FDR, but there was no way Roosevelt was going to lose in the middle of a war. Harry Truman, however, seemed weak and unpopular as Roosevelt's successor.

Dewey defeats Truman.

For months before the election, the Gallup and Roper polls showed Dewey with a solid, consistent lead. According to most pundits, Truman might as well close up shop. Roper even stopped polling, calling it a waste of time.

Before the election, reporters filed stories as if Dewey's victory were a foregone conclusion. *LIFE* ran a feature calling Dewey "the next President." Columnists such as Drew Pearson and the Alsop brothers filed early pieces designed to run the morning after the election that discussed the transition to a Dewey Administration.

GOV TO PREZ

New York Governors who ran for President:

1. John Jay
2. George Clinton
3. De Witt Clinton
4. Martin Van Buren
5. Horatio Seymour
6. Samuel Tilden
7. Grover Cleveland
8. Theodore Roosevelt
9. Charles Hughes
10. Alfred Smith
11. Franklin Roosevelt
12. Thomas Dewey

JUST NOT PRESIDENTIAL TIMBER

Two-time (or more) losers for the Presidency:

1. Charles Pinckney
2. John Quincy Adams
3. Henry Clay
4. Martin Van Buren
5. William Jennings Bryan
6. Eugene Debs
7. Norman Thomas
8. Thomas Dewey
9. Adlai Stevenson
10. H. Ross Perot

How many Americans, then, woke up, got their breakfast, unfolded the newspaper and spit out their coffee? Of course, not all papers said that Truman won. The *Chicago Tribune*'s early edition famously read DEWEY DEFEATS TRUMAN. The *Trib* may not have been the only journal to make this error, but it was the unlucky paper held up by Truman in the celebrated photograph.

How did this happen? "Give 'em hell, Harry" Truman waged an aggressive, nonstop campaign. His whistle-stop tour crisscrossed the nation, allowing millions to hear his message personally. Of course, four straight victories by FDR had trained the nation to pull the Democrat lever. Meanwhile, Dewey coasted his way into jumping the shark. He was more afraid of making a mistake than anything else, and when you play not to lose, it makes it hard to win.

There is another theory. Jimmy "The Greek" Snyder made his name on this election by predicting Truman's victory. His reason was that women were turned off by Dewey's mustache. Forty years later, Jimmy the Greek would jump the shark by voicing his racial views on the breeding of athletes. But that's another story.

When did

Michael Dukakis

1933– Governor of Massachusetts,
Democratic Presidential Nominee 1988

jump the shark?

He was so completely crushed in the 1988 presidential election—taking only ten states and losing the electoral vote 426–111—that it seems impossible so many Democrats could have been fooled.

The tank.

Sometimes you wake up the day after a wild party and are reminded of how you danced around wearing a lampshade on your head and nothing else. "I did what?!" These days you'll hear the same tone of voice when reminding Democrats that their candidate for president in 1988 was Michael Dukakis. "We nominated who?!"

How soon we forget. Democrats didn't just choose him, they were sure they had a winner. Coming out of their

LANDSLIDE

Dukakis was crushed in the '88 election. Here are the most electoral votes ever won:

1 Ronald Reagan 525 (1984)
2 Franklin D. Roosevelt 523 (1936)
3 Richard Nixon 520 (1972)
4 Ronald Reagan 489 (1980)
5 Lyndon Johnson 486 (1964)
6 Franklin D. Roosevelt 472 (1932)
7 Dwight D. Eisenhower 457 (1956)
8 Franklin D. Roosevelt 449 (1940)
9 Herbert Hoover 444 (1928)
10 Dwight D. Eisenhower 442 (1952)

convention, Dukakis was polling seventeen points ahead of Vice President Bush. It was Bush who looked bad, with people saying he reminded women of their first husband. What happened?

For one thing, Bush put on a full-court press. Bush attacked Dukakis for not supporting the Pledge of Allegiance because he wouldn't force people to recite it. Bush said Dukakis was a negligent governor because Boston Harbor was polluted. Bush even hammered Dukakis on an issue Al Gore had first brought up (of course)—the Massachusetts furlough program that let first-degree murderers out to commit new crimes. The attacks drew blood.

Some wounds were self-inflicted. Dukakis seemed to lack normal human emotion. When asked if he'd favor the death penalty for someone who raped and murdered his wife, Dukakis gave such a calm, measured response that you might have thought he was talking about land reform—except that land reform was the kind of stuff that actually excited him.

But Dukakis jumped the shark with a blown photo op. He was being shown a military tank, but before he got in to take a ride he wanted to wear the proper headgear. Bad mistake. Dukakis looked like an ineffectual dweeb in the silly Snoopy helmet.

MILITARY GEAR

Geeks just shouldn't wear:

1 Drill sergeant "campaign" hat
2 G.I. beret
3 White cotton sailor's cap
4 Army Ranger woodland fatigue cap
5 Tiger stripe boonie
6 One-hole face mask
7 French Foreign Legion kepi blanc
8 German WWI spiked helmet
9 Australian bush hat
10 Napoleon hat

Bush capitalized immediately, putting out ads showing Dukakis sticking out of the turret like a little kid in a big bad tank. The announcer said something about Dukakis not being ready to assume the position of commander in chief, but it was drowned out by America collectively exclaiming, "Who's that dork in the stupid hat?!"

We haven't heard from the former Massachusetts governor since.

When did

Florida

1845– The twenty-seventh state

jump the shark?

The recount.

Ah, Florida! The Sunshine State is home to Disney World, great college football, the Kennedy Space Center, and Key West, not to mention Spring Break and Elian Gonzalez (he moved). This capital of orange juice, humidity, and senior citizens has had its share of highs and lows, but when it comes to elections, look out.

There was this presidential election where the Democrat won the popular vote and the electoral vote came down to Florida, which had voting irregularities. The year? 1876. The ultimate winner, Rutherford B. Hayes, but any state can make a mistake. It could never happen again.

Election night, 2000. The networks called Florida for Gore and it looked like the election was over. Embarrassingly, the journalists got it wrong. So they reneged, calling Florida for Bush. But when the dust settled, Bush's lead was so narrow it set off a mandatory recount. When that was over, Bush led by 327 votes out of almost six million cast. (Did we mention that his brother happens to be the governor of Florida?)

NOT SO POPULAR

U.S. Presidents who failed to win the popular vote:

1 John Quincy Adams
2 Rutherford B. Hayes
3 Benjamin Harrison
4 George W. Bush
5 Alexander Haig
  (for a day)

There were claims of widespread ballot problems causing hundreds of thousands of votes to be tossed out. Palm Beach used a confusing butterfly ballot—designed specifically by a Democrat for ease of use by senior citizens—where perhaps thousands of Gore votes went to Pat Buchanan. The Democrats demanded manual recounts in four handpicked counties, which the Republicans sued to block. The Democrats sued to overturn votes in Seminole County and to stop irregular overseas ballots from being counted.

Katherine Harris, Florida's Republican secretary of state, certified the recounts (even though they weren't quite done) with Bush ahead. The Democrats sued. The state lower court upheld the decision but the Democratic Florida Supreme Court unanimously overturned the declaration and set a new deadline.

The counties utilized different methods for their manual recounts, using standards not seen before in Florida. The Republicans sued yet again, and the U.S. Supreme Court demanded the Florida Supreme Court write a new opinion. When the second deadline hit, even though not all counties were finished, Harris yet again declared Bush the winner. The Florida Supreme Court overturned the Harris decision, the lower court, and itself. It created yet a new deadline and ordered a statewide recount this time. But the U.S. Supreme Court declared it too late, calling Bush the victor.

And that's the *simple* version. The dirty secret is that every state has a certain percentage of ruined ballots and confused voters. The hope is that as long as the mistakes aren't based on fraud, they all even out. No one really notices unless the vote is extremely close. When that happens, you might as well toss a coin. Florida jumped the shark during that crazy recount, but it could have been any state.

Germany

98 A.D.–

jump the shark?

The Germanic people go way back. Over two thousand years ago, Julius Caesar defeated the Germanic tribes. This hearty people stuck around though, and sixty-odd years later prevented Roman expansion North of the Rhine. Today, Germany is a successful, democratic republic of over eighty-three million citizens. While there have been dark periods over the years, however, none has been so dark as 1933–1945—the era of the Third Reich.

Hitler becomes chancellor.

Adolf Hitler was born in 1889. Stung by Germany's loss in World War I in 1918, he fought against those he believed were destroying his land. In 1923, he was arrested for fomenting revolution during the Beer Hall Putsch. While in prison, he wrote *Mein Kampf*, where he outlined his philosophy regarding the greatness of pure German blood and the evil of Jews.

Hitler's Nazi party grew in popularity and by 1930 was the second largest party in Germany. However, as much as he tried to disguise his more extreme views, Hitler was still not popular with a majority of Germans. Aged Paul von Hindenburg easily defeated Hitler for the presidency in 1931.

There was a fear of communist revolution, though, and powerful people felt Hitler and his Nazi storm troopers could prevent it. Von Hindenburg was pressured into appointing Hitler as chancellor in January 1933, even though the Nazis had never won more than forty percent of the vote. No one could have known then that this act caused Germany to jump the shark, handing over power to one of the worst killers ever.

In February, the Reichstag, home of the German Parliament, was set on fire. Hitler blamed the communists and was able to exploit

MY WAY OR THE HIGHWAY

Twentieth century dictators:

1 Adolf Hitler
2 Josef Stalin
3 Mao Tse-tung
4 Pol Pot
5 Saddam Hussein
6 Idi Amin
7 Benito Mussolini
8 Nicolae Ceaușescu
9 Francois "Papa Doc" Duvalier
10 Marshal Tito

OH LORD, WON'T YOU BUY ME . . . ?

The Germans have always known how to make cars:

1 Mercedes-Benz
2 BMW
3 Audi
4 Porsche
5 Volkswagen

this incident to gain new powers. Communists were arrested, newspapers were shut down, and some candidates were murdered in the general election of 1933. The Nazis became the country's largest party.

By the end of 1933, Hitler had supreme power. There would be no more elections, no more opposition, no more freedom. His bellicosity eventually led Germany into World War II and its massive atrocities. All because, step by step, Germany allowed a madman to rule it.

The rise and fall of the Berlin Wall illustrates the changes Germany has gone through over the last half of the twentieth century. The country must carry the burden of Hitler's legacy forever. On Broadway, *The Producers* chronicles Hitler's rise to power in a brutally comedic way. This Tony winner cracks us up, but it also forces us to remember—and wish that, in this case, the shark could have devoured its prey.

When did
Newt Gingrich
1943– Speaker of the House 1995–1999

jump the shark?

A Congressman from Georgia, Newton Leroy "Newt" Gingrich, accomplished what many thought impossible. He masterminded a plan that made the Republicans the majority party after decades in the wilderness.

Newt flies coach.

Newt's brainchild in the 1994 election was the Contract with America, signed by Republican candidates. It promised to clean up government, hold down taxes, and get tough on crime. With President Clinton polling in the basement, Newt was able to nationalize the election and carry his party to victory. Newt became Speaker of the House, the first Republican to hold the position in forty years, and there was talk that he'd be the next president. Gingrich was flying high.

It was a trip on Air Force One where Gin-

LIZARD ALERT

Our five favorite amphibians:

1 Newts
2 Frogs
3 Toads
4 Salamanders
5 Caecilians

grich apparently let his success go to his head. Returning from Israeli Prime Minister Yitzhak Rabin's funeral, Newt complained that he'd been treated shabbily. He told reporters that neither Clinton nor his chief of staff Leon Panetta had spent much time talking to him. Worse, he continued, he was forced to exit from the rear of the plane rather than from the front with the president. Horrors!

There was a budget standoff at the time. Gingrich and Clinton engaged in a game of chicken and, in late 1995, the government was temporarily shut down. Gingrich seemed to be claiming that part of the reason for not budging on the budget was his Air Force One snub.

The floodgates opened and Gingrich was widely lampooned as a crybaby. He was the petty man who closed the government in a fit of pique. Not only did Newt jump, but his Republican Revolution took a leap as well. Clinton used this incident as leverage to help regain his popularity and sweep to a second term as president in 1996. Ultimately, when the Republicans didn't fare well in the 1998 election, Gingrich resigned.

LET'S NAME THE NEWT
Atypical political names:
1 Strom Thurmond
2 Orrin Hatch
3 Trent Lott
4 Arlen Specter
5 Wolf Blitzer

Gingrich isn't the first man to be brought down to earth by his ego. Too bad he didn't learn from Icarus: If you fly too high, you can get burned.

When did
Al Gore

1948– U.S. Vice President 1993–2001, Democratic Presidential Nominee 2000

jump the shark?

All the *Letterman* appearances in the world couldn't change the perception that Al was a stiff.

The public didn't warm to Al Gore. Michael Dukakis easily beat the Tennessee senator for the Democratic presidential nomination in 1988. Dukakis! That might have spelled the end of Gore's national career, but for Bill Clinton choosing him as his running mate in 1992. Gore served

Al and Tipper suck face.

faithfully as veep for eight years, biding his time, ready to reemerge as soon as his boisterous benefactor got out of the way.

Gore had little trouble outflanking Bill Bradley to gain the Democratic presidential nomination in 2000. The national convention was his big chance to bury the old, distant Al. Al Gore is dead . . . long live Al Gore. He was due for an upgrade.

The people breathlessly awaited his acceptance speech, but it turned out that something else would leave them breathless. His wife, Tipper, who wasn't wearing a warning label, introduced him to the cheering crowd at the Staples Center in Los Angeles. He took the stage and then he almost took his wife. He grabbed her, hard, and their lips locked in a passionate suction that clocked in at four plus seconds.

The next day, some discussed his speech, but most of the commentary was about "The Kiss." The pundits were perplexed by this prominent public pucker. Was he morphing from stiff to stud? Was this a new kind of "family values"? Was he saying "I'm not Bill Clinton—when I kiss someone, it's my wife"? Some thought it a magical moment; we thought he jumped the shark.

Regardless, there was a large contingent that simply found it the biggest "ewww!" moment since Michael Jackson publicly planted one on Lisa Marie. It just wasn't . . . right. We

discovered we preferred the wooden Al, dull but dependable.

Gore went on to lose a hotly contested election but continues in his quest for hipness with his recent beard. He's got all the time in the world to make out with Tipper. Take it away, Al.

When did
Alexander Haig

1924– U.S. Secretary of State 1981–1982

jump the shark?

It's not often that you get the chance to assume the presidency, but the general found his moment and seized upon it.

Al is in charge.

A highly decorated military man, General Alexander Haig served as the Nixon White House chief of staff. That administration crashed and burned over Watergate, but Haig survived to become secretary of state during Reagan's first term, where he went on to do some crashing and burning of his own.

On March 30, 1981, John Hinckley, Jr. shot Ronald Reagan as the president was leaving the Washington Hilton. The severity of his wounds was unknown for some time, and the nation was unsure who was President—except they knew it wasn't a guy named Al Haig.

Nevertheless, back at the White House, Haig was the highest-ranking official around. He nervously went before the cameras to reassure a worried nation, and left them wondering if a coup had just occurred. He let the public know, in no uncertain terms, that "I'm in control here." These words would follow him the rest of his life and vaulted the general over the shark.

Reagan was out of commission, but didn't that leave Vice President Bush in charge? And weren't there a few guys in line before Haig, even after Bush?

Haig would later explain that with Reagan shot and Bush temporarily absent, he merely was letting everyone know he was in charge over at the White House. In charge of what, seating for state dinners?

From that day on, many viewed Haig with suspicion for his seeming power grab. He resigned suddenly in July 1982, allegedly over foreign policy disagreements and complaints about his lack of authority. Little is remembered of his short tenure as Secretary of State beyond his unreassuring reassurance.

After leaving the Reagan White House, Al's political career was essentially over. He did attempt to run for the Republican presidential nomination in 1988, only to have then-Vice President George Bush show him who was really in charge.

When did Gary Hart

1936– U.S. senator from Colorado 1975–1987

jump the shark?

It's one thing to jump the shark. It's quite another to build the ramp.

In 1987, Gary Hart had the makings of a president. The Democratic senator from Colorado was a popular national figure. He had new ideas, but wasn't radical. In appearance he was more than presentable. He had many backers, from grassroot Democrats to Hollywood types like Warren Beatty. He had vigor and pres-

Monkey business with Donna Rice.

ence. There was just one problem—rumor had it he was a womanizer.

How'd he respond to the rumors? By throwing down the gauntlet. As he told *The New York Times*: "Follow me around. I don't care. I'm serious. If anybody wants to put a tail on me, go ahead. They'd be very bored." Smooth move, Gary. The press took him up on his offer and very quickly struck gold.

On May 3, 1987, *The Miami Herald* reported that Hart had been seen leaving his Washington townhouse with a woman who wasn't his wife. He tried to fight back, but far worse was to come. The *National Enquirer* published a photo of a young model, Donna Rice, sitting on Hart's lap on a yacht named *Monkey Business*. (Look, if you're gonna jump the shark, it might as well be on a yacht, right?)

In the photo, Donna and Gary had big smiles and were holding hands. The photo was reproduced everywhere and it had a devastating effect. It was a hall of fame jump the shark moment.

The press peppered Hart with questions about adultery, which he refused to answer. His wife came out and supported him, but it was too late. He lost almost half his support in a poll taken for the New Hampshire Democratic Primary.

On May 8, Hart withdrew from the race. His campaign had crumbled in less than a week. He left a bitter man, though he later admitted he'd made a huge mistake.

Since then, Hart has entered the private world of law, where adultery knows its place. He occasionally lectures and writes on events of the day, but in the Democratic Party, he's a pariah. Donna Rice got married and has become an antiporn crusader. Life goes on, but the shark never forgets.

jump the shark?

The hostage crisis.

The country formerly known as Persia has a long and varied history, with Alexander the Great, the Mongols, and many other visitors dropping by. But for the sake of brevity, let's skip all that.

Muhammad Reza Pahlevi became the shah of Iran in 1941. He was overthrown in 1953 by Iranian national hero Muhammad Mosaddeq, but was soon returned to the peacock throne with the backing of the U.S. He attempted to modernize his country, which did not go over well with fundamentalist religious leaders. Discontent grew and he used his brutal secret police (SAVAK) to stifle dissent. There was massive rioting, and by 1979 the jig was up. The shah fled the country, to be replaced by religious leader Ayatollah Ruhollah Khomeini, who'd been exiled in 1964.

FAMOUS IRANIANS

The Shah wasn't the only one:

1 Shahriar Pourdanesh, Washington Redskins offensive lineman
2 Vartan Gregorian, sixteenth president of Brown University
3 Pierre Omidyar, founder of eBay
4 Christiane Amanpour, CNN international correspondent
5 Ali "Al" Yeganeh, the real-life Soup Nazi

Khomeini declared Iran an Islamic republic and had a strong, anti-Western slant. On November 4, 1979, not long after the ailing shah was admitted to the U.S. for medical help, hundreds of Iranian students (many skipping classes) seized the U.S. Embassy in Tehran. All those inside were hostages. As far as America was concerned, Iran had jumped the shark.

President Carter tried diplomacy to get his people out. It failed. He tried economic pressure. It failed. He tried a rescue mission. It failed. He lost the election. That worked. The day Ronald Reagan took office, 444 days after the crisis started, the hostages were set free.

Ultimately, the hostage crisis was no good for anyone, except perhaps Ted Koppel, whose show *Nightline* got started due to the event. Iran got rid of its brutal leader for an even more

WHAT'S YOUR NAME?

Some countries go by two names:

1 Persia/Iran
2 Soviet Union/Russia
3 England/Great Britain
4 United States/America
5 Burma/Myanmar

brutal one. It also got into a nasty war with Iraq that lasted for eight years. Khomeini died in 1989, but his repression lives on. The fundamentalist version of Islam has been forced upon all. Whether known as Persia or Iran, the country remains both impoverished and unfree to this day.

When did
Iraq
3000 B.C.–

jump the shark?

The land between the Tigris and Euphrates, now called Iraq, was once known as the Fertile Crescent. It's been called the cradle of civilization, having given birth to the Sumerian culture about six thousand years ago. For you non-history majors out there, that's long before Greece and Rome flourished, and even before Egypt. Sadly, life there hasn't been too civilized since 1979.

The Republican Guard.

That's when Saddam Hussein took over. He'd already been involved in assassinations and revolutions, but it wasn't until he was endowed with complete power that he went hog-wild. He started a bloody war with neighbor Iran that lasted until 1988. He killed many of his own people, especially the Kurds, using chemical weapons. He also purged many of his top officials to keep the rest loyal, and to ensure there was no one around to replace him.

ARMY, NAVY, AIR FORCE, MARINES!

U.S. special forces include:

1 Army Special Forces (The Green Berets)

2 Army Rangers

3 Delta Force

4 Navy SEALs

5 Psychological Operations Groups

In August 1990, he turned his sights toward Kuwait, another neighbor. Saddam had built up a fearsome army, headed by the elite Republican Guard. Kuwait was overwhelmed, and Hussein declared the small, oil-rich country Iraq's nineteenth province. The United States, led by President George Bush and in coalition with the UN, decided to defend the loaded little guy and its black gold. The U.S. started with Operation Desert Shield, sending troops to the Middle East and giving Iraq a deadline of January 15,

1991, to leave Kuwait. Saddam predictably did nothing of the kind, and the actual war—Desert Storm—began.

For thirty-eight days, Iraq was pounded from the air with bombs, which destroyed its military infrastructure. Desert Sabre, the ground war, was next. While it was clear that the U.S.-led coalition was more powerful than Iraq, there was great fear there'd be huge casualties before the conflict was over. It was finally time to fight face-to-face, and that included taking on the vaunted Republican Guard.

It was no contest. The Republican Guard folded like an accordion and Iraq had jumped the shark. The ground war lasted all of one hundred hours. When these exhausted, dehydrated soldiers got tired of running away, they surrendered en masse—having been taught how by helpful leaflets dropped by the Allied forces. They surrendered to any soldiers they could find, and when they couldn't find any they surrendered to whatever was available, such as unmanned vehicles and CNN reporters. Meanwhile, the coalition forces suffered almost no casualties.

Having liberated Kuwait, the war was over. Saddam Hussein was still around—the coalition's mission was not to take Baghdad—but whatever reputation the Iraqi forces had as tough guys was gone.

OPERATION NICKNAMES

The U.S. names its military operations, like Desert Storm in Iraq. Some others:

1 Operation Indigo
2 Operation Victory
3 Operations Crossroads
4 Operation Killer
5 Operation Ripper
6 Operation Masher
7 Operation Niagara
8 Operation Golden Pheasant
9 Operation Urgent Fury
10 Operation Just Cause

John F. Kennedy, Jr.

1960–1999

jump the shark?

John F. Kennedy, Jr. was born only a few weeks before his father moved into the White House. Americans adopted him as their own. One of the most indelible images of the era was when little John-John saluted the casket of his slain father.

> **He failed the bar. Again.**

After that tragedy, mother Jackie tried to raise her kids out of the spotlight, but that was never entirely possible. Like a prince in a fairy tale, JFK Jr. grew up to be a handsome, decent young man, and one of the most eligible bachelors around. After seriously thinking about becoming an actor, the young Kennedy decided to take the path of least resistance and go to law school.

JOHN-JOHN'S GIRL GIRLS

Before getting hitched, JFK Jr. was spotted with:

1 Darryl Hannah
2 Madonna
3 Sarah Jessica Parker
4 Brooke Shields
5 Princess Stephanie

He attended NYU and graduated in 1989. Of course, to be a bonafide lawyer, you've got to pass the bar exam.

Let's lay our cards on the table. Being a Kennedy opens doors. People want to know you, want to help you, want to be next to you. If you're a young, handsome Kennedy, so much the better. The world was his oyster—certainly any elected political office short of president was his for the asking. JFK Jr.'s name was linked to some of the most beautiful women in the world.

Now that's all very well and good. But when you open that seal on the New York State Bar Exam, it's just you and your brain.

John-John failed. He was probably the most famous New York Bar flunker ever. One would think after such national humiliation, he'd really hit the books. Apparently, he still thought he could get by without proper preparation, failing it a second time. That's when he looked down at the shark. Anyone can flunk the bar

THE SEXIEST MAN ALIVE

Perennial *People* winners:

1 George Clooney
2 Sean Connery
3 Tom Cruise
4 Harrison Ford
5 Richard Gere
6 Mel Gibson
7 Harry Hamlin
8 Nick Nolte
9 Brad Pitt
10 Patrick Swayze

once—especially the tough New York Bar. But to know what to expect and allow it to happen twice, when the whole world is watching, takes some doing.

Already voted the Sexiest Man Alive, they now called him the hunk that flunked. His life got better (until his tragic plane crash): He ultimately passed the bar, worked as a prosecutor, married a beautiful woman, and published a political magazine, *George*. But for one brief shining moment, he was America's "himbo."

When did Ted Kennedy

1932– U.S. Senator from Massachusetts
1962–

jump the shark?

Chappaquiddick.

The sixties were tragic for the Kennedys. John was shot in 1963. Robert in 1968. Before the sixties were over, Ted, too, would be involved in tragedy.

Edward Moore "Ted" Kennedy was the youngest of the nine Kennedy children. Joe planned to create a political dynasty and just about achieved it.

John was elected president, Robert was named attorney general, and young Ted took over as a senator from Massachusetts. Ted probably wasn't the smartest of the clan—he had someone take his Spanish final for him at Harvard—but after his brothers were assassinated he would be the one to carry the Kennedy torch.

Robert was a front-runner for the presidency before he was struck down in 1968, so it only made sense that, in due time, Ted would run for the office. July 18, 1969, changed all that.

Returning from a party, Senator

Kennedy drove his car off a wooden bridge on Chappaquiddick Island and sailed right over the shark. He escaped with minor injuries, but his passenger, Mary Jo Kopechne, a campaign worker in her twenties, died. Kennedy left the area and didn't report the accident for hours.

Kennedy was only convicted of leaving the scene of an accident. Many felt he got off far too easily—that if he hadn't been a powerful man with powerful lawyers, he would have spent years in jail. Others investigated his story and felt he wasn't telling the whole truth.

Whatever happened, his presidential hopes were ruined. A decade later, in 1979, Kennedy tested the waters. President Carter was polling poorly and Kennedy announced he'd run for the Democratic presidential nomination. Carter said "I'll whip his ass" and went on to do just that. That was when Kennedy knew we hadn't forgotten, and never would.

Every six years, the citizens of Massachusetts vote for Kennedy, but it's a vote for "Camelot" rather than for Ted himself. He may be the liberal conscience of the Senate, but he knows if he ever tries to get any votes outside his state, the ghosts of Chappaquiddick will rise again.

ACCIDENTS WILL HAPPEN
These famous folk died in tragic accidents:
1 Will Rogers
2 Carole Lombard
3 James Dean
4 Buddy Holly
5 Ernie Kovacs
6 Jayne Mansfield
7 Duane Allman
8 Jim Croce
9 Stevie Ray Vaughan
10 Sonny Bono

When did

NASA

1958–

jump the shark?

In 1957, the Soviets launched Sputnik, the world's first artificial satellite, and the U.S. got scared. Did this mean America could be attacked from outer space? As a response to the threat, Congress created the National Aeronautics and Space Administration (NASA) to oversee rocket development and space travel.

Apollo 13.

MOON DANCE

Our moon doesn't have a name, but the others out there do:

1 Ariel
2 Caliban
3 Calypso
4 Cordelia
5 Europa
6 Ganymede
7 Io
8 Nereid
9 Phoebe
10 Rosalind

The sixties were a great decade for NASA. In 1961, Alan Shepard became the first American to pilot a spacecraft. The next year, John Glenn became the first American to orbit the earth. There were tragedies along the way, of course, such as *Apollo 1,* where three astronauts perished in a fire without ever leaving the launching pad. But by decade's end, America had done the impossible. On July 20, 1969, Neil Armstrong, of the *Apollo 11* mission, was the first man to walk on the moon.

After the moon landing, however, excitement lessened. The U.S. had scaled the heights and beaten the Russians to boot. But Mars was way too far, and other trips to the moon just seemed like more of the same. Nevertheless, there was still much to learn, and on April 11, 1970, NASA launched *Apollo 13.* The crew for this moon mission were James Lovell, Fred Haise, and John Swigert.

For the first two days, the mission was smooth sailing. But approximately fifty-six hours into the mission, an oxygen tank blew up, rupturing the line of another tank. The command module's supplies of electricity, light, and water were lost. Two of the three available fuel cells were threatened. The temperature dropped to near freezing. These conditions would be worrisome anywhere, but they're especially bad when you're 200,000 miles from Earth.

The astronauts were forced to move from the command module to the lunar module. Unfortunately, the lunar module was designed for a forty-five-hour mission and it would take ninety hours to get home, since the spacecraft had to go around the moon before flying Earthward. The crew had no choice but to heavily cut back on food and water consumption. In fact, they lost 31.5 pounds combined during the mission.

Now in a craft not built for the job at hand, the astronauts had to manually adjust their trajectory by sight, using the sun through the window for alignment. Amazingly, the crew managed to steer

NAME GAME

You thought naming hurricanes was fun. How about spacecraft?:

1 *Spider*
2 *Snoopy*
3 *Eagle*
4 *Intrepid*
5 *Aquarius*
6 *Orion*
7 *Enterprise*
8 *Discovery*
9 *Atlantis*
10 *Endeavor*

their ship back to Earth, and land safely. A major tragedy was averted. NASA may have jumped the shark, but that's nothing next to missing a planet.

Even before *Apollo 13,* space travel had taken a backseat to everything else going on during turbulent times in the U.S. Subsequent NASA missions lacked interest unless there was an unfortunate tragedy like the Challenger. Ron Howard's film *Apollo 13* does an excellent job of recreating the events of the mission, and if you look closely you'll see a shark fin swimming away at splashdown.

When did
Richard Nixon
1913–1994 U.S. Vice President 1953–1961, U.S. President 1969–1974

jump the shark?

No question about it, Dick Nixon was an up-and-comer. He'd been elected to Congress in 1946 by suggesting incumbent Jerry Voorhis was radically left-wing. He gained national prominence through his aggressive investigation of suspected communist Alger Hiss. He won a Senate seat in 1950 by calling his op-

Checkers.

ponent, Helen Gahagan Douglas, "the Pink Lady." It's no wonder Dwight Eisenhower picked him as his running mate in the 1952 presidential election.

Eisenhower looked like a shoo-in. He would, in fact, crush Adlai Stevenson, only losing states in the Democrat-controlled South (how times have changed). Before the election, however, his nominee for vice president ran into trouble.

Nixon was accused of receiving a secret fund of $18,000 from political supporters. As

NIXON CRISES

There was never a dull moment when Nixon was involved in politics. Our five favorites:

1 Almost dropped from Eisenhower ticket, 1952
2 Loses to Kennedy, 1960
3 Loses to Pat Brown ("You won't have Dick Nixon to kick around anymore"), 1962
4 Vietnam, 1969–1974
5 Watergate, 1972–1974

the scandal grew, some Republicans called on him to withdraw. In response, Nixon did something new—for 1952—and took his case to the public via TV. On September 23, he made his famous "Checkers" speech.

Nixon pulled out all the stops. He played the victim, a man whose reputation had been unfairly smeared. He said he was protecting the taxpayer. He suggested his opponent did worse things. He talked about his simple life and referred to his wife and family over and over. He implied the only people who'd attack him were soft on communism. Finally, and most famously, he admitted to receiving one gift—a cocker spaniel named Checkers, and he didn't care—"We're gonna keep him."

While some elites were repulsed, the mainstream was moved. The speech seemed to have saved his career. After this speech, Eisenhower had little choice but to keep him on the ticket. Yet, seen today, it's full of all the little Nixon tricks and mannerisms the nation would grow to mistrust.

The Checkers speech gave a glimpse of the chinks in Nixon's armor, and although he became president and had problems at a certain D.C. hotel, this was the moment that we knew Tricky would never be the same. Frantic attempts to control his image. A tenacious need for people to accept his side of the story. A bullying resentment of any and all opponents. A belief that the establishment was out to get him. The speech was a success that contained the seeds of his downfall. In Checkers, one can see both why he rose, against all odds, to be president, and why he was the first president to resign.

THE INVITATION

Visitors to the Nixon White House needed to be on "the list." Some classics:

1 Johnny Cash
2 Sammy Davis, Jr.
3 Olga Korbut
4 Elvis Presley (invited himself)
5 Grace Slick (invited, but not allowed in)

Oliver North

1943– U.S. Marine Lieutenant Colonel

jump the shark?

Oliver North was a military hero in Vietnam. In 1981, the decorated Lieutenant Colonel was moved into the White House to help on the National Security Council. While there he funneled private and foreign funds toward purchasing arms for the Nicaraguan resistance. Congress would have objected, so the operation was done in secret.

The noble officer finds a home on your AM dial.

ON THE RADIO

These radio voices like to stay to the right:

1 Rush Limbaugh
2 G. Gordon Liddy
3 Oliver North
4 Sean Hannity
5 Matt Drudge
6 Ken Hamblin
7 Michael Reagan
8 Armstrong Williams
9 Michael Medved
10 Bob Grant

Unfortunately for Ollie, it's hard to keep a secret in Washington. Before he knew it, the Iran-Contra investigation started and he was the main witness. At first North refused to speak, but once he got an immunity deal, he was ready to sing.

He arrived in full military garb, fruit salad on his chest. Voice quivering with earnestness, he stood before America, handsome and unashamed. He was a humble servant, helping his country as best he could. He personally thought taking money from Iran to support the Contras was a "neat idea." Ollie did state that the president had an idea of what was going on, but overall, he effectively wrapped himself in the flag.

His reputation changed from shady crook to great hero. He fought bravely for his country, let's leave him alone. Even the jury in his criminal trial saw him, as he put it, as a "pawn in a chess game being played by giants." He was acquitted on nine of twelve charges, and only convicted when the facts left the jury no choice. Even those three charges were later overturned.

So what should a great American hero who's just been through a criminal trial for his patriotism do? He became a TV commentator and a nationally syndicated radio host, and

SEMPER FI

The Marine Corps officer ladder is a tough one to climb:

1 General
2 Lieutenant General
3 Major General
4 Brigadier General
5 Colonel
6 Lieutenant Colonel
7 Major
8 Captain
9 First Lieutenant
10 Second Lieutenant

jumped the shark in the process. Suddenly, the graduate of the Naval Academy was all over the airwaves.

The fighting, the medals, the secret plans to protect the U.S . . . was it all just to become a star? There's a shallow gulf between selfless patriotism and self-promoting hucksterism, and swimming in between is a shark.

When did Jacqueline Lee Bouvier Kennedy Onassis

1929–1994 First Lady, 1961–1963

jump the shark?

Jackie gets the "O."

They were the first couple for a new age. After Ike and Mamie, a young dynamic power couple like John and Jackie Kennedy made the public swoon. There were even young kids, Caroline and John-John, bouncing around inside the White House. With movie star good looks, J&J turned Washington into the center of the fashionable world.

Just fourteen years earlier, Jacqueline Lee Bouvier had been "Debutante of the Year." Her wedding with up-and-comer Senator Kennedy was *the* event in 1953 Newport. And now they were in the White House, as if destined. But destiny had other plans, and JFK was assassinated on November 22, 1963. Jackie's courage in response gained her the admiration of the country.

She probably wouldn't have minded living the rest of her life raising her kids in semi-obscurity, but that wasn't possible. So when she married Greek shipping magnate Aristotle Onassis, twenty-three years her senior, on October 20, 1968, the headlines blazed across the world.

A DREAM PART

Jackie has been portrayed on the big and small screen by:

1 Joanne Whalley
2 Jaclyn Smith
3 Stephanie Romanov
4 Blair Brown
5 Herself

Jackie, how could you? America remembered her too well as the noble wife of a dead, beloved president. How could American royalty marry a commoner, no matter how rich? He seemed like a dirty old man grasping for prestige and connections. Worse, she seemed like someone who had money but wanted a lot more. Jackie had jumped the shark.

From the outside, the marriage did not appear to be that happy. He enjoyed her reputation and she enjoyed the shopping sprees, but where was the love? In 1973, when Ari's son Alexander died in a plane crash, he apparently lost the will to live and started drinking heavily. In 1975 he died of pneumonia. There was a struggle over the will, with an ugly lawsuit in which Ari's daughter Caroline sued Jackie for a larger share.

Jackie never remarried. She died too young, a victim of lymphoma, in 1994. She was buried in Arlington National Cemetery, next to President Kennedy. Perhaps, to all those who believed she'd jumped when she married Onassis, in the end she'd finally corrected that mistake.

> **RESTING IN PEACE**
>
> These nonmilitary personnel are buried at Arlington:
>
> 1 Writer Dashiell Hammett
> 2 ABC news anchor Frank Reynolds
> 3 Noted agnostic Robert G. Ingersoll
> 4 Actress Constance Bennett
> 5 Supreme Court Justice William O. Douglas
> 6 First Lady Jackie O.
> 7 Orator, "Monkey Trial" prosecutor William Jennings Bryan
> 8 City Planner Pierre Charles L'Enfant
> 9 Pianist Ignacy Jan Paderewski
> 10 The Lone Gunmen

When did
Tip O'Neill
1912–1994 Speaker of the House
1977–1987

jump the shark?

Thomas Philip "Tip" O'Neill, Jr. had a lengthy, distinguished political career. He was elected to the Massachusetts legislature in 1936 and became its youngest speaker. In 1953 he joined the U.S. House of Representatives and held the slot of Speaker from 1977 to 1987.

He was a big man—up to three hundred pounds—with a big heart. An old-style liberal, he fought for the New Deal and the Great

Everybody knows his name.

Society. He championed countless government programs. He fought against Vietnam and Richard Nixon. He was a national figure who believed "all politics is local." He guest-starred on *Cheers.*

A century from now, who knows what he'll be remembered for. Not too many people can say who was Speaker of the House in 1952, but they sure remember that episode were Lucy does a commercial for "Vitameatavegamin." It's quite likely Tip's fifty years of service will be forgotten, but the thirty minutes that he traded quips with Norm and Cliff won't.

Some politicians see TV shows as a stepping stone. Nixon's "sock it to me" on *Laugh-In* was part of his reintroduction to the American public. Next thing you know, he's president. Jimmy Carter appeared on *What's My Line?* and two years later he was president as well. Bill Clinton played the sax on Arsenio and talked about his underwear on MTV and the public liked what it saw. Boom, president.

Tip's appearance, however, seemed to be a winding down of his career. After years of fighting for more programs and more spending, the eighties brought the Reagan revolution, and a rethinking of big government. In 1983, when O'Neill did his guest shot, he seemed more a tired old man seeking refuge in a bar than a politician with plenty of victories ahead. *Cheers* wasn't even a hit yet—it ranked seventy-fifth that season. *Cheers* would definitely see better days, but Tip O'Neill—well, he was just another obsolete politician who had jumped the shark.

When did
H. Ross Perot
1930–

jump the shark?

H. Ross Perot founded Electronic Data Systems in 1962 and was a very rich man before the decade was out. Most rich people are content to count their money and vote Republican, but by the 1990s Perot felt there were problems with America that only he could fix. So he went on *Larry King Live!*

The NAFTA debate.

and announced he was running for president. He had neither the time nor patience to rise through the ranks, so he ran as an independent.

His timing was surprisingly good. Many felt that if George Bush and Bill Clinton were the best the two-party system had to offer, maybe it was time to take their business elsewhere. Some polling showed Perot beating Clinton and breathing down Bush's neck.

Perot spent a ton of his money on ads where he appeared with a bewildering array of charts to explain how to balance the budget.

Some economists questioned his arguments—his top-down solutions, his opposition to free trade—but when it was just Ross, a pointer, and a bunch of charts, how could he be wrong?

Mystifying everyone, Perot dropped out of the race in July. He claimed Bush was going to smear his soon-to-be-married daughter with phony photos of a lesbian relationship. He reentered the race in October, but had long lost his momentum. That he still managed to garner almost twenty percent of the vote is a testament to general voter dissatisfaction.

Most people would have recognized that they jumped the shark at this point and retired from public life, but the indefatigable Perot was

THIRD WHEELS

The most successful third-party candidates:

1 Theodore Roosevelt 1912, 27.4% (finished second)
2 Millard Fillmore 1856, 21.5%
3 H. Ross Perot, 1992, 18.9%
4 John C. Breckenridge 1860, 18.1%
5 Robert LaFollette 1924, 16.6%

YOU SAY TOMATO . . .

Classic political debates:

1 Federalists vs. the anti-Federalists
2 Lincoln vs. Douglas
3 FDR vs. the "nine old men" of the Supreme Court
4 Nixon vs. Kennedy
5 Chevy Chase (Gerald Ford) vs. Dan Aykroyd (Jimmy Carter)

now a public figure, and just because the election was over didn't mean he'd stop appearing on *Larry King*.

In 1993, he and Al Gore agreed to debate NAFTA. Perot, who claimed a free trade agreement with Mexico would create a "giant sucking sound" as jobs went south, was against it. Trouble is, it's easy enough to win an argument when the only other thing in the room is a chart. Gore cleaned Perot's clock and H. Ross had sailed over his charts *and* the shark.

Stung by his failure, Perot claimed Gore beat him because he was being fed answers via a hidden earpiece. At this point, even former supporters were embarrassed. Only Perot's stubbornness prevented him from admitting his moment was over. He did run in the 1996 election and support dropped to around eight percent. By 2000 he wasn't even the nominee of his own Reform Party, as the shark had moved on.

When did
Dan Quayle
1947– U.S. Vice President 1989–1993

jump the shark?

Up until 1988, J. Danforth Quayle led a charmed life. Congressional representative at twenty-nine, senator at thirty-three, the sky seemed to be the

Potatoe.

limit. And then George Bush picked him as his running mate.

Quayle was a deer caught in the headlights. Many claimed he wasn't prepared for the job of vice president, and his fumbling speeches only confirmed this impression. Opponent Lloyd Bentsen destroyed him in their debate by noting that he was "no Jack Kennedy."

Yet the Bush-Quayle ticket won. (See Mike Dukakis.) You might think that'd be the end of it, but things only got worse from there. The press had a field day exposing his misstatements and malapropisms, which he delivered on a regular basis. Talk-show hosts all over the country had four years' worth of prime material fall into their laps.

But nothing compared to the morning of June 15, 1992, when Quayle was presiding over a spelling bee/photo op at the Munoz Rivera Elementary School in Trenton, New Jersey. William Figueroa, twelve, correctly spelled "potato" on the blackboard, but Quayle's flash card read "potatoe." He helpfully advised the youth: "You're close, but you left a little something off—the e on the end." True, Quayle's staff had gone over the flash cards and not noticed anything amiss, and Mayor Doug Palmer watched approvingly as Figueroa changed the spelling, but it didn't matter. The vice president had just jumped the shark.

The media feeding frenzy began.

Quayle was the man who couldn't spell *potato*. One lousy error and his reputation as a national embarrassment was chiseled in stone. Even Figueroa called him an "idiot" and later told David Letterman on national television "He needs to study more. Do you have to go to college to be vice president?"

To this day, comedians use his name for easy laughs. Fair or not, his national career is over. Quayle has tested the waters to see if the populace is ready to accept him again, but apparently the power of the spud is too great.

When did

Ronald Reagan

1911– U.S. President 1981–1989

jump the shark?

The Iran-Contra affair.

Ronald Reagan was a late starter. After spending most of his adult life in front of a camera, he left the movies and went into politics. Never achieving the success of Jimmy Cagney or Errol Flynn, he fought back by making it to the top of his second career. In 1966, at fifty-five, he was elected governor of California. By 1980, he was president.

Reagan was as much a hero to conservatives as FDR was to liberals. Right-wingers delighted in Reagan's anticommunist "evil empire" rhetoric. At the time, Marxist Sandanistas ran Nicaragua. The Reagan administration backed the rebel Contras in their efforts to overthrow the ruling junta. This would ultimately lead to the biggest scandal the Reagan Administration would know, one that wouldn't be over until after Reagan's successor, George Bush, left the Presidency.

In 1982, the Democrat-controlled Congress passed the Boland Amendment, designed to prevent any aid from being given to the Contras. The Reagan White House did an end run around the rule by secretly funneling aid through the National Security Council, not clearly covered in the law. On top of that, the administration had been raising money for the Contras by covertly selling arms to Iran. They also hoped to swap these arms for American hostages being held in Lebanon by pro-Iranian forces.

The arms deal came to light in late 1986, Reagan admitted it was true, and the Gipper had jumped the shark. Special prosecutor Lawrence Walsh was assigned to investigate the whole tangled mess. Several administration officials, including Robert McFarlane, John Poindexter, and Oliver North, received criminal convictions.

Walsh, however, was after bigger game. He hoped to show that the involvement went all the way up to the big enchilada himself, Ronald Reagan. Reagan claimed to have been out of the room when all this stuff was discussed, and Walsh couldn't make anything stick. Nevertheless, in his final report put out in 1994, Walsh claimed the president was involved in some way, but he just couldn't prove it.

Anyway, before that, in 1992, President Bush had pardoned most of the principal figures in Iran-Contra. Many thought this odd, since Bush himself was under suspicion. But Bush was already on his way out and so didn't fear the political implications. As for Reagan, Iran-Contra marred his years in the White House. An administration that began with the promise of an American revolution spent its last few years fighting against jail time.

When did

The Republican Party

1854–

jump the shark?

Abraham Lincoln marked the start of a pretty good run for the Republican Party. In 1972, up to and including Richard Nixon, fourteen of the previous twenty-two presidents had been Republicans. Furthermore, although he couldn't know it at the time, Nixon would win forty-nine of fifty states in his reelection bid. Alas, some parties can't leave well enough alone.

Watergate.

On June 17, 1972, five men broke into the Democratic National Committee offices in Washington's Watergate Hotel. They were attempting to plant a bug and steal documents, but they bungled the job and were arrested, along with two accomplices, G. Gordon Liddy and E. Howard Hunt. All had connections to CREEP—the Committee to Re-elect the President.

This "third-rate burglary," as the Nixon people called it, blew up into arguably the biggest political scandal in American history. In February 1973, the Senate created a committee to investigate the break-in as well as other campaign irregularities as Woodward and Bernstein did their thing. In no time, the Nixon White House defense unraveled. It was soon apparent that this burglary and subsequent cover-up reached the highest levels.

Down they went. On April 30, 1973, John Dean (presidential counsel) was dismissed while H.R. Haldeman (chief of staff), John Ehrlichman (domestic affairs assistant), and Richard Kleindienst (attorney general) had to resign. Perhaps Nixon thought this would save him—a troubled sailor throwing off ballast—but it was just the beginning of his problems.

In May, Archibald Cox was appointed special prosecutor in the Watergate scandal. When he demanded secret White House tapes, Nixon had him fired. This led to calls for his impeachment, so Nixon appointed another special prosecutor, Leon Jaworski. Nixon also released his tapes, though two were missing and one had an eighteen and a half minute gap. In November, Nixon famously stated "I am not a crook." The public didn't buy it.

Next year wasn't any better. The pressure continued. Nixon was forced to release more tapes, tapes that proved he ordered the cover-up soon after the break-in. The writing was on the wall: Nixon resigned on August 9, 1974, before he could be kicked out.

It was all so unnecessary. Nixon probably could have done just as well with no dirty tricks. He just didn't trust others and felt he had to get them before they got him. When Reagan dominated the election in 1980, the Republicans were back on top, but never to be trusted again. One man's paranoia spoiled the entire party.

Al Sharpton

1954– Reverend

jump the shark?

The Don King of politics knows how to stir things up, provided he's got his facts straight.

In his early days, Reverend Al worked with James Brown and Don King. He apparently learned from them that if you're going to say something, you might as well say it loud. This strategy means you get heard. The problem comes when you say embarrassing things. Those get heard, too.

Whenever a racial incident occurs in New York, you'll find Al front and center, shouting louder than anyone. He led Bernie Goetz, Howard Beach, and Bensonhurst protests on behalf of African-Americans. It's been said his demands have led to boycotts, riots, and even murder.

His most famous involvement, however, came with the Tawana Brawley incident. In 1987, Tawana was a fifteen-year-old African-American who was found alive in a plastic garbage bag horribly abused with racial slurs written on her chest and torso. She claimed she'd been raped by a group of white law enforcement officers. Her story had discrepancies and didn't seem to fit the physical evidence, but that didn't stop Reverend Al.

Joined by lawyers Alton Maddox and C. Vernon Mason, Sharpton exploited the case for all it was worth. The three refused to participate with the authorities, though they were more than glad to appear on TV. They claimed there was a huge cover-up from a racist and corrupt system protecting the criminals. They didn't stop there. They named names. They said a district attorney named Steven Pagones, among others, was responsible for the crime.

It quickly became clear that Brawley's story was a hoax. Pagones understandably

> **Tawana Brawley.**

HOAXES

If you thought *The Sting* was good, here are some more classic cons:

1 Milli Vanilli
2 Orson Welles's *War of the Worlds* broadcast
3 The Hitler Diaries
4 Sidd Finch
5 Al Capone's Vault

GIVE ME BACK MY NAME

The celebrities strike back:

1 Carol Burnett vs. the *National Enquirer*
2 General Westmoreland vs. CBS
3 Jerry Falwell vs. *Hustler*
4 Tom Cruise and Nicole Kidman vs. *The Star*
5 Roger Waters vs. Pink Floyd

sued for defamation. In 1998, the trio of Brawley backers were ordered to pay Pagones $345,000. This hurt Sharpton's pocketbook less than his reputation, which had jumped the shark with Tawana more than ten years earlier.

Many feel Sharpton always knew it was a hoax, but he has never apologized. He continues to crusade against injustice, even doing jail time to promote his causes. Apparently Al hasn't noticed that we stopped paying attention to him a long time ago.

When did
The Soviet Union
1917–1991

jump the shark?

For its first century, the U.S. had plenty on its mind—Native Americans, the British, slavery, etc. But it at least knew it was a country born in freedom, and nothing was going to change that. Through the years, democracy spread. Ex-slaves could vote, citizens could vote directly for presidents and senators, even women could vote (although that took until 1920). At the same time, a specter was haunting Europe that would eventually frighten the pants off America—international communism.

Glasnost.

The most striking example of this phenomenon occurred in 1917. Communists took over Russia in a revolution that shook the world. It sure gave America the willies. In the Red Scare of 1919 and 1920, there were rumors of subversives who'd bring down the U.S. from within. Advocating communism could get you tossed in jail.

CCCPSTAN

The toughest former Soviet republics to spell:

1 Azerbaijan
2 Kyrgyzstan
3 Kazakhstan
4 Tajikistan
5 Uzbekistan

After a while, these fears subsided—somewhat. America was even willing to work with Stalin and the Soviet Union to defeat Hitler. But after World War II, fear of the red menace became greater than ever. Numerous anticommunist laws were passed. Congress held hearings to weed out reds. People had to sign loyalty oaths. Free speech was curtailed. Merely being accused of communism was enough to forfeit one's job.

Not that there wasn't a reason to fight a cold war. The Soviets were a real enemy and there were communists operating within the U.S. Khruschev was banging shoes and later, Brezhnev was building up the military. But destroying freedom to save freedom is not generally a successful tactic.

The Cold War continued through the Cuban Missile Crisis and the policy of mutually assured destruction. There were enough nuclear warheads on both sides to destroy each other many times over. Missile treaties heralded an age of détente, but the fear of communism continued.

Ronald Reagan was elected and he upped the rhetoric—the Soviets were evil, détente or no. His solution: "Mr. Gorbachev, tear down this [Berlin] Wall." Mikhail Gorbachev was the new ruler of the Soviets, struggling with a Union that was tired of being poor and unfree and of spending all its money on the military. Attempting to keep communism alive without violent suppression, Gorby promoted glasnost (openness), perestroika (restructuring), and demokratizatsiya (democratization). This only sped up the dissolution of the U.S.S.R.

In 1989, the Berlin Wall fell. In 1991, the Soviet Union fell apart, a victim of its inner contradictions. With the central tent pole gone, the Red Menace could not survive, and even Billy Joel ended up back in the U.S.S.R.

RUSSIA HOUSE

Leaders of the Soviet Union:

1 Vladimir Ilyich Lenin
2 Joseph Stalin
3 Nikita Khrushchev
4 Leonid Brezhnev
5 Yuri Andropov

And players on their great hockey teams:

1 Vladislav Tretiak
2 Slava Fetisov
3 Boris Mikhailov
4 Valeri Vasilyev
5 Alexander Yakushev

Clarence Thomas

1948– U.S. Supreme Court Justice 1991–

jump the shark?

After serving as chairman of the Equal Employment Opportunity Commission and sitting on the U.S. Court of Appeals in the D.C. Circuit, by 1991 Clarence Thomas was poised to become the second African-American to serve on the Supreme Court. When President Bush nominated him, some feared Thomas would be attacked for his conservative views and

> **Anita Hill reveals that Coke is it.**

unimpressive paper record, but no one foresaw the debauched battle his confirmation would become.

He squeaked through the Senate Judiciary Committee hearings with a 7–7 vote, but was expected to clear the whole Senate with little trouble until Anita Hill spoke up. A former employee of Thomas's at the EEOC, Hill said he had pressured her for dates, regaled her with dirty jokes, and talked at length about his favorite porno star, Long Dong Silver. Moreover, he once asked her "Who has put pubic hair on my Coke?" You can't pay for that sort of publicity.

> ### THE HONORABLE RON JEREMY
> Supreme Court justices whose names sound like porn stars:
> 1 Felix Frankfurter
> 2 Ward Hunt
> 3 Rufus W. Peckham
> 4 William Strong
> 5 Levi Woodbury

Conservative Senator Orrin Hatch was so unhinged by these dramatic accusations that he stated anyone who acted in such a manner would have to be a "psychopathic sex fiend or pervert." And while it's doubtful the public would have forgotten a jump-the-shark moment like the pubic-hair line, Hatch kept it alive by claiming Anita Hill stole it from *The Exorcist*.

Backed into a corner, Thomas denied it all. He claimed the whole thing was part of a "high-tech lynching for uppity blacks." This tactic worked well enough that he was voted onto the court, albeit by the narrowest margin ever—52–48. He's still the youngest justice on the court, and likely has many years left in his lifetime tenure, with many important opinions to write. Nevertheless, whenever we see him drinking a can of Coke, we're all thinking the same thing. He should strongly consider taking the Pepsi challenge.

> ### IT'S THE REAL THING
> Coca-Cola jumped the shark with New Coke. Here are its five most popular brands:
> 1 Coca-Cola Classic
> 2 Diet Coke
> 3 Sprite
> 4 Caffeine Free Diet Coke
> 5 Minute Maid

A Very Special Thanks...

To Steve Kurtz and Jason Allington—this book would not have been completed without their masterful writing. I am eternally grateful to these fine authors who really came through at crunch time, as well as Craig Neuman, Jay Goldstein, and Melissa Walker.

To Trena Keating, for believing in the concept and making this book happen; to Kelly Notaras, who went through the manuscript page by page and kept me on track while patiently answering questions like "what's a galley?"; to the Dutton team, especially Brian Tart, Lisa Johnson, Seta Bedrossian, and Robert Kempe (whose pop culture knowledge rivals my own . . . and that's frightening); and to all the great folks at Penguin Putnam.

To everyone who has volunteered their help with jumptheshark.com, including: Larry Abrams, for dealing with my "problems" and Thorn Communications for hosting; Melissa Walker, for keeping the site and stump going and never complaining; Tracy Carson, my first helper and newsgroup master; Dean Anderson, who runs the JTS Yahoo! Group with style and grace, and all the opinionated group members; Craig Neuman, who will always be the StumpMaster; H. Anthony Lehv for his patience, humor, and the law; Todd Anderman, dealmaker extraordinaire; Chris Henger, Bob Ferdman, Larry Carlat and crew for building and taking care of the Jump the Shark—The Music site; Mark Hallerman for bringing Shark programming into the twenty-first century, and the Internet Movie Database (imdb.com) and the All Music Guide (allmusic.com) for being the best places for online entertainment research.

To Todd Anderman, Keith Banks, Mark Seffinger, Peter Ginsburg, Eric Pomerantz, Frank Cernigliaro, Brian Lava, Scott Rosenzweig, and Todd Berlent for putting up with me since Chestnut Hill and sharing Luger's.

To Sean Connolly, Eric Champnella, Matt Schlein, Tim Snyder, Steve Doppelt, Kevin Hughes, Jon Glaser, Rob Marks, Dan Unowsky, Dan King, Craig, H, Roy, and all my Michigan pals (you know who you are) who have been there since '85. Go Blue.

To Jay Mandel, Lisa Shotland, Paul Furia, Howard Owens, and the folks over at William Morris for helping me sell out with such grace, and to Claudia Cross for initially getting the publishers interested.

To Jay Goldstein, David Epstein, Jason Banks, Chris Oliviero and Rob Capilli for making these sidebars even better. A very "very special . . ." thanks to Vinnie Favale, Mitch Semel, and Gary Dell'Abate, who have helped in countless ways and also happen to know that I'm a diabetic.

To Mark Efman, Joel Hodgson, Tiffany Hartsell, Lauren Pollack-Gellert, Fred Graver, Woody Thompson, Phil Olsman, Fred Klein, David Klein, Nancy Schuman, Vinnie Albanese, Michele Iglio, Barbara Kerbel, Marc Abrams, Judith Dutch, Alan Wurtzel, Heather Krug, Michael Kolbrener, Sibyl Goldman, Eric Weinstein, Howard Schochet, Evan Schnittman, Matt Timothy, and Lorin Prince for their invaluable professional advice.

To Howard Stern and crew who firmly established Jump the Shark on the pop culture map. Those guys will never jump (unless Cabbie keeps showing up).

To Maureen Dowd. She writes "Scrappy-Doo Spoiled It" in *The New York Times*, and offers from every publishing house in town pour in. Thank you, Maureen.

To Rob Owen, Don Kaplan, Mark Glaser, Adam Buckman, Meg Nesbitt, Aaron Berman, Rege Behe, Bonnie Vaughan, Jon Hart, Jaci Clement, Mike Watt, Janet Tegley, Leslie Gold, Butch Brennan, Kiri Blakeley, Brendan Conway, and Bill Simmons for putting the Shark out there for millions to find.

To Merrill Banks and the Lloyd family who have supported this "hobby" from day one.

To Steven Nalevansky, Vanessa Coffey, Marc Severino, Greg Heim, and the folks at King World for developing a show based on a website that chronicles the moments when things start to go downhill. Now *that's* faith.

To Julian Ham for his incredible artwork, Russel Mantell for his incredible accounting, Peter Goldring for his incredible T-shirts, and Steven Mark for his incredible protection to make sure no one screws me over.

To every person who has taken the time to surf on over to Jump the Shark. This book would be nothing without your contributions. Actually, it would be something, but just not as funny.

To Mom and Dad for having me and for their unflinching support; my brother Kevin for being a best friend; my in-laws Mel and Bette Ganz, who are a second set of parents; Lauren and Scott Hayden and Marc and Jodi Ganz, who help me wear jeans to Mill River; and everyone else in my family who knows there's too many of you to list without turning this thing into *War and Peace*.

To Rachel and Emily for making my life complete and understanding why Daddy spends so much time on his computer.

And finally, to my better half, Debbie, who knows me like no other, and whom I love more than TiVo itself.

Photo Credits

Photos on pages xi, 2, 15, 16, 21, 23, 34, 35, 43, 47, 59, 68, 70, 82, 91, 96, 99, 100, 112, 130, 137, 154, 167, 180, 181, 184, 193, 216, 227, 229, 273, 277, 317, and 324 courtesy of Photofest.

Photos on pages 10, 173, and 232 courtesy of The Everett Collection.

Photos on page 268 courtesy of Tom G. Lynn/TimePix, page 249 courtesy of Patrick Murphy-Racey/TimePix, page 288 courtesy of Time Magazine/TimePix, page 334 courtesy of Diana Walker/TimePix, page 310 courtesy of Steve Liss/TimePix, page 305 courtesy of Mansell/TimePix.